THE FAMILY AT WAR

Also by Mary Jane Staples

The Adams Books

Other titles in order of publication

MARY JANE STAPLES

THE FAMILY AT WAR

The Family at War

BANTAM PRESS

LONDON · NEW YORK · TORONTO · SYDNEY · AUCKLAND

TRANSWORLD PUBLISHERS LTD
61-63 Uxbridge Road, London W5 5SA

TRANSWORLD PUBLISHERS (AUSTRALIA) PTY LTD
15-25 Helles Avenue, Moorebank, NSW 2170

TRANSWORLD PUBLISHERS (NZ) LTD
3 William Pickering Drive, Albany, Auckland

Published 1998 by Bantam Press
a division of Transworld Publishers Ltd

Copyright © Mary Jane Staples 1998

The right of Mary Jane Staples to be identified
as the author of this work has been asserted in accordance
with sections 77 and 78 of the Copyright, Designs and
Patents Act 1988.

All the characters in this book
are fictitious, and any resemblance
to actual persons, living or dead,
is purely coincidental.

A catalogue record for this book is available
from the British Library.
ISBN 0593 041623

Printed in Great Britain by
Clays Ltd, St Ives ple

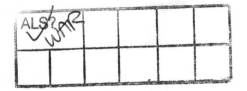

To Kelly
Whose hopes and dreams were once mine

THE ADAMS FAMILY

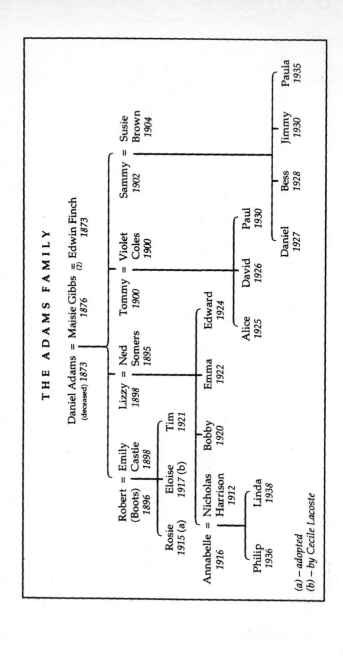

Daniel Adams = Maisie Gibbs = Edwin Finch
(deceased) 1873   1876   (2)   1873

Robert = Emily   Lizzy = Ned   Tommy = Violet   Sammy = Susie
(Boots)   Castle   1898   Somers   1900   Coles   1902   Brown
1896   1898   1895   1900   1904

Rosie   Eloise   Tim
1915 (a)   1917 (b) 1921

Annabelle = Nicholas   Bobby   Emma   Edward   Alice   David   Paul   Daniel   Bess   Jimmy   Paula
1916   Harrison   1920   1922   1924   1925   1926   1930   1927   1928   1930   1935
           1912

Philip   Linda
1936   1938

(a) – adopted
(b) – by Cecile Lacoste

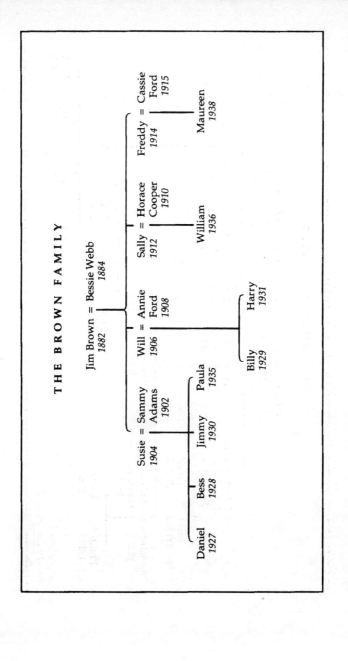

THE BROWN FAMILY

Jim Brown = Bessie Webb
1882   1884

Susie = Sammy Adams
1904   1902

Will = Annie Ford
1906   1908

Sally = Horace Cooper
1912   1910

Freddy = Cassie Ford
1914   1915

Daniel
1927

Bess
1928

Jimmy
1930

Paula
1935

Billy
1929

Harry
1931

William
1936

Maureen
1938

Chapter One

It was the second of June, 1940.

The dawn light of the awakening summer day fingered the closed curtains of the large handsome house in Red Post Hill, off Denmark Hill in South London. Mrs Maisie Finch, known to her family as Chinese Lady, came out of sleep and thought at once of absentees.

She thought first of those who were out in France. There was Boots to begin with, supposedly safe in being on General Sir Henry Simms's staff instead of in the front line. Well, that hadn't helped. The whole Army had been in the front line during the retreat to Dunkirk. Thousands of men had been brought home from the beaches, but there were still thousands waiting to be taken off. Why Boots was in the Army at all at the age of forty-three would have been an aggravating mystery to Chinese Lady if she hadn't known that behind his airy-fairy ways he was as adventurous at times as his late father had been. Then there was his son Tim, only eighteen, who'd volunteered as soon as the war broke out in September. Polly Simms had pulled some strings, with the help of her father, Sir Henry, and when Tim was sent to

France in February, it was to join the artillery regiment in which Lizzy's son Bobby was serving. Bobby was now a sergeant, and could look after Tim.

Then there was Jonathan Hardy, the young man to whom Lizzy's daughter Emma was very attached. He'd been called up in August, and at the end of his training was posted to a unit that left for France in January. That Boots and three young men of the family should all be at Dunkirk appalled Chinese Lady. As far as she was concerned, Jonathan Hardy was as good as family. She had met him several times, taken to him and spoken to Emma about him. Emma, self-possessed though she was, and much more in control of her emotions than her sister Annabelle, had nevertheless been unable to hide the depth of her feelings for Sussex-born Jonathan. Chinese Lady, never one to beat about the bush, asked her if Jonathan's intention was to marry her in due course.

'Granny love,' said Emma, 'I know what my intention is, and that's to cut his head off if he tries to marry anyone else.'

Accordingly, Chinese Lady regarded Jonathan as one of the family. Well, as good as. What Emma wanted Emma would get, and Chinese Lady was unreservedly in favour.

Reflecting on events now, she sighed at knowing neither Boots nor Tim, neither Bobby nor Jonathan, had arrived home yet. Last night the news on the wireless had referred to the possibility

10

that today would be the final day of the Dunkirk evacuation.

There were other absentees. Boots's daughters, Rosie and Eloise, were both in the ATS. Rosie had volunteered on the outbreak of war, Eloise in February. And Polly Simms, long a close friend of the family, was an ATS captain. Chinese Lady could not help having a considerable liking for Polly, even though she was sure Polly had a dangerous affection for Boots. But how any woman could be a soldier captain was beyond the comprehension of Chinese Lady, who simply didn't believe in that sort of thing. Nor did she think God approved. What some women had been getting up to since the end of the First World War wasn't natural. Daughter-in-law Emily, for instance, was now general manager of the family firm, Adams Enterprises. Chinese Lady was sure no good would come of such goings-on.

She thought of Emma again. Emma, soon to be eighteen, was herself thinking of volunteering for the ATS. And her parents, Lizzy and Ned, were wardens in the local ARP. For that matter, so were Tommy and Sammy. Chinese Lady wondered how long it would be before all her nearest and dearest were in the fight against that madman Hitler.

At least her husband Edwin was at home after spending months in France for the Government. He was sleeping peacefully beside her.

Chinese Lady slipped quietly from the bed and

crossed to the window. She drew the curtains back a little to look down at the silent road, palely touched by dawn's faint light. One might have expected some sign that the war had taken a chronic turn for the worse, and no-one could say it hadn't. But the residential thoroughfare was as peaceful as a sleeping dormouse. Not even the milkman was about.

She supposed Boots, Tim, Bobby and Jonathan would arrive home soon, along with the rest of the men still on the beaches. The phone would ring some time today, she was sure it would. It had rung at ten o'clock last night, and she'd thought it might be Boots, phoning to say he was on his way. But it had been Rosie, ringing from her ATS unit. Rosie had been phoning two or three times each day, asking if Boots or Tim had arrived. If Emma was self-possessed, Rosie was even more so. She was so like Boots in that she never showed alarm in a crisis. But when told last night that he still wasn't home, and nor was Tim, she became an anxious young woman. If anything happened to her adoptive father, or to Tim, Chinese Lady knew how much she would suffer.

Eloise had also phoned daily to ask for news of the absentees. Eloise had become devoted to her English family. And Polly too had been regularly on the line. Chinese Lady told her yesterday how much she appreciated her concern. Polly said a strange thing then. She said, 'I must be an un-deserving woman, Mrs Finch, or the fates would not have treated me so badly.' Chinese Lady did not ask her what she meant. She let it go.

She sighed again and turned from the window. Edwin was still asleep, so she put on her dressing-gown and went quietly downstairs to switch on the wireless to catch the early morning news. It was all about Dunkirk, about the men on the beaches and those still pouring into the port, and about the big ships and little ships that were rescuing British, French, Belgian and Polish troops from the bombed sands. Perhaps Tim and Boots would meet each other on one of those ships, together with Jonathan Hardy and Bobby. Lizzy was worrying about son Bobby, and Emma was getting anxious about Jonathan.

Chinese Lady said a little prayer for all concerned.

It was about this time, just as dawn broke that planes of the *Luftwaffe* took off from a forward station in France and caught a column of retreating British troops just outside Bergues, some seven miles from Dunkirk. They were the last British troops in the sector south-east of the port, the last of the men who, in this sector, had been fighting a desperate rearguard action against the German Panzers. Last night they had received orders to vacate their position and to make for Dunkirk. They began their march when darkness fell, and kept going through the night, weary, footslogging and silent, men of the infantry, artillery and tanks, guns spiked and abandoned, tanks and motor transport long since destroyed.

Among the artillerymen of what was left of one battery were Sergeant Bobby Somers and Gunner Tim Adams, both as weary as hell, but both determined to reach Dunkirk. Far ahead of them, in the van of the column, limped Jonathan Hardy, a gunner from a different regiment. The whole was a hotch-potch of companies, batteries, regiments and squadrons, the mixture thrown together by the haphazard and desperate nature of a tenacious fighting retreat. Jonathan had actually met up with Bobby and Tim two days ago, but was with the remnants of his own battery now. He knew Bobby and Tim were somewhere behind him, and that satisfied him. Bobby was Emma's brother, Tim her cousin. With luck, the column would easily reach Dunkirk before midday if it didn't sag and collapse on the road. And with a little more luck, they'd see the white cliffs of Dover before the afternoon was out. God, he could do with the comfort of a bed for a couple of days.

When the German planes caught the column, it disintegrated as the weary men, galvanized by the primitive need to survive, dived for the ditches, the verges and for whatever cover they could find. Officers shouted, NCO's bawled, and down went the men, tumbling and sprawling and flattening themselves on either side of the road. The noise of the oncoming planes was a scream and a roar. Within seconds they were strafing the road, coming one after the other, then flying on to ascend, to circle

14

and to come again. It was hell in a frenzy for five minutes, a lone Stuka dive-bomber joining in.

Away to the west, across the Belgian border, was a similar column of troops, heading towards Dunkirk on the road from Ypres. They were men of a corps commanded by General Sir Henry Simms, and they were the last of retreating troops from the Ypres sector. Near the van of the trudging column was an open, battered, staff car moving slowly, its engine occasionally misfiring. It contained Sir Henry himself, still spruce and vigorus normally, but now as weary as his men, and just as angry as they were at what they considered was a criminal lack of tanks per unit. The mere 200 supplied to the whole of the BEF had been crushed by the weight of the German armour. Defeat had been inevitable, despite the fighting resistance of the British.

Driving the car was Major Robert Adams, known to friends and family as Boots. Sir Henry was beside him, and squeezed in beside Sir Henry was the General's wounded sergeant-driver. In the back of the car were other wounded men, and Boots could only hope the damaged vehicle would hold out until Dunkirk was reached.

In the clear air of dawn the column trudged on, the staff car crawling. It was not what was expected of a general, to be with a retreating rearguard and risking capture. In the '14–18 war, few fighting units ever saw a general. Sir Henry, a soldier through and through, was not that kind of commander. He liked his men to see him, and it was completely in keeping with his character and his principles to have stayed with the rearguard in its fighting retreat to Dunkirk. He had sent all his staff officers except Boots to the port days ago. There were not many miles to go now before they reached it themselves.

Chapter Two

'Wakey, wakey!' The brisk voice of an ATS sergeant woke up sleeping recruits.

Private Eloise Adams opened her eyes. Sleep rushed away and she quickened. It was going to be Ramsgate Harbour again, it was going to be another emotional but exhilarating day. She thought of her father and of her half-brother Tim. They had to arrive today, they must, although it might not be at Ramsgate. Her English stepmother would be worried, and so would the grandparents.

Eloise, Anglo-French, had a British passport and a British National Identity card, and these had enabled her to volunteer for the ATS a little over three months ago. Along with other recruits, she was nearly at the end of the official training period, and if because of her French verve she had found British military restrictions a little irksome, everything about the Dunkirk evacuation had brought her to eager and pulsating life. She and other ATS personnel had been on duty by Ramsgate Harbour each day.

There had been some French soldiers among the British who had landed yesterday, the kind of Frenchmen prepared to fight on from Britain.

Eloise felt tingling pride in them. They were close to exhaustion, as were nearly all the returning soldiers, but they acknowledged the cheers of welcoming crowds with smiles and waves.

Eloise slipped from her bed in one of the barrack rooms of the training camp near Minster, five miles from Ramsgate, and began another exciting day. What did defeat matter when the Army lived to fight again?

Susie, wife of Chinese Lady's youngest son Sammy, rang up at nine o'clock.

'Mum, Susie here.'

'Yes, Susie?' said Chinese Lady, standing well back from the phone, and not letting the receiver make too close a contact with her ear. She still regarded telephones as unnatural, the kind of new-fangled contraptions likely to blow up just when a body wasn't ready for it, and there had been a lot of that kind of nervous anticipation lately.

'Any news of Boots or Bobby? Or Tim?'

'I haven't had none, Susie, but I expect we'll hear some time today. Or tomorrow morning at the latest.'

'Well, I hope so,' said Susie, 'I hope they're not among the soldiers who've been taken prisoner during the retreat. There's been an awful lot, it seems.'

'I'm sure Bobby wouldn't allow that to happen to him,' said Chinese Lady, 'and I can't believe Boots would be careless enough to. We all told him to leave his casual ways behind him when he went off.

And Tim's as sensible as his Uncle Tommy.'

'Oh, I'm sure we'll get good news before long, Mum,' said Susie.

'Well, it's all a terrible mess,' said Chinese Lady.

'Still, all those little ships are performing miracles,' said Susie.

'Where's Sammy?' asked Chinese Lady.

'He went off early to Luton,' said Susie, 'hoping to find the right kind of fact'ry he can buy, with a sort of dormit'ry for his machinists. Their children have all been sent to the country.'

'What's he want to have a fact'ry in Luton for?'

Susie could have said Sammy wanted to take precautions, that because of the way the war was going, the Germans might get themselves into a position to bomb London and its factories. Sammy wanted to move all his Shoreditch staff to Luton. The firm now had large Army and Air Ministry contracts for uniforms.

'Oh, he's lookin' ahead, Mum,' said Susie, not wanting to mention anything as frightening as bombs on London.

'I hope he's not profiteering,' said Chinese Lady.

'I'll see he doesn't,' said Susie.

'I don't want to suffer the shame and disgrace of havin' a war profiteer in the fam'ly,' said Chinese Lady.

'I don't, either,' said Susie. 'Well, I must get on, Mum, I've all sorts of things to do. I'll phone again later.'

'Yes, all right, Susie,' said Chinese Lady, who was expecting Rosie to phone next. Or Eloise. Or Polly.

19

Or Aunt Victoria, Vi's mother. Aunt Victoria had always had a soft spot for Boots. She was in a slightly complaining mood these days, mostly on account of the fact that Vi's dad, Uncle Tom, had gone and joined the ARP. He was too old at sixty-seven, she said. Chinese Lady pointed out he still looked hale and hearty. Yes, but he goes out on night duty, said Aunt Victoria. Well, never mind, said Chinese Lady, let him do it if he wants to.

In her home in Stead Street, Walworth, Mrs Jemima Hardy, Sussex-born, was preparing to bake a cake. She'd been saving up rationed ingredients for a suitable occasion, and a very suitable one was now due. Her son Jonathan was bound to be home any moment from Dunkirk, and nothing was going to make her believe otherwise, except a telegram. And she wasn't sure if she'd let any telegram into the house. In wartime, telegrams were the kind of thing people were better off without.

Her daughter Jane, seventeen, was at work, clerking in a London factory making war materials. Her other daughter Jennifer and her younger son Jonas were at school. They'd refused to be evacuated, although hundreds of other Walworth schoolchildren were now in the country.

Husband Job was at work for the council, and would be on ARP duty tonight as a warden. Job didn't like the war any more than she did, but wasn't going to shirk doing his bit as a civilian.

Jemima was going to spend the day listening to the wireless news and for the arrival home of

Jonathan, while getting on with baking the cake and other domestic jobs. Perhaps Emma would come round this evening. She sometimes did, and Jemima thought blessed if that sweet girl don't be acting now and again like a daughter-in-law.

Jemima also thought about a certain house in Lorrimore Square, Kennington. The family were moving there next month. She had insisted on leaving Stead Street because of a warning from a young Irishman of a mystic kind, a warning that implied war would bring down their present house. But it had taken some time for the family to find a place everyone considered right, and which was available for renting. The house in Lorrimore Square would be vacant next month and it had a small garden, much to Job's pleasure.

Jemima knew she would feel easier in her mind when the move was made. And when it was, she and Job would have to try to persuade the Stead Street landlord to let the vacated house stand empty.

Later that morning, a young woman, Helene Aarlberg, stood at the gate to a field of barley. The day was perfect, the farm a panorama of summery fields lush with produce. The sky was a canopy of clear blue, except for where it was stained by a pall of smoke above Dunkirk, six kilometres to the north. A little to the west lay the Belgian border. From there came the sound of guns.

The guns of the abominable Nazis.

'It's over for the British, mademoiselle,' said one

of the farm workers, and his fellow workers nodded in silent agreement.

'Yes, they're still running, running for home,' said Helene bitterly. She was disgusted with the British Expeditionary Force. It had been floundering, reeling and staggering from the moment the German Panzer divisions launched their attacks early in May. Helene Aarlberg, nineteen, was a strong and capable young woman, not a girl. Her thin grey jersey had never made any effort to disguise the firmness of her healthy bosom. A black serge skirt hung from her rounded hips, black lisle stockings sheathed her long legs, and black farm boots covered her feet and ankles. Her dark hair, auburn-tinted, was tied in practical fashion at the nape of her neck with an old black ribbon. Friends might have said that the prevalence of black meant Helene Aarlberg was already in mourning for France. Actually, she cared very little for tarting herself up, especially when she was working, and apart from spending some Sundays sailing her small boat off the Dunkirk shoreline, she was rarely not at work in summertime. She was invaluable to the owners of the farm, her parents.

She turned her eyes away from the distant pall of black smoke and looked at the barley field. The young shoots were fighting the encroaching weeds. Perhaps because of the war, weeds did not matter, and perhaps the shortage of farm workers was a small problem compared to the danger France was in from the iron hordes of Hitler. But overrunning weeds did matter. Land was eternal. It was also capricious. Farmland tolerated nothing that did not relate to good husbandry.

'See what Dunkirk means, mademoiselle, it means the British are leaving all the fighting to France,' said a grizzled worker. He and the others were all middle-aged or elderly.

'I know that.' Helene eyed them angrily. 'What are you standing about for? There are a thousand things to do. Go and do them.' She swung herself aggressively over the gate instead of opening it, such was her mood. Her skirt rushed up. The labourers blinked. She had superb legs, and the plainness of her lisle stockings could not hide that fact. Landing on her feet, she looked scorchingly at the workers. A grin or two showed. 'Men!' she said bitingly, and strode away.

Eyes followed her. She was something to talk about, apart from the war.

'Men, yes, but she only needs one, one who can stand up to her,' said the grizzled farmhand.

'Henri Barnard, perhaps?' suggested another man. 'He's big enough.'

'Just over-sized marshmallow. Helene Aarlberg would eat him.'

Chapter Three

The black smoke rising above Dunkirk spoke of Stukas pounding the town, beaches and harbour. The crump and boom of bombs launched from the air were a sign that the Stukas were enjoying another field day. The flurries of aerial combat between the *Luftwaffe* and French-based RAF fighter planes had died away. The last retreating remnants of the BEF were swept by rumours that every RAF squadron had been recalled. Much as he disliked leaving the BEF without cover, Prime Minister Churchill had yielded to the necessity of preserving the fighting wings of the RAF now that the larger part of the BEF had been successfully brought home. It was from home airfields that RAF fighters were taking off to engage the numerically superior enemy over Dunkirk.

More than three hundred thousand men, including groups of French, Belgian and Polish soldiers and airmen, had been taken off the beaches by the big ships and little ships. But there were several thousand still there, and the Germans, after a brief pause, were preparing to move again, determined to close Dunkirk down consequent on the *Luftwaffe*'s expected final reduction of the port.

The evacuation that had been going on for days was in its final stages. The beaches were still crowded with columns of men under the control of marshals, and the columns spilled into the sea as the soldiers and other servicemen waded out to boats. And there were still a thousand and more rearguard men limping into Dunkirk from every road and lane.

The ragged lines of exhausted men on the road from Bergues had four miles to go to reach the beaches. They had picked themselves up and resumed their footslogging march after being strafed at dawn outside Bergues. Dunkirk offered them their only chance of escape.

It was at this point that Gunner Tim Adams came out of the mind-blotting effects of concussion. He found himself moving automatically. His uniform was filthy, his underclothes clammy, his rifle slung, his dusty steel helmet an uncomfortable weight on his head. That was because he had a horrible headache. On top of that his eyes were playing him up, and he had difficulty in focusing. Double vision kept recurring. Behind and in front of him men were trudging wearily. They filled the sunlit road like a dusty and straggling crocodile that constantly changed shape as exhausted men wandered and wavered.

Where were they? How far to go now? Where were the guns, the transport? Where was Bobby? Where was Jonathan Hardy?

He remembered the dawn attack from the air then, the cannon-fire from *Messerschmidts* and the bombs from a Stuka that had scattered a thousand men, killed some and wounded others. He himself, buffeted by the blast of an exploding bomb, felt as if he had run into a brick wall. It knocked him out. He could not remember, but he supposed he had picked himself up along with all the other survivors to automatically resume the march. But he remembered now that Jonathan had been in the van of the column along with other members of his unit. Tim hoped he was still there. As for Bobby, Tim had no remembrance at all of how they had become separated, and he had no idea, either, of whether or not Bobby was now a casualty. A dead weight of depression settled on Tim, and the effects of severe concussion made it difficult to concentrate. But something jerked him into thinking he ought to look for Bobby. He halted. Men lurched past him. He stopped several of them in turn, those he recognized as belonging to his regiment, including an officer, asking if any of them knew what had happened to Sergeant Somers. The answers were tired negatives.

A weary officer called to him to keep moving, but Tim stayed where he was, turning to look back at oncoming men. He had a flesh wound at the side of his right thigh where a bullet had cut through his khaki trousers and badly nicked him. Beneath the field dressing, the scored flesh was sore and painful.

The column trudged by as he strained his aching eyes. Emma would want him to look out for Jonathan as well as Bobby.

On the exhausted men came, some with rifles, some without, and all of them rid of their webbing equipment. Any amount of personal equipment had been discarded to lighten loads, and the road to Bergues and beyond was littered. Tim blinked in an effort to keep his eyes open as the column gradually thinned and there were only stragglers to be seen.

From the lee of a hedge divided by a five-barred gate fronting the road, a man had been watching this last rearguard of limping, shambling British soldiers heading for Dunkirk and the beaches. He knew from a succession of French radio bulletins that the Germans would almost certainly be in control of Dunkirk by tomorrow at the latest. And in this clear morning air he could hear what many of these British Tommies were probably too far gone to hear, the low but perceptible sound of German planes flying in formation above other retreating soldiers on the road from Ypres, just across the nearby Belgian border. They were undoubtedly heading for Dunkirk, fighters and Stukas, probably, to take their turn to strafe and bomb the beaches and the ships.

Sadness took hold of Jacob Aarlberg. He had fought with the Belgian Army alongside the British Tommies in the last war, and had always held them in great respect. These exhausted men were the sons of those Tommies. He had watched them as they passed by, eyes red-rimmed, faces grey and dusty, some weary to death from the ferocious battles they had fought in trying to contain the

27

heavily armoured Germans. There had been hundreds of them, lurching and reeling but still staying on their feet.

They had disappeared now, all but a few stragglers and a man who had turned his back on Dunkirk and was squinting painfully into the distance. Jacob Aarlberg did not move. The tragedy of an army beaten into the ground held him there. He looked to his left, in the direction of Dunkirk, and saw the pall of black smoke rising thicker over the town and its beaches.

He looked at the motionless Tommy again, wondering about him as the last of the stragglers passed by.

Tim strained his eyes. The road was empty now. There was no sign of Bobby or anyone else.

'Tommy?' It was a man's voice, quiet but clear.

Tim turned. From behind the hedge a man appeared, regarding him from the other side of a five-barred gate. He was middle-aged and healthily brown. He wore a dark blue shirt, black breeches and a black beret.

'What?' asked Tim vaguely.

'Where are you going, Tommy?' The spoken English was excellent.

'I'm looking for a cousin, my sergeant,' said Tim. He crossed the verge to the gate, and Jacob noted the look of exhaustion and the forward tilt of his steel helmet to keep the sun out of his eyes, eyes that were cloudy with pain. 'He's my height, but broader. Have you been watching this road?'

'I have been watching all of you go by,' said

Jacob. 'Now I am waiting, stupidly perhaps, for the Boche and their tanks to arrive. Tommy, go on to Dunkirk. Your sergeant would not want you to fall into the hands of the Germans.'

'God knows where he is,' said Tim. 'We got separated early this morning.' With an effort, he spoke of the dawn attack on the column by German planes. 'I can't go on without him if he's somewhere back there and wounded.'

'Perhaps he is far ahead, looking for you,' said Jacob.

'I'd like to think so,' said Tim, feeling a lot older than his eighteen years. 'D'you think you might have seen him? No, that's a daft question.' He adjusted his slung rifle, grimacing a little. 'Sorry about the war. We've made a mess of it.'

'You have fought as well as you could,' said Jacob, 'so go on to Dunkirk and your ships, which will give you the chance to fight again. The German armies will be resuming their advance any moment. That warning is being spoken in every radio bulletin.'

'Well, damn that,' said Tim tiredly, but made no attempt to move, and Jacob felt strangely affected by this British soldier's reluctance to give up the hope of finding his sergeant, his cousin.

'Go, Tommy. Today is your last day.'

'Damn that too,' said Tim. He searched the road with aching eyes again. It was still empty. 'Well, perhaps he is ahead of me, perhaps I've got to settle for that. He's the last kind of bloke to have given up. If he's still back there somewhere and he does come by, he's Sergeant Somers. Tell him to get a move on.' Tim smiled faintly. 'That's if you'll still be watching.'

'Yes, I will stay here a while,' said Jacob. 'You must catch up with your comrades – wait, take this.' He disappeared behind the hedge. Reappearing, he lifted a bicycle over the gate. 'Take it. It belongs to one of my farm workers. He will understand and I will make it up to him. It will get you to Dunkirk quicker and a little more easily than on your legs. So take it. I fought with the old Tommies, your fathers, in the last war. They were my friends, my comrades.'

'My father's in this one as well,' said Tim, 'but God knows where he is, either.' He hesitated a moment, a moment of wrenching finality, then he said, 'Thanks. I'd like to think I can bring the bike back to you one day. I'm Tim Adams. Will you tell me who you are?'

'My name is Jacob Aarlberg. I am Belgian. Go, my young friend. Good luck and cheerio, as the old Tommies used to say.'

Tim nodded. He wheeled the bike onto the road and mounted. Jacob thought he could have made things easier for himself by throwing his rifle away. But despite what had happened to him during the dawn attack by the *Luftwaffe*, he had somehow recovered his rifle and tin hat. The instincts of discipline, perhaps, a discipline strengthened by the teachings of his sergeant, who was also his cousin? His rifle was still with him as he pedalled away. He looked back for a second, lifting one hand in a gesture of thanks and goodbye. Jacob returned the gesture. He saw the bike waver for a moment, then it straightened and went steadily on. He would catch up with his comrades now, thought Jacob, and reach the beaches. He was obviously concussed and exhausted, but very enduring. Jacob kept watching until he disappeared.

The silence was almost eerie. It seemed to presage a greater storm, a storm that would engulf Dunkirk and perhaps France as well. He had a feeling that the conquering Germans of today would not be the same as the Boche of 1914–18. Their politics were based on violence as well as arrogance.

The defeat of the British was a sad and bitter thing, and a tragedy for France, which had lost its taste for war because of the carnage of the '14–18 conflict. One could only hope the British would return. He felt they would want to have another go at the Boche. After all, they had lost battles in many wars, but had lost very few wars.

Jacob stood there, behind the gate, listening for what might come next, the sound of German Panzer divisions on the move. Not far away was Belgium, where he'd been born. He lived here now, the joint owner with his French wife of a French farm. Soon it would make no difference whether one lived here or over the border, for the new Boche had found a different way of making war, a way that would result in their occupation of both France and Belgium unless a miracle happened.

What was there to do at the moment except wait

for the arrival of the German tanks and take a look at these formidable fighting machines? His heart was not in farming this morning. But no, the Germans might not resume their advance until tomorrow. It was said that Hitler had given Goering permission to reduce Dunkirk and the British Army to ashes with his *Luftwaffe*, so leaving the Panzers on the sidelines for a few days. All the same, Jacob stayed where he was, although not in any hope of catching sight of a certain British sergeant, who was probably a casualty of that dawn attack from the air.

It was quite some time before he decided he must do the sensible thing and return to his farmhouse, to tell his wife the last of the British troops must now be very close to Dunkirk. However, he did take a final look at the road that had been empty of troops for at least thirty minutes. A lone figure caught his eye. A British soldier. His helmet dangled from its strap in his left hand, and in his right he carried his rifle. His walk was painful but dogged. He lurched after each few steps. He recovered each time. He came on in this unsteady but resolute way. His forehead was bandaged, his dark hair thick and dusty, his uniform torn in places. On each sleeve were the three stripes of a sergeant.

The morning was hot, the sun climbing, the smoke above Dunkirk a malevolent black against the blue of the sky, and Jacob was intensely curious. A sergeant? Could he be the one in question, the cousin of the soldier who had thought of going back to look for him? What was his name now? It had been mentioned. Yes, Sergeant Somers.

Jacob spoke.

'Sergeant Somers?'

Bobby Somers lurched to a stop, pulled himself upright and said, 'That's me. Who's asking?' He saw him then, a brown-faced man behind a gate.

'I am asking, Sergeant, and on behalf of a soldier whose name is Adams,' said Jacob.

'Adams?' Bobby shook his head in an attempt to clear it. 'Tim Adams?'

'Yes.'

'You've seen him, spoken to him?' said Bobby, eyes rimmed and strain showing.

'Yes. He should be close to the Dunkirk beaches by now.'

'Well, thank Christ for some mercies,' said Bobby. The sun and the heat were cooking him, and he was fighting it, and fighting his exhaustion. He was not a sergeant for nothing, he was born for the job, resolute, decisive and with a natural sense of responsibility. Major Carter, officer commanding his battery, had marked him down as officer material. At the moment, however, Bobby felt on close terms with a sack that had had all the stuffing knocked out of it. Keeping on his feet was an effort of willpower. When the Stuka dive-bomber had struck the column at dawn and bombs rained down, his tin hat jerked free, something struck his temple and he had known nothing more until he came to. He was lying on the verge, two dead men close by, men left for the Germans to see to. His field dressing, held in place by a bandage, tightly clasped his wounded head. He guessed a medical orderly had dressed the wound, but had been unable to arouse him. So he had been left too, perhaps because he was considered to be on his way out. That was how it had to be when most transport had been destroyed and the remaining vehicles used to carry casualties to Dunkirk overnight. Dead or dying men had to be left. Well, he didn't intend to wait for German medical assistance. He made the greatest physical effort of his life. With his head thumping and his limbs feeling tortured, he climbed to his feet, retrieved his rifle and helmet, and began walking in the direction of Dunkirk. In an atmosphere of brooding quiet, he left the scene of minor devastation, passing dead men on the way. He experienced the kind of strain that continually drained him, but he kept going by gritting his teeth, talking to himself, thinking of home and of a compulsive need to get there along with Jonathan, Tim, and Tim's father, Uncle Boots – wherever he was.

Bobby shook his head again, trying to make sense of this sudden appearance of a man who looked like a farmer and had spoken of cousin Tim.

Jacob regarded him compassionately. His bandage was stained and grimy, the dressing thick. His face, firm-fleshed over strong bone, and tanned from many weeks of sunshine, was touched by the grey of extreme exhaustion.

'Sergeant—'

'Sorry – can't stop – must get on – must catch up with cousin Tim.'

'Sergeant—' Jacob was again interrupted, this

time by an invasion of thunder. The peaceful sky seemed to burst with the noise. A flight of Messerschmitts, heading towards Dunkirk, broke formation as Hurricanes of the RAF came out of the sky above them and screamed downwards. It was one more final gesture of the RAF Fighter Command to protect men still on the beaches. Exhaust trails streamed across the blue, and the aerial fight was on. It did not take place in any fixed area. The German and British machines used the limitless sky in flight and pursuit. A plane fell out of the azure blue, smoke pouring from its fuselage, and plunged to destruction near Ypres. For a few minutes only, Jacob and Bobby stood listening, faces turned upwards, and the thunder rolled away as planes chased planes north, south, east and west.

'I'm—' Bobby found it an effort to dredge up words. 'I'm not the only one having a bad day. They're shooting each other to pieces up there. Must get on,' he said again.

Jacob stiffened as his ears picked up new sounds.

'I think not, Sergeant Somers,' he said quietly. 'Listen.'

Bobby, swaying, stopped trying to move forward. He listened. The sounds were of motorcycles, slowly powering along the road some way behind him, the machines, probably, of German scouts, sent forward to reconnoitre and report on the Dunkirk defensive perimeter manned by British and French troops.

'Christ, that's done it,' he said.

'Quickly,' said Jacob, and opened the gate. He

came through, and took Bobby by the arm. 'Quickly, Sergeant, for the sake of your cousin, your comrade. And for yourself.'

Bobby, instinct for survival surfacing, made his effort. He jerked forward, Jacob assisting him and getting him through the open gate as the noise of the motorcycles became a steady roar. The farmer slammed the gate shut, then he and Bobby plunged down on their stomachs behind the stone-based hedge. The motorcyclists arrived, moving at no more than ten miles an hour like cautious foragers, some machines with occupied sidecars attached. Jacob and Bobby lay still and silent. The machines passed the gate. When their engine noises faded, Jacob lifted his head to listen for other warning sounds. He heard nothing.

'Sod it,' breathed Bobby, 'they've caught me up and passed me. That's made my day, I don't think.'

'Then one more effort, Sergeant, to my farmhouse?' said Jacob. 'Their tanks and infantry may be on the move. You can rest while you consider your situation.' He did not think this man capable, in any case, of getting to Dunkirk in his present condition.

Bobby gritted his teeth and climbed painfully to his feet, and Jacob rose with him. He took Bobby's tin hat and rifle, and led the way. It was 150 metres to the farmhouse, and he kept close to the hedge that fronted the road. If the road was quiet again, there was no telling what or who might next appear. He reached another hedge, one that divided this fallow field from a second.

Bobby, wounded head thumping, followed. Jacob took him through another gate, then turned left towards the farmhouse, using the dividing hedge as a further screen. Bobby, soldiering on, continued to follow. His aching feet felt like lumps of hot dough in his boots, his legs protesting fretfully at what was being asked of them, and his head felt worse. But he refused to fall over. Jacob, moving with sympathetic slowness, turned his head.

'You are managing?' he asked.

'Carry on,' said Bobby, husky from a dry throat.

Jacob carried on, and Bobby followed on. Images danced in his mind, images of home and family that alternated with images of the awesome concentrations of German armour.

From the farmhouse, eyes watched the approach of the two men. Jacob chose to bring Bobby over a rutted path to the side of the forecourt. The rear of the house could be seen by any of his workers who happened to have it in view. As he led Bobby to the front door, it opened. They entered a large tiled hall, Bobby unsteady on his feet. The door closed and a woman spoke.

'Jacob, what are you doing, bringing a soldier here?' asked Madame Estelle Aarlberg, a well-preserved and full-bosomed woman of forty-three, with smooth black hair parted down the middle. Her brown eyes were gently critical.

'I know what I've done,' said Jacob ruefully. 'I'm not sure I know what to do next.'

'How silly you are,' she said. They were speaking French, assuming it was unknown to this British soldier. 'Aren't things bad enough?' She was not accusing, merely reproving. Jacob was a good man, an estimable husband and a fine farmer. She had married him early in 1916, when she was nineteen, he a handsome young Belgian officer on leave in France. She inherited the farm on the death of her father when she was twenty-one and Jacob was still with the Belgian Army under the command of King Albert. After the war, she had deeds drawn up that made her and Jacob joint owners. A good wife could not have done less for a kind-natured husband who had been a valiant soldier. His own home near Ypres had been obliterated during the Great War. The compensation he subsequently received he invested in the farm by acquiring more land. 'Look at the dreadful trouble France is in,' she said, 'and now the trouble we are in. The Boche will be at our door tomorrow.'

'Tomorrow or soon after,' agreed Jacob. 'But this English sergeant has marched through the night and by himself most of the morning. He's wounded, and if I hadn't brought him here, German motorcyclists would have caught him. Their armoured divisions must be on the move.'

'I can hear them,' said Madame Aarlberg. 'The house can hear them. The farm can hear them. All France can hear them.'

In fact, everything was strangely quiet at the moment, but Jacob knew precisely what she meant.

'Well, a cognac and a chair for the sergeant shouldn't mean any extra trouble for us,' said Jacob. 'He's close to collapse.'

Madame Aarlberg glanced at Bobby, her expression not unsympathetic. He was holding himself up as resolutely as he could, but his exhaustion was as obvious as the significance of his bandage.

'Yes, I see he is,' she said.

The conversation had, for the most part, penetrated the cotton-wool barrier to Bobby's brain. His school French had profited from the fact that his father, his Uncle Boots, his cousins Rosie and Eloise, and his step-grandfather, Edwin Finch, all spoke the language excellently. And his time in France had perfected it.

In French, he said, with a mental effort, 'Madame, you can believe me, once my legs are working again, I'll be on my way.'

At his fluent use of her language, Madame Aarlberg gave him a longer look.

'A rest, then, and a cognac,' she said, and led the way to the living-room. It was square and expansive, and to Bobby's heavy eyes it looked as if it had been invaded by a prodigious army of furniture. It crowded the room in Victorian fashion. There were armchairs, uprights, sofas, pot plants, cabinets, bookcases, a piano, a large round mahogany table covered by a fringed velvet overlay, and a huge log container of iron by the stone hearth of an enormous fireplace. A hand gently pressed his shoulder, and for all his sense of inner urgency, he sank gratefully into an armchair. He accepted its comfort and stretched his suffering legs.

'Thanks,' he said.

A balloon glass appeared in front of him.

39

'Cognac,' said Jacob.

'Thanks, good as a port in a storm,' murmured Bobby, and took the glass. He drank the fiery spirit in two mouthfuls. It rushed burningly into his system and spread its reviving factor through his tired body. A hand took the empty glass from him, and he heard voices whispering, 'Give me ten minutes or so,' he said, 'then I'll be off.'

Jacob turned to him and said, 'Will you be able to, Sergeant?'

'Have to. Got to.' Another mental effort. 'Could you point me to a route that would keep me off the road? Anything. A path, a lane, anything. Dunkirk's not all that far, is it?'

'Nearly seven kilometres and too far for you, I think, in your present condition,' said Jacob. 'There is a way over fields and through woods, but that is even longer. I regret the German motor-cyclists have cut you off from the direct road route, so I must ask you, would you consider giving yourself up?'

Bobby blinked heavy lids.

'The answer's no,' he said. 'I'm not cut out for digging ditches as a prisoner of war. I'll risk finding a way as soon as my legs have straightened out. What do I do, keep going over fields towards the smoke? That's Dunkirk, isn't it, the smoke?'

'Frankly, Sergeant, I don't think you'll get very far, not as you are at present,' said Jacob, his wife hovering. 'The cognac was to revive you a little, not to make you believe you're fit enough to escape the Germans. You need rest. Give yourself until this

40

evening at least. You are welcome to stay here until then. I'm sure your cousin, if he knew you were here, would advise you not to risk capture because of your condition. He would have taken the risk himself of going back to find you, but I persuaded him to go on to Dunkirk.'

'Glad you did.' Bobby lapsed into English. 'That was his job, to get to Dunkirk, not to muck about with percentage factors. I'll let him know that when I catch up with him.'

Jacob let a faint smile show. Madame Aarlberg, whose English was limited, supposed that something amusing had been said, which was surprising under the circumstances. Her husband spoke again.

'I am Jacob Aarlberg, and this good lady is my wife,' he said.

'Pleasure,' said Bobby. 'Name's Somers, Bobby Somers.'

Madame Aarlberg looked at him with new eyes, seeing him now not simply as a problem, but as a wounded and exhausted soldier who was trying to drag up a smile, and who had a fine firm mouth and very fine shoulders. His brown eyes were direct and frank, although surrounded by the dusty blue shadows of extreme fatigue.

'It is some help to us that you speak French and can understand our worries,' she said. 'I have agreed with my husband that you can rest here for a while. You are not fit enough to leave yet.'

'Oh, I could be worse,' said Bobby, his weakness a frustration to a man of his character. He was

41

twenty, but he did, of course, look older at the moment. The shattering nature of the Nazi blitzkreig had put years on him. He was the same age as Boots had been just prior to the first battle of the Somme. Boots too had looked older then. 'Are you sure that if I do stay for an hour or so, it won't mean trouble for you?'

'The Boche won't trouble too much with civilians until they've taken Dunkirk,' said Jacob. 'You are safe here for today, I'm certain. They will come here eventually, yes, and write down the names of everyone. They're always very thorough about names. But perhaps their main army might not commence its final move until tomorrow, perhaps their motorcyclists are already on their way back.'

'We've been fighting a forward formation,' said Bobby, the effects of the cognac already giving way to an overwhelming need to simply fall asleep. Along with the other rearguard men, he had slept very little during the last few days. Everyone had expected the Germans to launch a whole army group at them.

The main thrust of that force, commanded by General Rommel, had been halted some days previously by a small formation of British Matilda tanks which counter-attacked and completely destroyed a German Panzer unit close to Arras. The Germans had lost all of thirty tanks, and Rommel, quite shaken by this reverse, insisted on regrouping before resuming the offensive. The action, which was totally in keeping with Sir Henry Simms's concept of how the British should have used their armour, had been an isolated one. But it saved the BEF from being cut off in its attempt to reach an escape port, and allowed Goering to ask for permission to finish the British off by use of the *Luftwaffe*.

'Let us hope the road will open up again for you,' said Jacob.

'I'd like to think it will,' said Bobby, eyelids now as heavy as lead.

'French troops west of it are still helping to keep Dunkirk open,' said Jacob. 'Perhaps that will mean you might still have another day, perhaps you will still have tomorrow. I think my wife and I will be happy to have you stay until then.' He looked up as the door opened and a young woman came in. Her dark hair was tinted with auburn. There were similar tints in Jacob's hair. She was pleasant-looking, and might have been more so with make-up. Her complexion was healthy, her skin tanned. Her most attractive features were her dark blue eyes and her long sooty Latin lashes. She had a good body, and gave the impression, when she was working, that she was as physically vigorous as a man.

She stared at Bobby, at his uniform and his bandaged forehead, and she took note of the rifle and steel helmet Jacob had placed on a sofa. Her face stiffened. Helene Aarlberg was extremely French, extremely frank and currently very angry. Her anger was mainly directed at the inept British Expeditionary Force that was running away.

'What is this man doing here?' she demanded.

43

'Resting,' said Jacob.

'Do you mean skulking?' asked Helene.

'No, I don't mean that,' said Jacob, 'I mean resting.'

'I see.' Helene was not in the least impressed. 'And when he's rested, he'll go and run with all the others?'

'Helene, they have fought all the way,' said Jacob.

'But they are running, all of them,' said Helene. 'Why has this one stopped? Because he wore himself out running too fast?'

Bobby made himself heard.

'No, because the Germans got in front of me,' he said. That, although delivered in lucid if husky French, did nothing to mollify Helene. She looked, in fact, as if she resented his command of the language.

'I am sorry, but we do not want you here.'

'Helene, that is not the way to speak,' said Madame Aarlberg.

'He should not be here,' said Helene.

'You will excuse us a moment, please, Sergeant Somers?' said Jacob.

Bobby nodded. The little movement made him realize his head was on fire. He was left to think about the complications of his situation as Jacob took his sympathetic wife and simmering daughter out of the room to the nearby kitchen.

Chapter Four

From the Ypres road and the Bergues road, the last columns of British troops, together with some French and Belgian men, converged on Dunkirk. They met and mingled on the approach to the beaches of the devastated port. The smells of war were still pungent here, fires burning in the port area, smoke rising in every area.

Jonathan had stepped out of line, escaping the weary eye of a lieutenant in charge of twenty men of his battery. Ahead, the still trudging soldiers were being marshalled into something approaching good order. Here, Jonathan stood waiting. He felt he had to wait, that he could not go forward to join a beach file until Bobby and Tim caught up with him. He could hardly believe his luck when Tim actually appeared only a short while after he had stepped out of the moving column. He looked as much of a mess as anyone else, and he was limping and lurching. But he gave a little yell as he saw Jonathan. He fell out, and Jonathan slapped his shoulder in greeting.

'You bugger,' said Jonathan, 'you've been hiding.'

'Riding a bike, if you must know,' said Tim, 'and

it's crippled me. Listen, have you seen Bobby?'

'Not a sign of him, not a—'

'Get into line, you two men!' shouted a sergeant-major.

Tim and Jonathan stepped into line and moved slowly forward, with Tim recounting the air attack that knocked him out, and the fact that he remembered nothing until he came to and found himself footslogging. Where Bobby was and what had happened to him, he had no idea.

'Jesus,' breathed Jonathan, 'how the hell do we go back without him?'

'I'm hoping he got in front of us,' said Tim. 'I'm laying money on his single-mindedness. His one idea since we were ordered to make for Dunkirk has been to get home and start all over again. And he doesn't let go of ideas like that very easily. Then there's my father. Where the hell is he, I wonder? Back home by now, or what?'

Boots was actually close to the beach, still in company with Sir Henry, the staff car an expired piece of old iron half a mile back on the road. Boots was wondering about Tim and Bobby, and about Jonathan too. He was wondering if they'd been evacuated or not. Today was the last day of an operation that represented both a miracle and a disaster.

The *Luftwaffe* put in another appearance then. A stream of fighter planes hurtled in to strafe the streets, the beaches, the scattering troops and the suffering sea, on which rescuing craft danced and warships blazed away at Goering's marauders.

Ramsgate

The big ships and little ships were still running the gauntlet, despite all that the Germans were throwing at them from the skies. Many of the little ships had been making repeated rescue sallies, picking men out of the shallower waters, taking them to home ports, then turning round and going back for more.

Skippers reported that there always seemed to be more, despite the many thousands already safely landed. Prime Minister Churchill, of course, wanted every man brought home before a new onslaught by the Germans closed Dunkirk down. The weather was superb, the skies an incredibly clear blue, and if such conditions were an immense help to the little ships, so they were to the *Luftwaffe*.

The fine Victorian seaside resort of Ramsgate on the coast of Kent had been a favourite with cockney holidaymakers for years. Its cockles and whelks rivalled those of Margate and Southend. Now its harbour was a scene of hustle, bustle and urgency. From there had sailed Ramsgate's own small armada of little ships in the fight to save the British Expeditionary Force. And, like other small armadas elsewhere, they were still coming and going. Into the harbour they came, crammed with as many men as each craft could safely hold. Here, the human cargoes were unloaded, to be received by official and volunteer personnel detailed to welcome them, revive them and to send them home on leave until they were recalled to their units.

These were the men who knew now just how

formidable was Hitler's war machine. They were tired to death, as their fathers had been on the long fighting retreat from Mons to the Marne in 1914. But their fathers had turned at the Marne and driven the German hordes back, earning themselves fame as the imperishable Old Contemptibles. For the men of Dunkirk, however, there was only the sea in front of them and the unstoppable German military might at their backs. So they had to be taken off the beaches, beaten, bitter and disillusioned.

Coming ashore at Ramsgate in their scores, their gratitude to the men of the little ships was evident, and many were able to smile and wave at cheering people all round the harbour. But the smiles hid their true feelings. What they thought of the way they had been asked to fight was unprintable. Long before the German onslaught began on France and the Low Countries, they had been ordered to dig trenches, as if it was to be the same kind of warfare as in '14–18, for God's sake. The Dunkirk soldiers wanted War Office heads to roll. What a hope. War Office heads never rolled.

Personnel from the Red Cross, the police, St John Ambulance Brigade and the Army were hard at work around the harbour. Cigarettes, mugs of tea, a variety of sandwiches and essential instructions were given out, and ambulances were on hand to take any wounded men aboard. An ATS unit was providing sterling help, as on previous days. The girls felt for the bitter and defeated men. They knew the defeat was more than that. It was a

48

disaster. The old sweats among the survivors were particularly bitter, and it showed. The ATS girls did all they could to cheer them up. One or two even offered to meet particular men under a Ramsgate street lamp that night.

'Nice of yer, girl, but I couldn't make it, not on these legs, and even if I could, what could I do for yer that a naughty Boy Scout couldn't do better?'

'All right, soldier, leave it till Christmas, then.'

Private Eloise Adams, a very competent young lady of twenty-three, with a dash of French *élan* about her, regarded the evacuation as splendid and heroic. Her one worry was about her father and her half-brother Tim. They were still not home, according to a phone call she had been able to make from the public phone box just outside the ATS training camp before the company left for Ramsgate. Today, they would land today, she told herself. Her father, having survived the other war, would never let this one beat him. Nor would he allow Tim to fall into German hands. Somehow, they would have found each other and probably be in Dunkirk now, together. Perhaps they would even land in Ramsgate. Eloise buoyed herself up with hope and optimism.

An officer appeared among new arrivals, an artillery captain. Eloise, casting a glance, thought him the grimmest of all the officers she had seen during these last few days. His head was bare, his battledress filthy, his face grimy and his right eye heavily bandaged. A Red Cross worker approached him, and spoke to him about getting him to Officers' Reception and then to an ambulance.

'Bugger the ambulance,' he said. The Red Cross lady, understanding and tactful, spoke to him again. He took no notice. He caught sight of an attractive ATS private, a young woman who looked bright and vital. She had just given a mug of tea, a sandwich and a cigarette to a limping soldier. The officer liked the look of her and the fact that she wasn't a mere girl. He waved Red Cross assistance aside. 'Not now, not now,' he said, and advanced on Eloise. He took her by the arm. 'You'll do,' he said. 'At least, I hope you will. Find me a place where I can use a phone, and then get me a whisky.'

Eloise looked at him, at his stained bandage and his grimy, rugged face. His sound eye held a threatening glint.

'Sir, you have to report to your reception, but you can have hot tea first,' she said. There was a French lilt to her English.

'Christ,' he growled, 'you don't think the bloody Jerries are drinking hot tea, do you? They're fighting a war, we're playing tin soldiers. Where's a phone? I need to spit into an ear or two before the military bureaucrats here get their hands on me and tie me up in red tape.'

'Yes, sir,' said Eloise, and felt instinctively responsive to his kind of fighting talk. 'I'll see what—'

'Excuse me.' Bossy Lieutenant Raleigh pushed in. 'Excuse me, sir, but Private Adams has very specific duties. If you'll come with me—'

'I don't want tea and biscuits, Lieutenant,' said

the rugged and aggressive artillery captain. He correctly read her as an earnest junior officer who would always go by the book. 'I've had some of that, and it doesn't work, except in a vicarage. Go and look after some of my men there. I'll take charge of Private Adams. I'm Captain Lucas, 23rd Heavy Field Artillery. I'll report to reception in a few minutes.'

'Captain Lucas, we must keep to procedure.' Lieutenant Raleigh looked around in search of a senior male officer from reception. 'We have to see—'

'You keep to procedure, I'll keep to what's necessary,' said Captain Lucas, his left eye bloodshot. It glinted redly. 'My immediate responsibility is with the War Office. That's confidential, by the way. Come on, Private Adams.' He took Eloise by the arm again and walked away with her, steering her clear of soldiers and bustling helpers.

'I'm not sure, sir, if I'm going to be allowed to get away with this,' said Eloise, her English fluent and easy.

'Don't pussyfoot about, Private Adams,' said Captain Lucas, 'or I'll chuck you into the harbour.'

'Pardon?' Eloise was taken aback. Men friends admired her and exhibited very good manners. She was not used to being spoken to as if she was an ordinary young lady. She was not ordinary. She was enchanting, even in an ATS private's uniform. Her latest admirer, a desk officer in the Ministry of Defence, swore she was the most enchanting of all young ladies. And her stepmother had lately said it

51

was a wonder she wasn't already married to a lord. Of course, she wasn't going to marry anyone until she was in love, as much in love as her late lamented mother had been with her father. 'Sir, I refuse to be thrown into the harbour.'

'Quite right,' said Captain Lucas. 'Now, where's a private phone?' He was intent on delivering some home truths before military protocol took hold of him, lectured him on the necessity of keeping his mouth shut, and then placed him back in his appointed slot.

Eloise decided that the spirit of the occasion called for a procedure-breaking response.

'There's a phone in an office at the back of the harbourmaster's building, sir,' she said. 'But, of course, it's out of bounds, you understand.'

'Well, let's not give a damn about that. Lead the way, Private Adams.'

'Yes, sir,' said Eloise. He might look a battered hulk of a man, and he might not have quite the nice manners of some men, but he was the most determined soldier who had landed at Ramsgate. She felt very responsive to that. Because she had become devoted to her English family, she was very patriotic, and the bringing home of so many British and Allied soldiers from Dunkirk exhilarated her. No, she was not going to protest about Captain Lucas's aggressive defiance of procedures.

She veered in her walk until she and the grimy captain were well clear of the ruck around the harbour. She led him to the rear of a building and to a short flight of wooden steps. No-one shouted at them, no-one bawled for them to come back. Everybody had too much to do, thank goodness. She went up the steps, Captain Lucas beside her. A door confronted them. He opened it, although a notice said, 'Strictly Private'.

'There's a phone in here?' he asked.

'Yes, sir,' said Eloise. He stepped in. 'Now I must go back,' she said.

'Not on your life you won't, not yet,' he said. 'Come in.'

She followed him in and closed the door, standing with her back to it. She was not naturally designed for military life, but she looked smartly on guard. A little grin touched Captain Lucas's hard mouth. He crossed to a desk. That, with a chair, a phone and shelves of files, was all the office contained. He sat on the edge of the desk and picked up the phone. Eloise saw that his brown boots and battledress trousers were sea-stained, and she guessed that like so many other men he had waded out up to his hips from a beach.

He dialled and waited. He spoke.

'Hello? George? Lucas here, Bill Lucas. Yes, it's me. No, it wasn't luck, it was a bloody miracle on top of an almighty cock-up. Just landed. Now listen – no, hold on a moment.' He turned his bloodshot eye on Eloise. 'Where's that Scotch you promised me?'

Eloise had promised nothing of the kind, but she didn't argue, she was beginning to like the atmosphere he was creating. He was shockingly filthy, yes, and not at all what one would call handsome, but he had the kind of dash to appeal to the French side of her nature.

'Oh, the whisky?' she said, and thought of the pub that was close to the harbour. 'I'll try, sir.'

'Knew you would,' he said, 'you've got the look of a trier. Hop off, then.' Eloise, opening the door, heard him speak into the phone again. 'Listen, I want to see your number one. What? Yes, him, for Christ's sake.'

Eloise slipped out, closed the door, looked around and descended the steps. Supple, she began to run. An ATS sergeant called to her as she emerged from the shelter of the building, but she affected not to hear. She ran on. Silent laughter ran with her. So, Eloise Adams, you look like a trier and have been told to hop off. Shall I tell him my father is a major on the staff of a general? No, I think that would not impress him at all. I think from what I heard him say on the phone that he knows certain important people and means to make their ears ring. He is disgusted and angry with the Army's defeat.

Approaching the pub, she halted. Two military policemen, sergeants in red caps, were coming out of the place. Eloise knew what they were about, they were checking the town and the pubs for soldiers who might have managed to dodge reception in favour of getting drunk as soon as they landed. Some were in that kind of mood, but of course the Army authorities had to note down the details of every man who landed, British or Allied. She herself was disobeying the special duty rules and regulations at the moment.

The two Redcaps glanced at her, then walked away. She entered the pub. It was crowded with all kinds. The soldiers there were obviously men who'd checked in officially and were now treating themselves to English beer before going home on special leave. Some newspaper reporters were also present, taking in their own kind of liquid refreshment while talking to the soldiers.

Eloise had to push her way through to the bar, where the proprietor himself gave her his attention, noting her uniform, the smartness of her peaked cap and her bright, engaging smile. She let him know she wanted some whisky for a wounded officer who had just come ashore. In a glass? To be taken off the premises? A bit tricky, said the proprietor, and illegal as well. But liking her and liking, too, the sound of a wounded officer sitting up and asking for a Scotch, he suggested selling her a half-bottle from his little off-licence, otherwise known as the Jug-and-Bottle. And at a special price. Five bob only to the Dunkirk gent. Eloise thought a half-bottle much more practical than a glass, and said she could carry that very easily.

'Well, bless you, young lady, go round to me Jug-and-Bottle, then,' said the proprietor, and Eloise went. He served her himself, with a half-bottle of Johnny Walker Red Label. She put it in her shoulder bag, and handed over five shillings.

'Thank you, I am very obliged,' she said.

'You English?' he asked.

'Of course,' said Eloise proudly. 'Also French,' she said, as she left.

She walked fast, keeping clear of the milling reception areas, and watching out for Subaltern Raleigh. She ran when it was safe to. Reaching the rear of the harbourmaster's building, she ran up the wooden steps and entered the strictly private office, empty except for Captain Lucas. He was still on the phone, but she thought he was speaking to someone else now.

'A triumph? Bloody rubbish. Not for the Army, not for you and not for any bugger in Whitehall. Just for the Navy and the little ships – hello, you're back, are you, Private Adams? Thought you'd gone home. Don't go away – no, not you, Gus. Here's one final message for you to pass on. I've got NCO's and gunners ready to blow up the War Office, the Houses of Parliament and Buckingham Palace as well, once they've got their legs in working order again. Got that? Right. I'll be on my way shortly. Get the gates open. Right, and sod you too, old man.' Captain Lucas put the phone down and looked at Eloise. She had the bottle of whisky in her hand. 'What the hell's that?' he asked, bloodshot eye glinting again.

'It's a half-bottle of Scotch, sir.'

'That's a fact? The genuine stuff?'

'Yes, of course, sir,' said Eloise. 'I thought a bottle would be easier to bring than a glass.'

Captain Lucas gave her a look of distinct approval.

'Thought I was right, thought you looked a

winner,' he said. 'Well done. Care to hand it over?' Eloise gave him the bottle. He broke the red wax seal and pulled the capped cork. He put the bottle to his mouth and swallowed a good measure. Then a second. 'Private Adams, I'm obliged. What's your full name?'

'Eloise Cecile Adams.'

'Come again?' said Captain Lucas, thick bandage as grubby as he was. 'Did you say Eloise Cecile?'

'My mother was French, sir.'

'I see. That accounts for it, I suppose.'

'For what, sir?'

'The way you speak and your commonsense,' said Captain Lucas. 'They're a practical people, the French.'

Eloise did not think much of that. It was not her idea of a compliment.

'If you say so, sir,' she said.

'Well, let me tell you, Eloise Cecile Adams, you're a great improvement on a large number of people.' Captain Lucas sat down in the chair, the bottle still in his hand, his eye quizzing her. In her cap and uniform, worn with natural flair, she looked both smart and engaging. 'Why are you only a private?' he asked.

'I'm still at a training camp,' said Eloise, who thought she ought to go. 'Sir, I think you should have your eye seen to.'

'It's been seen to. It's just a gashed eyebrow. A bit bloody, but nothing to worry about.'

'But you should have a fresh dressing,' said Eloise.

'Stop fussing.'

'Sir, I do not have the fault of being fussy,' said Eloise, 'and I must go now.'

'Stay where you are,' growled Captain Lucas.

'Are you an important officer, sir?' asked Eloise.

'What you're looking at, Private Adams, is a bit of a wreck,' said Captain Lucas. 'Aside from that, I'm a bloke with three pips, acquired because I'm a regular Army man and a bit pushy. Because I'm pushy, I've got to know a few people, including those I've just been talking to. Pushy isn't the same as being important.'

The door opened then, and a man in a blue uniform appeared, a harbour official. Eloise put herself in his way.

'I am sorry,' she said, 'but you can't come in. Captain Lucas is waiting for the War Office to phone him.'

'Eh?' said the official.

'Yes, so sorry if it's your office,' said Eloise, 'but Captain Lucas has important connections. Please come back later.'

The official looked at Captain Lucas, who gave a brusque nod.

'Right, see what you mean,' said the official, all in favour of a Dunkirk man giving the War Office brasshats something they needed to hear. He left, and Eloise closed the door again while wondering if she was going to be severely dressed down by Lieutenant Raleigh when she finally returned to her duties.

'You're a bright young lady, damned if you're

not,' said Captain Lucas, and suddenly looked tired. Eloise regarded him with sympathy. The girls had a feeling for all these beaten men. They had quickly found out that although many of them responded cheerfully to the welcome given them on landing, they didn't like knowing how resoundingly they'd been defeated. Eloise suspected Captain Lucas positively hated it. He was about thirty, she thought, with a strong mouth, firm cheekbones and a determined jaw. 'How long have you been in the ATS?' he asked, stirring himself.

'I'm into my fourth month,' said Eloise, and thought of something then. 'Captain Lucas, would you know my father, Major Adams?'

'Major Adams? What regiment?'

'He's on the staff of General Sir Henry Simms, sir.'

'Is he, by God. That's a prize job. But no, I don't know him. Why'd you ask?'

'He hasn't arrived home yet,' said Eloise.

'He will, Private Adams, he will,' said Captain Lucas. 'There's no way General Sir Henry Simms is going to allow the Jerries to put himself and his staff in the bag.'

'In the bag?' said Eloise.

'Taken prisoner,' said Captain Lucas. 'They'll be landed somewhere today, so keep smiling.' He grimaced then, and Eloise suspected his wound was paining him.

'Sir, you really should report your arrival,' she said.

'Later,' he said. For all his aggression, his

tiredness was showing, and Eloise experienced a little tug at her sympathetic heartstrings. He swallowed another mouthful of whisky. 'What're you being trained for, Private Adams?'

'Admin duties,' said Eloise, thinking that if she didn't go soon, Lieutenant Raleigh would charge her with desertion of her post.

'Admin duties? Is that a fact? Good. Have you got a pencil and a piece of paper?'

'There's a notepad and some pencils on the desk, sir,' said Eloise.

'Missed 'em, did I?' Captain Lucas grimaced again. 'Can't see for looking, can I? Damn being one-eyed. Well, there we are, Private Adams.' He pushed the pad across the desk. 'Help yourself to a pencil.'

'To write down a message?' enquired Eloise.

'Information,' he said. He was very direct. 'I've just phoned all the messages I care about at the moment. Write down your name, number and unit. You're going to be posted.'

'Posted?' said Eloise. 'But, sir, our Commandant hasn't—'

'Don't argue, Private Adams. My regiment is going to be reorganized, retrained, and have its guts put back into it after it's been made up to full strength again. We'll need ATS personnel in admin. You'll be one of them. You're competent, aren't you?'

'Yes, sir, I am,' said Eloise, 'but—'

'You'd better be competent,' said Captain Lucas, 'I'm up to my ruddy eyebrows with incompetence.

Private Adams, they licked us all ends up, they blew us apart and shot us to pieces because we thought we were going to fight another trench war, a defensive one, by God. We let them come at us when we should have gone at them while they were still putting themselves to right after their Polish campaign. Write down your details. Or don't you want to be posted to guns? Take care how you answer that.'

Eloise knew nothing about artillery. She did know that some ATS units were being trained to serve with ack-ack batteries, but that her own unit specialized in turning out administrative personnel. She had nearly finished her training. However, ignorant of artillery or not, she was sure Captain Lucas was a man of action, and she felt a sudden willingness to go along with his wishes. She used a pencil to write down her number, rank, name, unit and the unit's address.

'Will that do, sir?' Eloise had accepted the rules that required her to address male officers as sir, although she was quite unused to feeling second best to any man. She was used to feeling the other way about. It amused her father, who asked her once if it was a requirement in her men friends to acknowledge they were second best. No, she said, only to acknowledge they are not as fascinating as I am. Boots laughed, so she laughed too. 'Those are my details, Captain Lucas.'

'They'll do,' said Captain Lucas, 'so will you, Private Adams. Well, I think you will. God help you if I'm wrong. How much was the whisky?'

'Because of Dunkirk, I don't need payment,' said Eloise.

'Good of you, but it's up to me,' said Captain Lucas, who knew pay for an ATS trainee was pretty puerile. 'But I'll have to owe you unless you'd like soggy Belgian francs. No, that's not a good idea, is it? Write down that I owe you a quid.'

'But it was only five shillings, sir.'

'Worth a quid at least,' said Captain Lucas, and made a note himself on the pad. Ripping off the top sheet, he folded it and put it into his pocket. His sound but bloodshot eye quizzed her again. Eloise did not lose her poise, nor her confidence in her looks. Her dark brown hair, rolled at the nape of her neck, was healthily glossy, her grey eyes showing a hint of blue, her fine features classically oval. He saw how self-assured she was in the way she held herself, straight of spine, her khaki jacket trimly buttoned. It did not, however, disguise the excellent figure beneath. The little grin touched Captain Lucas's firm mouth again.

'Sir?' said Eloise, slightly aloof.

'Time to go,' said Captain Lucas, and shook himself out of oncoming torpor. He came to his feet, put the cork back into the whisky bottle and slipped the bottle inside his battledress.

'Yes, it is time for me, sir,' said Eloise, 'if I'm not to be charged and given seven days CB.'

'Can't have that, Private Adams, can we? Not after all your help. Come on.' He followed her out. 'If you can find me a sandwich, I'll demolish it and then report.'

Eloise led the way back to reception, which was still bustling and busy, men still being landed. The noise was a minor uproar, the excited people of Ramsgate unable to divorce themselves from the spectacle. Outside the roped-off area of disembarkation, they raised their voices in demonstrative welcome. Eloise made for the table that contained huge platefuls of sandwiches. A voluntary organization worker, a woman, smiled at her. Eloise picked up two sandwiches. A voice called sharply to her.

'Private Adams! A word with you!'

Eloise made a face. Lieutenant Raleigh was on the warpath. Arriving, she placed herself in front of Eloise.

'Yes, ma'am?' said Eloise, who disliked playing second fiddle to women even more than she disliked being made to feel second best to men.

'What are you doing, where have you been all this time?' demanded Lieutenant Raleigh.

Such a silly woman, thought Eloise. Didn't she have any sense of occasion? Even a backward peasant would know history was being made, yes, even here in little Ramsgate. Imagine anyone being so dull-witted as to get worked up about what an ATS private was doing on a day like this.

'I'm providing Captain Lucas with sandwiches, ma'am. He's been in telephone conference with the War Office, and it's made him hungry.'

'The War Office?' said Lieutenant Raleigh, put slightly off-balance. 'He's been speaking to the War Office?'

'I think he has important connections,' said

Eloise. She had no real idea what they were or to whom he'd spoken. 'He told me to make sure he wasn't disturbed. I thought you'd approve I should do that, ma'am.'

'Approve?' Lieutenant Raleigh was rapidly losing ground. 'Yes, I see, but there are rules to observe, you know.'

At that point, Captain Lucas materialized. Nothing about his grimy and rugged appearance had changed. He still looked like a man who wanted to quarrel with the Chief of the Imperial General Staff on behalf of the routed Army. However, on the fringe of organized hustle and bustle, he addressed Lieutenant Raleigh mildly.

'I'm obliged, Lieutenant, for your co-operation in allowing Private Adams to assist me,' he said. 'A credit to you. And the ATS. Can't speak too highly of her, damned if I can. Private Adams, many thanks. And for these as well.' He took the sandwiches from Eloise. 'Goodbye. Goodbye, Lieutenant.' He left, going towards Officers' Reception, tucking into a sandwich on the way.

Lieutenant Raleigh, now all at sea, said, 'Well, I – oh, very well, Private Adams, I must excuse your long absence, I suppose.'

'Thank you, ma'am,' said Eloise.

'What was it he said to the War Office?'

'Mostly swear words,' said Eloise.

'Pardon?'

'And very loud ones, and some in terrible French, I think,' said Eloise, 'so I stopped listening.'

'Don't be ridiculous, Private Adams. Return to your duties.'

Eloise did so. The atmosphere was still of an exhilarating kind, the success of the prolonged evacuation giving the people of Ramsgate a chance to behave as if disastrous defeat had been turned into a famous victory. Eloise thought that perhaps in time to come it could and would be seen as such. However, despite the continuing excitement of deliverance, she felt just a little flat. She had not met many men like Captain Lucas. In fact, she had not met any. He was hardly a young lady's idea of D'Artagnan, of course, but he was a very masculine and invigorating man. One could not ignore that he seemed to project vibrations. Would he really arrange for her to be posted to his regiment? Would it matter if he didn't?

For some reason, Eloise felt it would matter, and that it would be mortifying if he actually forgot.

A small fishing boat sailed in to disgorge more men, and she was delighted to see a few French soldiers among them, soldiers who had decided to carry on the fight from England rather than give themselves up. The crowds gave them an extra cheer, and they took off their helmets and waved them.

She thought again about her father and Tim. As soon as she was given a little time off, she must phone home. Perhaps they were there now. The morning was fast falling away from the day, the day that everyone was saying would be the last.

They must arrive today, they must, and cousin Bobby, too.

Private Eloise Adams, a Catholic, crossed herself.

Ramsgate was not the only place where ATS personnel were at work. A dozen NCO's and privates, selected from three platoons attached for administrative purposes to an infantry training camp in Sussex, were at Hastings. There, fishing boats packed with survivors kept arriving. The soldiers, landing, were swallowed up by Army men, ATS girls and other helpers, to be given cheerful directives as to procedure.

'You must report, but have a cup of tea while you're queueing, have a cigarette, try a sandwich, then report, they want your details, any wounded come this way, welcome back, all of you, glad you made it, but you must report.'

Report, report. Number, name, rank and unit.

In charge of the ATS team was Captain Polly Simms, as elegant in her peaked cap and tailored khaki as in any of her civvy creations. Forty-three, she had always fought the wrinkled demon of time in his envy of youth and beauty by refusing to let him lay his destructive hand too maliciously on her. She had consistently exercised vivacious defiance to keep him at bay, and looked now as if she was still a few years short of forty, the dread year for all women who regarded its advent as unnerving and demoralizing. She was as willowy as ever, a fascinating woman and a popular officer, but she dealt swiftly and in a no-nonsense fashion with susceptible young subalterns of the ATS who imagined they were in love with her. That sort of thing sent her into fits of suppressed laughter. Polly was not the kind of woman to be censorious or disapproving, she simply saw outlandish behaviour as something to ridicule, not condemn.

Her immediate assistant today was Rosie, Lieutenant Rosie Adams, twenty-five years old, strikingly lovely, and a woman whom Polly cherished more than any other in the realms of deep abiding friendship of an undemanding kind. Polly, who had the right connections, had ensured that, after being commissioned, Rosie was posted to her own company. They had one very special thing in common. They both regarded Boots, Rosie's adoptive father, as their favourite person, Rosie as a never-failing daughter, Polly as a would-be lover. Polly had been that for many years, and swore sometimes that the Almighty would cast the man onto a thousand sharp swords if he spurned her for ever. That always made Boots laugh, which in turn always made Polly want to spit, in a manner of speaking.

As for Rosie, while she acknowledged the Dunkirk evacuation was a tremendous feat all round, she couldn't help feeling there had to be certain people in high places who were mainly to blame for what had befallen the BEF. She was never going to believe a whole army of stalwart men could have been beaten so badly unless complacency or obstinacy in high places had let them down to begin with. A veteran northern soldier, a sergeant, had hardened her suspicions when he landed yesterday.

'Bloody old General Haig and his gormless lot all over again, lass. Fixed us up for diggin' trenches, by heck. Didn't know t'other war was over, didn't know what tanks were for. Gormless, aye, all on 'em.'

'Well, let's hope there'll be new generals, Sergeant, when you go back.'

'Aye, we'll go back, one day. We've got to, but I'm thinking we'll bury generals on way, new or old.'

There were casualties here and there, ambulances standing by for the serious cases. Rosie was searching the faces of all the men, wounded or otherwise, hoping to spot Tim or Bobby, or Emma's young man, Jonathan. Or Boots, of course. She was worrying badly about him now, and about Tim and Bobby. She had phoned home this morning to find out if any of the missing ones were back, for they could have landed at any of the Kent or Sussex ports being used. Grandmother Finch had had to say that so far there was no news of any of them, and the whole family was becoming very anxious.

Something of a lull occurred, and the ATS personnel were able to take time off for coffee or tea. Polly, coming out of the improvised reception area, drew Rosie aside.

'Have you managed to phone again, Rosie?' she asked, and Rosie thought her concern was plainly visible. She could usually hide serious emotions with a joke or with her brittle laugh.

'No, not yet,' said Rosie.

'Well, pop across the road and phone now,' said Polly. 'I'll stand in for you if there's a rush.'

Rosie went. She got through to Chinese Lady from a public phone box.

'Nana, any news?'

'No, Rosie love, not unless Lizzy's heard. If she has, she'll let me know. I don't like nothing happening, it's not like Boots to leave things as late as this, and I can't think he's lost his way over there. Sammy might. He'd be so set on selling something to the French that he'd forget where he was. But not Boots, nor Tim, and nor Bobby, neither. You don't think they could all of got on a boat that's takin' them the wrong way, like to Spain or somewhere?'

'No, of course not, Nana. You know Daddy. He'd soon put the captain right, or take the ship over without hardly trying.' Rosie spoke in a light, reassuring way, although her heart was beginning to sink.

'On the wireless they keep saying this is the last day,' complained Chinese Lady.

'Oh, no-one can be sure, Nana,' said Rosie.

'Boots was supposed to have a safe job workin' for Sir Henry,' said Chinese Lady, 'but I don't know what's safe about it if he's still over there.'

'I think everything got mixed up during the retreat,' said Rosie, 'but I'm sure he'll be putting things to right now and taking his place on some ship, along with Tim and Bobby, and Emma's young man. I'm sure they're all together.'

'They'd better be,' said Chinese Lady, 'or I'll say something they won't like.'

'I must get back on duty now, Nana,' said Rosie, 'the troops are still coming in. But I'm sure our missing ones will turn up some time today. Hope and faith, Nana. I'll phone again later.'

Polly, on receiving negative news, bit her lip. Wherever Boots was, she desperately wanted to be with him. She would have been if only the stuffed shirts of Whitehall had allowed the ATS to serve with with BEF in an administrative capacity. Or as transport mechanics once they'd been taught how to service engines. Polly, like Eloise, was against playing second fiddle.

Chapter Five

In the huge kitchen of the Aarlberg farmhouse, where the family took all their meals unless there were visitors, Helene faced her parents defiantly.

'I am sorry,' she said, 'but that man shouldn't be here. If the Germans find him, they'll shoot you, Papa. You know that. You know it too, Mama.'

Jacob said, 'It was expected of me to let him fall into German hands? That, Helene, I couldn't do. He was wounded and exhausted, but still on his feet. I fought with the fathers of these men in Flanders. There have been reunions. There will be reunions again, when this new war is over. If I give this man up to the Boche, the Nazi Boche, how will I be able to look into the faces of the old Tommies?'

'The old Tommies were different,' said Helene. 'They never ran, never. They didn't leave France to fight by herself. These new Tommies are all running, and where to? To what they think is the safety of their island. What a joke that is. Hitler will bomb it as he has bombed Warsaw and Rotterdam. Then he'll cross the Channel and their island will go up in flames. There'll be no more reunions, Papa.'

'You are worried about France, Helene,' said

Jacob. 'We all are. But you don't know the British as I know them.'

'It's enough to know they're deserting France,' said Helene, and her mother gave her a sad look. Who could not be sad when the Boche were almost on their doorstep and a wounded British sergeant posed such an unhappy problem for them?

'This man has a comrade, a cousin, who would have risked walking into German tanks to find him,' said Jacob. 'A man who has that kind of comrade must deserve better of us than to be handed over to the Boche.'

'That isn't fair,' protested Helene. 'I didn't say we should do that, only persuade him to go. Let him begin running again, with all the others.'

'They have to save their army, Helene, they must,' said Jacob. 'Their defeat has shocked us all, but they will learn from it, I'm certain they will.'

Madame Aarlberg said, 'Helene, your father and I have agreed the sergeant may stay at least until tomorrow morning. We must give him a chance to recover. We could not do less for him.'

Helene fidgeted.

'He'll go as soon as he's recovered?' she said.

'He talked about going after a short rest,' said Jacob, 'but he's cut off from Dunkirk. By this evening, perhaps, or first thing tomorrow morning, the road may be clear again. I think the motor-cyclists we saw may only have been part of a reconnaissance unit.'

'Well, let him try this evening or early tomorrow morning, then,' said Helene.

'If the British evacuation finishes today,' said Jacob, 'he may miss his chance of being taken off. I wonder, can he sail a boat? If we could get him through at night, before the Boche have occupied the port, he could take our boat. It would be his best chance, if he's done any sailing.'

'Papa, are you crazy?' breathed Helene. 'Get him to Dunkirk tonight and give him our boat? It's my boat.'

'I doubt if you'll be able to use it until the war is over,' said Jacob. 'Perhaps no-one can, perhaps it's been taken, or smashed to pieces by bombs, along with all the other little weekend boats and yachts.'

'Papa, you can't sail any of those weekend boats across the Channel, only the big yachts,' said Helene, 'and the British are bound to have taken those. In any case, why should I let that man use my boat? Even if I did, he'd drown himself before he was halfway across.'

'I'd risk that.'

Helene swung round. She saw the sergeant standing just inside the half-open door. She flushed.

'You've been listening,' she accused angrily.

'Only for a moment,' said Bobby, looking grey. He'd tried to rouse himself by getting up from the armchair, and had actually keeled over. That knocked alarm back into him, the alarm of a man in danger of being left behind and put into the German bag. 'Sorry to interrupt, but I've been trying to stay awake and it's made me thirsty. Thinking about it, I believe I've been thirsty

73

for a week. Is there a glass of water going spare?'

Jacob supplied one immediately, and Bobby downed a glassful of tapped spring water, clear and cold and fresh. Helene regarded him with no softening of mood. He was an intruder, an unwelcome one, and probably far more concerned for himself than for them. He was English, yes, one could see that. Coming to the kitchen to eavesdrop, asking for water and inviting himself in to drink it, that was typical of the thick-skinned, arrogant English. As for his wound, she suspected it was no more than slight, for he showed no sign that it was paining him. She conceded, however, that he looked exceptionally drawn and tired, but perhaps that was simply because he had been running too fast from the triumphant Nazis. He returned the glass to her father and thanked him. That was something, she supposed, to hear him say, '*Merci, m'sieur.*'

Madame Aarlberg, not given to flapping her hands or losing her head, said, 'Please sit down, Sergeant.' It was obvious he could hardly stay on his feet. She could not help liking him. He was very calm, very uncomplaining, and was making no demands.

'I was wondering—' Bobby gritted his teeth and started again. 'I was wondering if there's any chance of getting away now.'

'Sergeant,' said Jacob in his quiet way. 'I thought you had accepted you're in no condition to leave yet. You've taken no rest, and in any case, this evening would be better. The Germans will almost

74

certainly have finished their reconnaissance by then. Be sensible. Sit down.'

Bobby gave in to exhaustion again. He sat down at the table. The kitchen was even larger than the living-room, its huge range alight. Shining pots and pans hung from hooks, chairs clustered around the table, and an enormous dresser held a variety of china and earthenware. The sun slanted in through three windows, filling the kitchen with warm June light. On the dresser stood a radio, silent at the moment. Vaguely, he supposed it fed only bad news to the family whenever it was switched on. He wanted to sleep, desperately, but his sense of urgency fought the need.

'Kind of you not to kick me out,' he said.

'That is the last thing we would do,' said Madame Aarlberg gently.

'I am Belgian,' said Jacob. 'My wife is French. My daughter Helene chooses to be very French.'

Helene made no comment. She seethed in silence. What were her parents doing, making this unwelcome man at home? Everyone knew the danger France was facing, but her mother was now actually asking the sergeant if he would like some English tea.

Tea? Bobby, disorientated, had to give the offer some thought. He also had to fight to stay upright in his chair.

'Tea, did someone say?'

'If you would like,' said Madame Aarlberg, trying to shut her ears to the noise of more planes over-head. 'We don't have it often in the mornings—'

75

'We never have it any morning,' said Helene. 'But what does that matter? Let everything stop for tea. Let us tell the Germans, then perhaps they will stop too and make their own tea.'

'There's nothing we can do about the Germans, Helene,' said Jacob.

'Make tea, then,' said Helene. 'Yes, why not?' She would have walked out, for there was a huge amount of work to do, but she suspected her parents might commit themselves very foolishly to the welfare of this man if she left them alone with him. It was not like her father to neglect his responsibilities, especially at this time of the year, and more especially now that the war had left them short of labour. But no, perhaps it wasn't unusual, for who could work normally when the invading Germans were swarming into France? Her father had gone out early to the fields, returned for breakfast, listened to the news, then gone out again to watch the defeated British troops filling the road to Dunkirk. He was absurdly in favour of the British, all because of the Tommies he had known in the last war. She had come in herself from the fields because she was as restless as he was worried. To discover he had let this English sergeant into the house alarmed and infuriated her.

She glanced at the man. His head was drooping. Her father spoke again then, decisively.

'Sergeant, I think what you need most of all is rest,' he said.

'Yes,' said Madame Aarlberg, 'go upstairs with my

husband, Sergeant, and he will show where you can sleep for a while.'

'Legs,' muttered Bobby in English, 'I can't find my ruddy legs.'

Jacob helped him to his feet, Bobby shook himself into a state of consciousness, and left the kitchen in company with the farmer, who took him upstairs to a spare bedroom. Once on the bed, he simply fell asleep. Jacob removed his boots.

In the kitchen, Helene paced about.

'It's foolish,' she said, 'foolish.'

'We can't turn him out,' said her mother.

'We are going to keep him?'

'I didn't say that, Helene.'

'It's dangerous having him here at all,' said Helene. 'Who's to know the Germans won't be here in five minutes?'

'They'll be too busy to bother us yet,' said Madame Aarlberg.

Jacob returned.

'He's sound asleep,' he said.

'You've made him comfortable, of course?' said Helene with a note of sarcasm.

'He's on the bed.' Jacob eyed his prickly daughter tolerantly. 'Helene, is it fair to blame one man for the defeat of a whole army?'

'Who is blaming him?' asked Helene. 'I am not. I have only made it plain that I'm disgusted with all of them.'

'Have no fear, my infant, that you have not been heard,' said Madame Aarlberg a little drily. Her daughter, very much a strong-willed young woman

77

at nineteen, made an impatient gesture, then crossed to the dresser and switched on the radio. At once, war news came pouring forth. It had been like that for many days, ever since the Germans had attacked the Low Countries, and very little of it was comforting. It was worse now. There were, of course, the usual Government-inspired references to tactical dispositions that would turn the tide, but such references were now suspect. And there was an admission that German armies were poised to make an all-out assault on France.

'The situation is hopeless, then, but not desperate,' said Jacob wryly, quoting a Russian general of the last war.

A new voice on the radio called for the people of France to stand firm. Helene switched it off in disgust.

'We must pray,' said Madame Aarlberg.

'And we must hope,' said Jacob, 'we must hope that one day the British will come back, better equipped and with better ideas of how to deal with the German Panzer divisions.'

Which were precisely the sentiments of most of the men of Dunkirk.

Chapter Six

Worrying, that's what it is, thought Job Hardy on his way home from his Saturday morning's work. He didn't like what Dunkirk meant. In the first place it meant the Army had taken a nasty bashing, never mind how many men were rescued. In the second place it meant the country itself might take a bashing if the French got licked. Be very upsetting to my friends and neighbours, that would, he thought. Bombs all over the durned place, and then an invasion. Hitler would fancy himself as another William the Conqueror, even with a name like Adolf.

It's all upsetting to Jemima as well, Dunkirk and our Jonathan not come home yet. Apple of her eye, our first-born.

He let himself into the house and walked through to the kitchen. Jane, Jennifer and young Jonas were all there, with their mother.

'Any news?' he asked.

'None,' said Jane.

'Strikes me Jonathan's cutting it a bit fine,' said Job. 'Anything on the wireless, Jemima?'

'Only that the evacuation don't be finished just yet,' said Jemima.

'But the blessed Germans be getting nearer,' said Jennifer.

'Up to Jonathan to knock their heads off if they get too near,' said Job cheerfully. 'Got good shoulders, Jonathan has.'

'There's still plenty of time,' said Jemima.

'Plenty, Mum,' said young Jonas.

'Jonathan won't let us down,' said Jemima.

'Course he won't, Mum,' said Jane, 'especially as you've baked a cake. We could have invited Joe Morgan in if he hadn't been called up.'

'Months ago, that was,' said Jennifer, 'soon as he was eighteen.'

'I reckon our Jane be missing Joe a mite,' said Job.

'And him getting handsomer and our Jane getting prettier,' said Jemima.

'Rotten old war,' said Jane.

Earlier that morning, Emma, working at the office, had been taking dictation from her Aunt Emily, now the general manager in place of Uncle Boots. She thought Aunt Emily very efficient but just a bit too businesslike, and she had a feeling it was because she was set on proving she really could do the job as well as Uncle Boots. Emma thought she didn't need to prove what she, Emma, considered obvious, that women were as good as men. It was just that men somehow managed to wangle all the best jobs for themselves. One thing about a war, it pushed women into important jobs vacated by called-up men, and gave them the chance to prove their worth, which they did very easily. Aunt Emily ought to relax more because she was very good at the job, anyway. As it was, you couldn't chat to her like you could to Uncle Boots during dictation. However busy he was, Uncle Boots always had time to listen to little confidences, whereas Aunt Emily would say talk to me later, Emma, say at lunchtime, we must get on with the letters. Of course, that was right and proper, work came first, but all the same, Emma missed Uncle Boots and his smile, the smile that always seemed to be lurking about in his eyes, even in his nearly blind one. She never lost the feeling that he had a deep affection for her and Annabelle because they were the daughters of his sister, with whom he had shared a very close family friendship during their years of growing up. He also had a very special relationship with her father, and Emma knew it was the relationship of old comrades of France and Flanders. Grandpa Finch had told her once it was something all the men of the trenches shared with each other, and that it would last all their lives. Emma supposed Jonathan was forging similar relationships with men of the BEF, the men now desperately clambering into the big ships and little ships.

Aunt Emily was dictating briskly and rapidly, and Emma's shorthand pencil was having to fly. Aunt Emily changed tack then.

'I'm fed up with all these letters from Government departments,' she said.

'Do I put that down?' asked Emma.

'No, of course not,' said Emily, 'I was just makin'

a remark. Anyone would think that's all we've got time for, attendin' to forms and circulars.' The restrictions on materials and the necessity of quotas seemed to have given the Civil Service a chance to go in for making mountains of paperwork.

'It's the war, Aunt Emily,' said Emma.

'Don't I know it,' said Emily.

'Are you getting badly worried about Tim and Uncle Boots not being home yet?' asked Emma.

'Yes, we all are, Emma, and about Bobby too,' said Emily. 'It's not doin' my concentration any good, so let's get on before I start really worrying.'

I'm worried myself, about Jonathan as well as the others, thought Emma, and then her pencil had to fly again.

Emma was actually getting very upset about Jonathan. She had said goodbye to him on the last day of his embarkation leave, and he had made some of his barmy remarks to lighten their parting. She had begun to miss him badly only a few days after he'd gone, and it occurred to her that she was actually in love with him. Not given, like Annabelle, to being demonstrative, she had never mentioned anything like love to him. Well, not yet eighteen she didn't think a girl that age could really know her own mind. She would be eighteen in twelve days. Was that old enough to be definitely in love? She must be because of how upset she was that her Sussex-born young man was still among the missing.

'Aunt Emily, you're going a bit too fast for me.'

'You'll have to concentrate a bit more, Emma, or

we'll never get through these letters,' said Emily.

Get the war over and come back quick, Uncle Boots, thought Emma wryly.

Come back, Jonathan.

'Susie?'

'Sammy? Where are you?' asked Susie.

'Just about to leave Luton, I'm at the station,' said Sammy, who had caught a very early train to the town to make the most of the Saturday morning. 'Thought I'd let you know, and to ask if Boots and the boys are home yet.'

'No, they still haven't got back,' said Susie.

'I don't feel too happy about that,' said Sammy.

'No-one does,' said Susie, 'but your mum's goin' to ring as soon as she hears from any of them. I've been speakin' to Lizzy about Bobby. She can't believe he's goin' to be near to the very last.'

'Well, I can appreciate her concern,' said Sammy, 'but as long as he gets home, with Tim and Boots, being last won't matter. I'll catch my train now and be with you later.'

'Well, don't be too late,' said Susie, 'little Paula wants to know where you are.'

Five-year-old Paula was their youngest child. The other three, Daniel, Bess and Jimmy, were all at school in a Devon village, along with other evacuees from the Denmark Hill area.

'I'm on my way,' said Sammy, and hung up. Blow that, he thought, making for a platform, it's going to turn the family inside-out if Boots, Bobby and Tim don't make it home. Who the hell had thought it a good idea to go to war? Someone who was seriously off his head. Adolf Hitler.

'There's still no news,' said Lizzy to her husband Ned on his arrival home from the City.

'Well, damn that,' said Ned. Forty-five, he was showing his age a bit, and Lizzy tried not to notice there was just a little hint of grey showing at his temples. 'There's not much time left, Eliza.'

'The wireless said the last men will leave before dark as long as the Germans can be held off,' said Lizzy.

'Held off?' said Ned. 'What with, spades and sand buckets?'

'Don't make jokes, I'm not in the mood,' said Lizzy.

'No joke, Eliza, a stark staring fact,' said Ned.

'Well, I don't want to hear,' said Lizzy. 'I just want to know if Bobby's safe. I can't understand it, all those thousands of men brought home, and yet our three, Bobby, Tim and Boots, still missing.'

'There could be a good reason why you can bracket them,' said Ned. 'They could all be with the divisions fighting a rearguard action. If the whole Army had melted away in the direction of Dunkirk, the Germans would have been right on their tails.'

'But it's hardly fair that all of our three should be caught up,' said Lizzy. 'And there's Emma's young man too, we haven't heard from him yet, either.'

'Where is Emma?' asked Ned.

'She's home from work and a bit sad that Em'ly

84

seems to be more concerned with the business than with Dunkirk,' said Lizzy.

'I'd say Emily's using her work to take her mind off what might have happened to Tim and Boots,' said Ned. 'We all know Emily and how she likes to be doing things, she's not the sort to sit about and bite her nails when she's worried. Where's Emma now?'

'In the front room, with Edward,' said Lizzy. 'They're glued to the wireless, and Emma's not very happy about anything. She asked as soon as she came in if Jonathan had phoned. I think she's a lot more attached to that young man than we realized. She doesn't show her feelings as much as Annabelle does, but she's gettin' very worked up now.'

'Well, make a wish that the phone rings some time this afternoon,' said Ned. 'As for Emma's feelings, you've noticed, surely, how often she's been to Walworth to visit Jonathan's family, haven't you, Eliza? That was pretty demonstrative in my book.'

'I don't know why our two girls have both managed to fall in love at only seventeen,' said Lizzy.

'There's a simple answer to that,' said Ned, 'they both take after you and me.'

Lizzy found a smile.

'Well, I hope that's goin' to turn out as well for them as it did for us,' she said.

Tommy and Vi Adams, bereft of their three children, evacuated to Devon, felt incomplete and gloomy without them, and when Tommy arrived home from work, Vi was forced to add to his unsettled state by telling him that Boots, Tim and Bobby were still not back. It spoiled Tommy's homecoming. He considered the Adams family was showing three gaping holes at the moment, and he and Vi weren't in favour of that, neither was Chinese Lady, not by a long shot. He rang her.

'Hello, who's that?'

'Tommy. Stand a bit closer to the phone, old lady, I can 'ardly hear you.'

'Now you know I don't hold with these things,' complained Chinese Lady, 'they could give a body an electrical shock, and I'm not goin' to stand any closer to it than I am now.'

'Listen, about Boots and the boys not bein' home yet,' said Tommy. 'I've heard on the wireless that there's thousands more still waitin' to be taken off, so I thought I'd phone and tell you to keep smiling.'

'Tommy Adams, I don't know that anyone should smile on any account when things are so bad for the Army,' said Chinese Lady. 'It's like smiling at sinkin' ships.'

'They're not sinkin',' said Tommy, ignoring the fact that the Germans had bombed some to destruction. 'They're steamin' or sailin' forwards and backwards, goin' like the clappers.'

'Goin' like what?' said Chinese Lady.

'Like merry hell,' said Tommy, 'and doin' a marvellous job.'

'I don't like you bein' common,' said Chinese

Lady, 'and if that's what comes of workin' in Shoreditch, you'd better get Sammy to buy some fact'ries with a nice respectable view of Brockwell Park or Camberwell Green.'

'I'd fancy a fact'ry by Brockwell Park,' said Tommy. 'Anyway, keep your pecker up. Vi and me feel sure everyone'll get home, and we want you to feel sure too. Give us a ring as soon as Boots and Tim arrive. No, tell you what, we'll come round this afternoon and keep you and Dad company.'

'Yes, do that, Tommy,' said Chinese Lady, who welcomed visits from any members of her extensive family. 'We'll have tea in the garden while we're waitin' for Boots and Tim. I haven't seen Vi much lately, it must be all of two or three days, so it'll be nice havin' you and her to tea this afternoon.'

'Be with you in a couple of hours, old girl.'

'Don't call me old girl, it's what Boots does. Still, I won't say anything if he calls me that when he does turn up—oh!' Chinese Lady let go a little exclamation. 'There, I knew it,' she said.

'What's 'appened?' asked Tommy.

'This thing just give me an electrical shock or something,' said Chinese Lady, and hung up in a hurry.

'It's come,' said Mrs Cassie Brown to her husband Freddy.

'What's come?' asked Freddy, just in from his work as assistant manager to Tommy Adams.

'Your call-up notice,' said Cassie's dad, who lived with them.

87

'Yes, here it is,' said Cassie, mother of two-year-old Maureen and Lewis, just two months. 'I opened it when it came by the midday post. I could see it was from the Government. Freddy, you'll have to tell them you can't be called up. Well, you can't, you're the father of a little girl and a little baby boy. Yes, and you're a husband as well.'

'I'd like to tell them I'm too busy, Cassie, believe me I would,' said Freddy, reading the call-up command that required him to report in two weeks time to a training camp of the East Surrey Infantry Regiment. He had had his medical over a month ago. 'But I don't think they'll wear it. They're a grim lot when there's a war on.'

'I don't care if they're as grim as a workhouse laundry on a wet winter Monday,' said Cassie, 'they've got to understand about your fam'ly responsibilities.'

'All right, Cassie, see what you mean,' said Freddy, and gave her arm a little pat. They looked at each other, and Freddy knew that she knew what he knew, that nothing could be done about it. It was the turn of men in his age group, twenty-five, to be called up, whether they had family responsibilities or not, and only on the most extreme of compassionate grounds would the War Office give them dispensation. The turn of their close friends Nick Harrison, Horace Cooper and Danny Thompson would come, and they too were all husbands and fathers.

Mr Ford, Cassie's dad, known as the Gaffer, spoke up.

'It's 'ard luck, Freddy,' he said, 'but I'll be staying put, don't you worry, I'll keep an eye on Cassie and the little 'uns.'

'I know you will, Gaffer,' said Freddy.

'As a matter of fact,' said Mr Ford, 'I've 'ad a communication meself today, from me sister Win that lives in Wilts. Win's the one that married a market gardener just before the last war. She and 'er better 'alf, Ben, live in a fair-sized country cottage near the market garden, and seeing their sons and daughters all 'appen to be married, she's been so kind as to say there's room for Cassie and the little 'uns if things get a bit – well, a bit difficult 'ere. I showed the letter to Cassie only a few minutes ago. What d'yer think, Freddy, d'yer think when you're called up that it might be a good idea for her and the little 'uns to go and live in Wilts?'

'Don't answer that, Freddy,' said Cassie.

'Why not?' asked Freddy, as little Maureen, called Muffin, came and cuddled his legs. He picked her up and gave her a smacker on her snowy forehead. 'Why not?'

'Because I've already said no.' Cassie sounded as if she wasn't going to tolerate an argument.

'On account of your dad?' said Freddy.

'Yes,' said Cassie. 'He's been invited as well. But there's his job. He can't leave his job, so he can't leave here.'

'Gaffer, you're a railway ganger,' said Freddy.

'Well, I don't recall I've ever said I wasn't, Freddy,' said the Gaffer.

'Get a transfer to Swindon,' said Freddy, 'there's

a big works buildin' railway engines there. There's a large network of sidings too. I've read about it. With the labour market as it is now, with thousands of blokes bein' called up, a transfer should be easy.'

'That's a prize piece of talk, that is,' said the Gaffer. 'Freddy, blowed if you don't 'ave an 'ead on yer shoulders.'

'But what about all our friends and neighbours?' asked Cassie.

'Unless your Aunt Win invites them as well,' said Freddy, 'they'll have to stay behind, won't they, Muffin, eh?'

'Tickle,' said Muffin, so Freddy gave her the lightest of tickles. It still gave her the shrieks.

'Freddy, d'you really think we should go?' asked Cassie. She had her funny little ways, but wasn't short of commonsense. She was quite aware, as were many other people, that the defeat and evacuation of the British Expeditionary Force could lead to an attempt by the Germans to bomb Britain into surrender.

'Yes, I think you should, Cassie,' said Freddy, 'and I also think your Aunt Win knew what she was about when she offered to have all of you.'

Cassie made a little face. She hated the thought of Freddy's departure into the Army. Since the age of ten, she had never known a time when he was absent from her life. He was an essential part of her existence, as she was of his. In the eyes of wives and mothers, war was a thief of one's nearest and dearest. It ought to be outlawed once and for all.

'Well, I'll think about it, Freddy,' she said.

'Best if you accept, Cassie,' said Freddy.

'Tickle,' said Muffin, so he tickled her again. More excited little shrieks.

'Freddy, where're you goin'?' asked Cassie a second later.

'Somewhere quick,' said Freddy, 'Muffin's wet 'erself and me as well.'

That's a welcome bit of light relief, thought the Gaffer.

Elsewhere in Walworth, Jemima and her family tried to make light of the fact that as the day wore on Jonathan still wasn't home. By six o'clock in the evening, there weren't too many more hours to go. Jane said perhaps he was on a slow boat to China. Jennifer said she'd never heard him say he fancied going to China. Young Jonas said more like he'd landed in Scotland and was waiting for a train. Job said there was still plenty of time for him to get home, even if it meant in the middle of the night. Leave the kettle warming on the hob for him, he said, he's bound to fancy a cup of tea as soon as he gets in. Jemima said she supposed she ought to leave him a slice of the cake as well.

No-one laughed at any of this, however. Jemima and her family had stopped laughing for the moment.

Emma turned up at seven-thirty, and it was Jemima who opened the door to her.

'Well, here you be, Emma, come to see us again.'

'Jonathan?' said Emma.

'No, still not yet, Emma.'

Emma made a face as she stepped in.

'Nor my brother Bobby, nor Uncle Boots and cousin Tim,' she said. 'I'm—' she swallowed. 'I'm very unhappy.'

'Well, bless you, my dear,' said Jemima, 'but no-one's going to lose hope yet. That Jonathan of ours, leaving it so late, it's not like him to be a worry to us. He's like my Job, kind and thoughtful.'

'He's like you too,' said Emma.

'Like me?' said Jemima.

'He makes people feel happy,' said Emma, and a little sigh escaped her because she was far from happy at the moment. 'I thought I'd come and be with you and your family for a little while. You don't mind?'

'Emma, there don't be anyone more welcome in this house,' said Jemima. 'It's never but a pleasure to see you. Come into the kitchen, everyone be there, and Jane's just put the kettle on for a pot of tea.'

The atmosphere of warm hospitality and affection embraced Emma as she entered the kitchen.

'Hello, Emma, come and sit here,' said Jane.

'No, here, with me,' said Jennifer.

'Being a feller,' said young Jonas, 'I'm best for you, Emma.'

Job, coming to his feet, said, 'All one, Emma, wherever you sit, it just be fair comforting to see you.'

I really wouldn't mind if they were my family too, thought Emma.

Do I mean my in-laws?

Come home, Jonathan, and then I'll know one way or the other.

Chapter Seven

'Are you awake?' The question was asked coolly, and in English.

Bobby opened his eyes. The bedroom was warm with balmy evening light. Instinct told him he'd slept for far longer than he should have done, that every hour asleep had been an hour of opportunity lost. Not very clever, he thought. In a detached kind of way, he analysed his condition. His wound was sore, very sore, but bearable, and the thumping ache in his head was far less bothersome. Still sleepy, he slowly took in the figure of Helene Aarlberg. She was standing beside the bed, looking down at him. His mind browsing, he frowned. Helene thought what a mess he was in his filthy battledress and his grimy bandage. His face was in need of a wash, his thick untidy hair in need of a barber. She made herself heard again.

'Are you going back to sleep?' She spoke in French this time. Her English was good enough, but she resented the language at the moment.

'What?' He came to, using French. 'No, I'm awake. Just pulling myself together. What's the road like, do you know? Is there any chance I can get away now?'

'You can leave whenever you like,' said Helene. Reluctantly, she added, 'But you won't get very far. The road is blocked. It's full of German vehicles. They aren't moving, they're stationary. The radio says our General Gamelin expects Rommel to commence his advance on Dunkirk at dawn tomorrow, that he delayed it because of the presence of a French army on his flank, and that this army has now taken up a more advantageous position.'

Bobby, coming fully to, said, 'What's more advantageous than being on your enemy's flank?'

'Ask the people who compose these communiqués,' said Helene, 'but don't ask again if you can get away when you know you can't, unless it's to give yourself up. Officially, it's expected that Dunkirk will be fully occupied by the Germans by midday tomorrow.'

'I wish you hadn't said that,' remarked Bobby. 'It's not my idea of good news.'

'Is that a joke?' asked Helene stiffly.

'Not to me,' said Bobby, finding relief in the fact that talking now had a less painful effect on his head. 'You sure it's official, or was it a guess?'

'It was what was said on the radio.' Helene was aloof rather than out of temper. 'I have come up to ask if you would like something to eat.'

'Eat?' Bobby gazed up at her. She stared him out. He thought her not a bad-looking young woman. Good figure too. The Scots would have called her bonny. 'There's food?'

'If you wish.'

'I'll come down. Thanks for the offer.'

'You must thank my mother,' said Helene. 'She is the one who is offering. I am only her messenger.'

'With wings?' said Bobby, mind beginning to apply itself to his problems again.

'Excuse me?'

'Angels of mercy and so on,' said Bobby.

'I am not in the mood for silly conversation,' said Helene.

She watched as the inconvenient guest swung himself off the bed, sat on the edge of it and pulled his boots on. She noted the sorry condition of his grey socks.

'You're a suffering young lady, aren't you?' he said.

'I've good reason to be, I—'

'Oh, I understand, don't think I don't,' said Bobby, and stood up. 'France has its back to the wall, and I'm an embarrassment. Nobody could expect you to feel like dancing. I don't feel much like it myself. If it's possible to make a dash for Dunkirk some time this evening, I'll risk it.'

'I would not stop you, but the Germans will,' said Helene. One of the things she resented about him was his lack of humility. He ought to be abject with it at the resounding way the British had been defeated and forced to run back home. However, she only said, 'I think you should have a wash before you come down.'

'Yes, sorry about how I look,' said Bobby. 'Sorry about my socks too.' He hadn't missed her disdainful glance at them.

'You need not feel, when you've gone, that I shall remember what your socks were like,' said Helene. Her father came in then. 'He's coming down,' she said.

'Good,' said Jacob, 'but shall we first take a look at your wound, Sergeant? I can give you a fresh dressing, if necessary. We have a large first-aid box in case of accidents on the farm.'

'Thanks,' said Bobby.

Jacob unwound the bandage and carefully peeled off the dressing. It was thick with dried blood. Its removal disclosed a jagged wound at the right temple. Swollen, it looked ugly with dried blood, and was surrounded by deep purple bruising.

'Ah, not too bad, Sergeant, not too bad,' said Jacob.

Helene compressed her mouth. The painful look of the wound made her feel uncomfortable.

'I think a bomb shattered the road,' said Bobby, 'and that a large lump of it came up and hit me.'

'I am sorry, of course,' said Helene, 'but there are French soldiers worse off, and dead ones too.'

'I know,' said Bobby, and she went down to the kitchen then, leaving her father to attend to the wound. Jacob made an unfussy job of cleaning it, disinfecting it, and applying a new dressing and bandage. Bobby thanked him and asked if he might have a wash. Jacob showed him to the bathroom. 'I'm owing you a lot more than I can repay at the moment,' said Bobby.

97

'Think nothing of it,' said Jacob. 'Come down as soon as you're ready.'

The evening meal was served in the kitchen, the table laid with a blue-and-white-check cloth, lightly starched. One might have thought that with France in crisis, food, or at least an appetite for it, would have taken a back seat. However, despite every worry, or perhaps in a gesture of defiance, Madame Aarlberg had prepared a casserole of veal, the vegetables cooked with it. She was very French in her enjoyment of cooking, and was excellent at it. But she preferred to concentrate on a satisfying main course following a modest starter, and not spend all evening, as many French housewives did, providing a variety of different courses. She always said she was against participating in a domestic marathon every evening. Not that she was burdened with too much housework. She had a daily maid who cycled in from Dunkirk to help her. But the girl had not been seen for days, and she did not need to ask why.

She first served sardines in a deliciously appetizing sauce, a favourite with Jacob, and followed with the casserole, bringing it steaming in its crock to the table. The long June day had far from run its course, and the kitchen was still flooded with light. The arrival of the casserole coincided with the roaring sound of one more flight of German planes heading for Dunkirk. The kitchen windows vibrated. Madame Aarlberg bit her lip. Jacob eyed the steaming crock.

'Serve it, Estelle,' he said, 'it's too good to take second place to the Boche.'

It proved very good, and there was, of course, a bottle of dry white wine to go with it. But it was impossible to enjoy the meal in light-hearted fashion. Jacob had switched the radio on again, the need to listen compulsive. The mood of France over the departure of the defeated British came through as one of dismay and incredulity, which did nothing, of course, to improve Helene's prickly relationship with Bobby. He made no attempt at conversation, except in exchanging little pleasantries with Madame Aarlberg about the excellence of the meal.

Nothing could hide the obvious, that the Aarlberg farm was situated in an area surely destined to be overrun by the Germans within twenty-four hours unless a miracle happened. Bobby was all too aware of the family's worries, but despite that and his own difficult situation, he ate well. A practical young man, he saw the need to put food into himself if he was to attempt to break through to Dunkirk before it was too late. His appreciation of Madame Aarlberg's cooking quite pleased her. She was a more philosophical person than her daughter.

At the end of the meal, Helene got up and switched the radio off in her angry way.

'Hitler is gobbling up Europe,' she said.

'A man of greedy ambition,' said Jacob.

'A pig,' said Helene, sitting down again.

'One meal too many might give him fatal indigestion,' said Bobby.

'That is funny?' said Helene.

99

'No, a serious hope,' said Bobby, who felt caught between the unreality of the moment and the urgent necessity of getting away. At home, his family would be waiting for a phone call from him, announcing he had landed. Tim had probably arrived by now, along with his father. And Jonathan Hardy too. Damn being stuck here, he thought. But he addressed Madame Aarlberg cheerfully, complimenting her on the meal.

'You enjoyed it?' said Madame Aarlberg, smiling.

'Every mouthful,' said Bobby, who hadn't missed the slight flavour of garlic or been put off by it. His hunger had won that little battle for him. He smiled. 'I'm as good as new,' he said.

'Yes, you do look much better,' said Madame Aarlberg.

'Well, I had a wash and a scrub, your husband gave me a new dressing and now I've enjoyed your very welcome food,' said Bobby. 'All that must have improved me.'

'I cannot argue,' smiled Madame Aarlberg. 'Your head doesn't feel too bad now?'

'That's improved too,' said Bobby.

What an idiot, thought Helene. The Nazis had blown the British Army off the map of France, and were about to savage France itself, and here he was exchanging small talk with her mother. Ingratiating himself, of course. True, he did not have the look of an ingratiating man, but the English were like that. They could wear an air of superiority even when holding out a begging bowl.

Jacob said, 'It's remarkably quiet.'

'But the road isn't,' said Helene, 'there are German vehicles lining it.'

'I know,' said Jacob. He and Helene had each taken a look before ceasing work.

'What sort of vehicles are they?' asked Bobby.

'Mostly troop carriers,' said Jacob.

'Full of German infantry?' said Bobby.

'Would you expect them to be Greeks?' asked Helene.

'They're in my way,' said Bobby, 'and that's upsetting me.'

'You think it's not upsetting us?' said Helene.

'It's even worse for you,' said Bobby.

'It's far worse,' said Helene, quarrelsome.

Jacob sighed. Sergeant Somers was up against a Tartar in Helene. She could not be blamed for her mood, although some things she had said were to be deprecated.

'We must pray for the best, not the worst,' said Madame Aarlberg, and poured coffee for all of them, the cups small because of rationing.

'Thank you,' said Bobby, receiving his. It was a strange atmosphere here in the farmhouse. Outside, farmland was bathed by golden evening light, and apparently wrapped in quiet. It made him feel he could make some kind of a dash for Dunkirk. He offered a comment of an unexpected kind. 'I suppose,' he said, 'that good cooking does far more for civilization than gunpowder.'

Madame Aarlberg stared at him. Sergeants to her were men with bawling voices, and it astonished her to hear this British sergeant say something like that.

Helene, however, cried in exasperation, 'Listen to the man! Who would think the British are running for their lives and that France is going to be set on fire? Cooking and gunpowder, what is he talking about?'

'Civilization,' said Jacob.

'Yes, in a crazy way,' said Helene. 'He'll be talking about chickens and cows next.'

'All likeable creatures,' said Bobby.

'We have cows, and many chickens,' said Helene, 'and I'm sure they will all be happy to have you fall in love with them.'

'What a thought,' said Bobby. The assertive nature of his tongue was backed by his belief in his opinions. 'But I won't be here long enough for that. I'm sorry about being here at all. But I'll be away fairly soon now that I've got my legs back. Have you ever had a feeling that your legs have gone missing?' He asked the question of Jacob.

'Many times in the last war,' said Jacob.

'Worrying, in a way,' observed Bobby. 'Well, we all like to feel everything's in place. Better than feeling you've been operated on without giving your consent.'

'Mother of God,' breathed Helene. 'What a crazy one the man is.'

'Can I help with the dishes?' asked Bobby. In feeling physically improved, apart from soreness and a headache, he had elected to be optimistic, to convince himself he'd still get to the beaches in time to be taken off. He got up and began to clear dishes from the table and to stack them beside the sink.

'What are you doing, please?' asked Madame Aarlberg.

'I thought I'd wash the dishes,' said Bobby. 'Is this the hot water tap?' He turned a brass faucet. The water streamed warm, then hot. 'Well, that's not a bad start.' He turned the flow off, then listened. He heard an ominous, vibrating rumble from the road. Twilight had arrived, and with it some heavy German armour, probably. The rumbling lasted only a few seconds. They're massing for a dawn advance, he thought, but I'll still try my luck in about thirty minutes, say. 'Are there any soap flakes?'

'No, no, there is no need,' said Madame Aarlberg. 'In the morning, when our maid—' She stopped and shook her head, reminding herself that Marie, their maid, had not turned up for several days, not since the war had shown its frightening face to the people of Dunkirk and made it impossible for them to come and go. They were living in their cellars. 'No, no, Sergeant, we will see to them.'

'I'd like to give a hand,' said Bobby, 'I'm better to live with when I'm doing something, as the elephant said to his keeper. There wasn't much the keeper could do about that without getting sat on.'

'Excuse me?' asked Madame Aarlberg, astonished again that a sergeant could be so whimsical, and at a time like this.

'He's saying, Estelle, that it doesn't pay to argue with an elephant,' said Jacob.

'Ah,' said Madame Aarlberg, 'does he mean a soldier with a rifle can't argue with a German tank?'

'He's joking, Mama, that's all,' said Helene. For his benefit, she added, 'Nothing is a joke to France at the moment, but that doesn't worry him.' Look at him, she thought, he's taking over. He had located the tin of soap flakes on the window ledge, and was shaking some into the sink, where the running hot water was rising.

'Shall I wash, mademoiselle, while you dry?' he suggested, at which Helene gave him an icy look.

Jacob smiled. Helene was a strong-willed young woman, and was not taking kindly to the sergeant's attempt to be cheerful. His long hours of sleep had made a new man of him. Helene's mood, of course, continued to be understandable. She was suffering for France. She hated the Nazis, and was disgusted with the British. That side of her which was warm, generous and affectionate was in limbo. Her dislike of Sergeant Somers was plain to see. But since the outbreak of war, her opinion of men was that most of them were idiots. Only idiots went to war, she said. She really should have a suitor now, a farmer, for she had a born love of the land. Jacob could not see her as other than a farmer's wife, providing the farmer in question could match her intellectually. She had once said yes, she was willing to marry, but it was questionable whether she was serious or not, for she never made much of her appearance. To her, time spent in front of a mirror was time wasted.

She thought Parisian women vain and shallow. Jacob had asked his wife why Helene did not make herself more attractive. His wife replied that Helene would when she fell in love, to which Jacob said he had a feeling she did not think love as important as the farm.

He noted the cold look she gave Sergeant Somers as she said, 'I am not in the mood for drying dishes.'

'I believe you,' said Bobby. 'I'm in a bad mood myself at my own stupidity. I made the mistake of not getting my head down this morning. Black mark, I can tell you. Got myself knocked cold at just the wrong time.' He was placing clean plates on the draining-board, and Madame Aarlberg was regarding him much more tolerantly than Helene was. 'There's always tomorrow, of course. We'll be back.'

'The British?' said Helene. 'When?' she asked sceptically.

'There'll come a day,' said Bobby.

'If France should beat the Nazis, you won't need to return,' said Helene. 'If France loses, you won't be able to. You could not invade German-occupied France from across the Channel.'

'We'll have to,' said Bobby, 'to make up for this mess.'

Jacob got up and began to dry the dishes. Helene gritted her teeth, feeling that by the time they all retired to bed this unwanted sergeant would probably have made himself one of the family.

When the domestic chore was finished, Bobby

asked Jacob if he had a map of the area. Jacob produced one and laid it out on the table. They pored over it. Jacob, with a pencil, traced the route of rural paths that could take Bobby to the eastern outskirts of Dunkirk, showing him he could not avoid having to cross the road soon after leaving the farm. Helene looked on, restless and fidgety. Her mother sat listening. Nothing could be heard, however. The Germans on the road were at a standstill.

'Sergeant,' said Jacob, 'when are you thinking of leaving?'

'In a few minutes,' said Bobby, scanning the route and attempting to memorize it.

'A few minutes?' said Jacob. 'With the Boche everywhere?'

'But Dunkirk's still open,' said Bobby. 'I think I'll have to make a sketch of this route.'

'No need to,' said Jacob, 'the map is yours.'

'Thanks,' said Bobby, 'I'll take a chance.'

'Excuse me?' said Madame Aarlberg.

'He means he'll make an attempt to get to Dunkirk through the woods and fields,' said Jacob.

'I wish him luck,' said Helene.

'If you don't succeed, Sergeant,' said Jacob, 'come back here and I will see how much help I can give you for another attempt tomorrow.'

'The Nazi pigs will be swarming tomorrow,' said Helene. 'Next it will be the day after tomorrow for the attempt, then two days, then three, then a week. And then a firing squad. For you, Papa. The Nazis will shoot everyone who hides British soldiers.'

'Helene, it isn't good to talk like that,' said Madame Aarlberg.

Bobby said, 'If the Germans do come while I'm here, it'll be better for me not to give myself up, but for you to hand me over. Make them welcome, thank them for coming.'

Helene looked at him in amazement, her mother in shock.

'What are you saying?' asked Madame Aarlberg.

'That if the Germans search your house and find me,' said Bobby, 'we all know what that will mean. So we've got to be sensible. Hand me over as soon as they arrive. Tell them I've only just got here. Best to work this sort of thing out in advance. But with any luck, I'll be away and in Dunkirk in a few hours from now.'

'Excuse me, if you please,' said Madame Aarlberg, 'but you are saying we are to give you to the Germans?'

'If they come, you've got to do just that,' said Bobby. 'Best thing for all of us.'

'I am shocked,' said Madame Aarlberg.

'I could not agree to it myself,' said Jacob.

Helene was silent.

'It still makes sense,' said Bobby who, in any case, was determined not to get himself into a situation as dramatic as that.

Helene came to angry life.

'You are an idiot,' she said.

'I can't agree with that,' said Bobby.

Helene glared at him, at his firm, resolute features, and still saw only an idiot.

'Our friends would get to know,' she fumed, 'they would get to know we delivered a British soldier into the hands of the Nazis.'

'Oh, I'll explain to your friends,' said Bobby.

'Explain? When?'

'When our armies come back,' said Bobby.

'In a thousand years?' Helene was stinging. 'That is how long Hitler has said his Greater German Reich will last.' She turned to her father. 'See what you have done, Papa? Out of all the thousands of British soldiers running for their lives, you have brought the craziest. He will explain, he said—' She was interrupted by a roar of sound as yet another formation of German fighter planes swept over the farm towards Dunkirk and the medley of ships in the lingering twilight, to strafe the escaping Allies for the last time that day. The noise engulfed the farmhouse in thunder for long, unbearable moments, during which Bobby and the French family stayed silent. They all had their own thoughts concerning the formidable might of Nazi Germany.

The noise abating, Bobby said, 'More trouble for the lads on the beaches. Hope my cousin and his friend are aboard a boat by now, and lending a hand with the oars.'

'Oars?' said Madame Aarlberg, limbs trembling, and the fate of France a constant worry. 'The soldiers from the beaches are in rowing boats?'

'He is crazy, don't you understand, Mama?' said Helene.

'The old Tommies, they made jokes too,' said

Jacob, wondering how heavy the heel of Germany would be. He had little faith in the French commanders. He thought them defeatist.

'I'll slip out in five minutes and see what the road looks like,' said Bobby. 'If I could cross it tonight and lie low, I could head for the beaches at first light. There's bound to be a ship or two waiting to pick up latecomers while the port's still open. I don't fancy sitting here and doing nothing. And I'm not keen on making things more difficult for you by hanging on.'

'Good,' said Helene. 'Yes, go and see what chance you have. You heard the news for yourself, and you know Dunkirk is expected to be in German hands by tomorrow. So you will have to get there tonight.'

Bobby gave her a thoughtful look, and decided she was indeed a fine, robust young woman. Her physique was the kind he admired in her sex. Pity about her animosity. Still, it was all of understandable. Who wouldn't be sick at what the Germans were capable of doing to the French Army after making mincemeat of the British?

'You're right,' he said, 'that's my best bet.'

Helene, wanting him out of the way for her parents' sake, said, 'I agree, but first you need a change of socks.'

Bobby laughed then. If he was committed, body and soul, to getting back home and starting again, in common with the better part of the BEF, his appreciation of Helene's mood was still wholesome.

Jacob thought him a young man of resilience. Madame Aarlberg thought him unusual in being able to laugh at all under the circumstances. Helene thought he was laughing too soon.

As far as young women were concerned, Bobby was responsive to two kinds. Those who were rattling good sports and game for healthy adventure, and those who could make up their minds without taking all day. He placed this young Frenchwoman in the second category, particularly as most Frenchwomen considered themselves too sophisticated to be regarded as good sports. He had discovered, before the blitzkreig hit the BEF, that some Frenchwomen thought most English girls played hockey and defended their virginity ferociously. But that wasn't his idea of good sports. Hockey had nothing to do with it, or virginity. It was an attitude in the main.

'I need a bath as well as a change of socks,' he said. 'But I'll give that a miss and save time.'

'Sergeant, I will give you socks,' said Jacob, 'but not to help you walk into the arms of the Germans. I can't agree that you should try to cross the road tonight.'

'Don't discourage him,' said Helene.

Jacob shook his head. While he had made up his mind to do what he could for Sergeant Somers, he was not prepared to help him commit suicide.

'Helene,' he said, 'I must discourage him from taking foolish risks.'

'Whenever he leaves, this evening or in the middle of the night or tomorrow morning, he'll be taking risks,' said Helene. 'He can please himself as far as I'm concerned. My worries are only for France.'

'Understandable,' said Bobby. 'As soon as it's dark I'll take a look at the road.'

'Very well,' said Jacob, quite sure nothing would come of it. 'First I'll find you clean socks.' He and Bobby left the kitchen together.

Helene began to walk restlessly about.

'Mama,' she said, 'it's necessary for this man to go as soon as possible.'

'It's necessary to you, Helene, I see that,' said Madame Aarlberg, 'but I would not myself wish to be responsible for pushing him into the arms of Hitler's Germans.'

'The Germans have taken thousands of British prisoners,' said Helene. 'Are we to consider it a tragedy if they take one more?'

'You are very angry with the British, Helene, but their defeat isn't the fault of this man alone.'

'I didn't say it was.' Helene made an impatient gesture. 'What is he doing now, finding a hiding-place in the attic?'

'I think, my infant, he's probably washing his feet,' said Madame Aarlberg gently.

Chapter Eight

London, the old grey heart of the British Empire, had for several days been alive with wonder at what was being called the miracle of Dunkirk. So had the rest of the United Kingdom, so had the Empire itself. It was twenty-minutes-past-nine that evening, with London still bathed in light and the whole country glued to its wireless sets, when the phone rang in the senior Adams household. Emily rushed to answer it.

'Hello, Em'ly Adams here – who's that?'

'Boots,' said a very tired man.

'Boots? Oh, thank the Lord. Where are you? Oh, you're not still at Dunkirk, are you? Only you sound far away.'

'I'm at London Bridge station,' said Boots, 'in a public phone box. Sir Henry's on his way home, and I'll be catching a train in about five minutes.'

'Oh, yes, get home quick,' said Emily. 'We've been so worried. Eloise phoned a little while ago, and then Rosie, and I could only tell them to keep hopin'. Are you all right?'

'I'm still standing up at the moment.' Boots sounded whacked. 'Has Tim arrived, or Bobby?'

'We haven't heard yet, not from either of them,' said Emily.

'Well, damn that,' said Boots, and thought of the fact that he'd been in the last major contingent of men to arrive on the beaches. 'I was hoping they were home.'

'Oh, I'm sure they'll turn up, lovey. I'll get a meal ready for you.'

'That and a bath and bed,' said Boots.

'Yes, I won't talk any more,' said Emily, 'I'll save it till you get home, except I'm so relieved to hear you, it's been like a miracle, so many of you bein' brought back.'

'You can call that a miracle, Em. The rest was a prime example of how not to fight the modern German Army. See you in twenty minutes or so. Keep listening for Tim.'

Boots hung up.

Emily rushed to let Chinese Lady and Mr Finch know Boots was on his way. Then she phoned Lizzy in the hope that Bobby had made it too. Lizzy was demonstrably touched to hear about Boots, but had to say there was no news of Bobby, or of Emma's young man, Jonathan Hardy. Emma had just come in, she said, after spending time with Jonathan's family in Walworth.

'Oh, we've got to believe they'll all get back, Lizzy.'

'Yes, we've got to believe,' said Lizzy.

Only ten minutes later, Emily had to answer the phone again. This time it was Tim, sounding as tired out as Boots. When told that his dad had just

113

preceded him, he said, 'Well, good old Dad, but what about Bobby?'

'Oh, I was speakin' to your Aunt Lizzy a little while ago,' said Emily, 'and they haven't heard yet from Bobby.'

Tim, who was at Charing Cross station, was silent for a moment, then he said as lightly as he could, 'Well, I hope he hasn't missed the boat.'

'Oh, he won't do that,' said Emily. 'Bobby's too sensible to miss any boat.'

'Anyway, Jonathan ought to have arrived,' said Tim, 'he was in front of our lot getting off Dunkirk.'

'And where was Bobby?' asked Emily.

'Farther back, in the rear of our column,' said Tim, and felt it was going to be difficult to tell the family he suspected Bobby was among the casualties of the day. 'Well, I'll go and catch a train, Mum, and be with you as soon as I can.'

'All right, Tim love, everyone's goin' to be glad to hear that you're safe and sound,' said Emily.

Having acquainted Chinese Lady and Mr Finch with the further good news, she set about preparing food for the homecomers, leaving Mr Finch to answer the phone when it rang yet again.

It was Rosie calling, and for the third time in three hours.

'Grandpa, don't tell me they're still not home yet.'

'Your father and your brother are,' said Mr Finch, 'they're on their way here now, Rosie.'

'Well, bless you for that,' said Rosie, hugely

relieved. 'But tell that airy-fairy father of mine to buck his ideas up and not to leave something like this until the very last minute. It's not good for our peace of mind. But wasn't Bobby with them?'

'They arrived separately,' said Mr Finch, 'and Bobby wasn't with either. Tim said he was some way behind him, which means he'll be among the last to be taken off, I imagine. We're waiting for Lizzy to ring us when he does turn up.'

'But why weren't Tim and Bobby together?' asked Rosie. 'They're in the same battery.'

'We'll find out when Tim gets here,' said Mr Finch.

'Well, we can rely on Bobby to make it, even if it means he really will be the last,' said Rosie. 'He's got stamina and stuffing, and he's positive as well. Is Boots – is my father all right?'

'His only complaint to your mother was to the effect that someone had blundered,' said Mr Finch.

'Yes, did you know that during the months of the phoney war, the BEF commanders had our troops digging trenches, as if it was going to be the Great War all over again?' said Rosie.

'Sometimes, Rosie, I despair of unimaginative leaders who never learn,' said Mr Finch.

'You and me both, Grandpa,' said Rosie. 'Never mind, let's be thankful for all the glad news. Give our two heroes my love, and tell Daddy I'll phone again in an hour to talk to him and to find out if Bobby's made it. No, wait, what about Emma's young man?'

'He should have landed by now,' said Mr Finch,

'Tim told Emily he was well in front of him at Dunkirk.'

'Oh, good for Emma,' said Rosie, 'that girl's a sweetie and a star turn.'

'Somewhere along the way of life,' said Mr Finch, 'this family acquired several star turns of the feminine gender.'

'Love you, Grandpa,' said Rosie.

'I cherish that,' said Mr Finch. 'By the way, if Polly's around, let her know her father is also back, according to Boots.'

'In the beginning, Grandpa,' said Rosie, 'Boots my dad was born to be the bearer of good tidings. He brought them to me when I was five years old. Give him my special love.'

Off the phone, Rosie delivered to Polly the kind of news that stopped the elegant ATS officer biting her lip. They were back in camp and in the officers' mess. Polly was halfway through a cigarette and a much-needed gin and tonic, and discouraging the company of other officers.

'Your father and mine, they're both back,' she said.

'Both,' said Rosie.

'And is that supposed to do something for us?' asked Polly.

'Well, after days of racked nerves, it is supposed to cheer us up,' said Rosie.

'I thought so,' said Polly, 'but I must be getting some kind of complaint, because I feel like a bloody good cry.'

'Not in here, please, Captain Simms,' said Rosie.

'I appreciate your embarrassment, Subaltern Adams,' said Polly, 'let's get drunk instead.'

'Well, thanks, Polly,' said Rosie, 'I'll have a large gin and tonic to start with.'

'So you shall, ducky,' said Polly. 'Who do we toast on our way to inebriation?'

'You and me,' said Rosie, 'and your dad and my dad.'

Polly's smile was not as brittle as usual. She knew Rosie meant Boots, her adoptive parent, not Major Charles Armitage, her natural father.

'Shall we include the big ships and little ships, Rosie?'

'Yes, let's go the whole way,' said Rosie, 'let's include the Polish soldier who somehow lost his trousers climbing into a fishing-boat, and the Scots lieutenant who wanted to show us saucy picture postcards from Paris.'

'Did he?' said Polly, signalling to a steward. 'Did he get them from Paris?'

'No, from somewhere up his kilt,' said Rosie. 'I like the Scots.'

'I like their kilts,' said Polly, and thought about when she might be able to see Boots.

It was Chinese Lady who opened the door to Boots. If she was shocked by the state of his uniform and his unshaven look, she did not say so.

'Well, you're here at last, Boots.'

'Hello, old girl,' he said.

'You left it a bit late,' said Chinese Lady, 'we've all been on tenderhooks.' She meant tenterhooks.

'Still, you're home now, so I won't go on at you. Tim's been on the phone, and he'll be here soon.'

'Well, I'm damned glad to hear it,' said Boots. Carrying a small valise containing his most personal items, he stepped in. He put his left arm around his mother's shoulders, gave her a squeeze and kissed her cheek. He was forty-three, she was sixty-three. He felt drained, and she looked sprightly, showing not a single grey hair or furrow. 'What's the idea?' he asked.

'Oh, you've got something to say, have you?' she said, keeping her feelings to herself.

'Yes,' said Boots, 'why have you been growing younger while I've been growing older?'

Chinese Lady actually laughed.

'Go on with you,' she said, 'you're still not improved with those remarks of yours.'

Emily appeared, Mr Finch behind her. Emily darted, wound her arms around Boots's neck and kissed him.

'Thank goodness someone's home,' she said.

'I understand you've all been on tenderhooks,' said Boots, shaking hands with his stepfather.

'Well, and I should think we 'ave,' said Emily. 'We – wait a minute, what d'you mean, *tenderhooks*?'

'Em'ly, it's no good pretendin' we haven't been worryin' and hardly able to sit still,' said Chinese Lady. 'It's been a very fidgetin' time for all of us, what with Boots and Tim and Bobby all leavin' it so late. But I've told Boots we're not goin' to go on about his – his—'

118

'Tardiness?' suggested Mr Finch.

'No, well, he's home now, and lookin' like he needs a good meal and then his bed,' said Chinese Lady, 'and I don't know why we're standin' here when I expect he needs a sit-down.'

'And a whisky,' said Boots.

'I'll join you,' said Mr Finch who, along with Emily and Chinese Lady, thought it out of place to make any comments on Boots's tired and dishevelled appearance. Nothing better could have been expected.

'Oh, a meal's nearly ready, Boots,' said Emily, 'and we're hopin' Tim will be home himself any moment to share it with you.'

'Come along,' said Chinese Lady, 'come along. Oh, I think I'll have a little drop of port, Edwin.'

'Perhaps a full glass, Maisie?' suggested Mr Finch.

'Well, all right, Edwin, just this once,' said Chinese Lady graciously.

Just before ten, a taxi pulled up outside the Hardy home in Walworth. The driver tooted. Jemima heard it. She ran from the kitchen to the street door. She pulled the door open and saw Jonathan alighting from the taxi. He looked like the rag-tag and bobtail of old Fred Karno's army, and all he had with him was his rifle and tin hat.

'Hello, Mum,' he said.

The taxi driver called, 'Good luck, mate, hope yer do 'em next time round.'

'Thanks,' called Jonathan, and away the taxi

went. 'Free ride, the cabbie gave us, Mum, self and another squaddie.'

'Jonathan, I be a happy woman this moment,' said Jemima. From the kitchen surged the rest of the family, Job, Jane, Jennifer and young Jonas. They surrounded Jonathan on the doorstep. Jennifer hugged him.

'Durned if this don't call for getting a bit tiddly,' said Job.

'Mum's baked a cake,' said young Jonas.

'There's a funny smell,' said Jane.

'That's me,' said Jonathan. 'I tried to get to a phone at Victoria railway station, to ring Emma, but there were great queues.'

'Jane, run to a public call box and phone Emma,' said Jemima. 'Go quick. Jonathan be too worn out to go himself. Run, Jane, time's getting late.'

Emma, receiving the call, went off her head and said she'd come and see Jonathan at once. But it's gone ten, said Jane, and he's so worn out I think he'll be asleep by the time you arrive. Emma asked if he was all right otherwise. Oh, he's glad to be home, said Jane, but he smells a bit. Smells a bit? Yes, said Jane, he's one of the great unwashed just now, and smelling like a farmyard. I don't care if he's public enemy number one as long as he's all in one piece, said Emma. I didn't see anything missing, said Jane. Let's be thankful, then, and not mind about his smell, said Emma. Tell him I'll come and see him tomorrow morning. We'll have him washed all over by then, said Jane. Oh, terrific, said Emma.

'Emma, what about your brother Bobby?' asked Jane.

'He's still not home,' said Emma.

'Oh, he will be, though,' said Jane, 'we're all on your side, you can be sure.'

'Did – did Jonathan ask after me, Jane?'

'You were his first mention,' said Jane, 'he hoped to ring you from London, but there were great big queues at all the phone boxes.'

'I think the whole country's on the phone,' said Emma. 'My Uncle Boots and cousin Tim called to say they were on their way. Thanks for coming out to phone me, Jane. I'm really grateful for that.'

'It be a downright pleasure, Emma.'

Tim had arrived home and found his dad there. He'd have enjoyed the reunion with his mum and his grandparents much more if there'd only been news of Bobby.

In Sunrise Avenue, off Denmark Hill, Lizzy and Ned were still hoping to hear from Bobby. They knew now that Boots and Tim had made it, and so had Emma's young man. What they didn't know was that Tim was keeping to himself the possibility that Bobby might be among the dead of Bergues.

He did speak to Boots, however, in the bath-room. Boots was having a welcome soak, Tim sitting on the bathroom stool and recounting the events that took place at dawn and afterwards.

'You were with Bobby up to the time of the air attack?' said Boots, who might have gone to sleep in the bath if Tim hadn't come in to talk to him.

'All the way,' said Tim. 'When I came to, I was heading for Dunkirk with all the other survivors. I've still got a head that hurts a bit, but that doesn't bother me. What does is what might have happened to Bobby. I think he must have been a casualty, or he'd still have been with me.'

'Yes, I see that,' said Boots. 'If he hadn't caught a packet himself, he'd have looked for you, helped you to your feet and been with you when you came to.'

'I can't help thinking he did catch it,' said Tim. 'I asked several blokes and one of our officers if they'd seen him since the attack or knew what had happened to him, and got no infor-mation at all from them. It's something I don't want to mention to the family, that I think he's a casualty.'

'No, keep it under your hat, Tim old lad,' said Boots. 'You don't know what happened, in any case. It might be serious, and it might not. Your Aunt Lizzy's going to phone any moment, just as soon as she thinks you've arrived. She'll want to talk to you about Bobby if he's still not home.'

'I'll just have to keep her optimistic,' said Tim. 'Rotten bad show over there, Dad. Where the hell were our tanks?'

'All over the place,' said Boots. 'The Jerries used theirs in concentrated formations, like battering rams.'

'French people were chucking things at us during our retreat,' said Tim.

'Yes, we had some of that in places,' said Boots. 'Feeling fed-up, are you, Tim old lad?'

'Yes, I am, Dad,' said Tim, 'and I'm well and truly whacked, and depressed about Bobby.'

'Join the club,' said Boots soberly, 'but outside the club try to spread optimism.'

Lizzy did phone, and she did speak to Tim, and Tim told her that although he didn't know where Bobby had got to, he was the kind of bloke who, having made sergeant, wasn't going to get left behind, even if it meant he finished up as the last man aboard the last ship. Lizzy and Ned had to be content with that.

Jacob and Bobby returned to the kitchen, Bobby wearing a pair of Jacob's clean socks and his tin hat. The tin hat was slightly tilted to keep it clear of his bandaged temple. And he was carrying his rifle.

'What is that for, to shoot all the German Army?' asked Helene.

'Hardly,' said Bobby, 'but I can't leave it behind, it's against the regulations.'

Helene knew then he had made up his mind not just to take a look at the road, but to cross it and go on his way. If he could. Good, she thought. It was madness, of course. He would lose himself in the darkness or run into Germans, but that was his own affair.

'Sergeant,' said Jacob, 'take care when you reach—' He stopped and stiffened. His wife and daughter held their breath. Bobby's jaw tightened. The sound of an engine swelled until it seemed to be loudly harsh outside the front door. Then it ceased abruptly.

'That's a truck,' said Bobby.

'It can't be looking for you,' said Jacob.

'No,' said Bobby, 'but if it is, you know what to do. But right now, I won't stand and wait.' Taking the map and his rifle with him, he disappeared into the farmhouse scullery, where Madame Aarlberg made her cheese and butter. It had a back door.

Someone knocked thunderously on the front door.

'That's a Nazi knock,' said Helene, her face stiff.

'If anyone is nervous, that's quite natural,' said Jacob, and left the kitchen to answer the summons. Helene was tense, her mother apprehensive. They heard a guttural voice, a demanding one.

'*Das Wasser, mein Herr.*'

Water.

Jacob was facing two German artillerymen, helmeted. One was a sergeant, carrying a large metal container that was capable of holding many litres of water. On the dark forecourt loomed the bulk of a German Army truck. The men had driven up to the farmhouse by way of a lane that led from the road.

'*Das Wasser?*' he said. He knew a fair amount of German. 'Ah, water, yes.' He reached, indicating his willingness to take the can and fill it. The sergeant declined the invitation by pushing Jacob's hand aside. He gestured. Unmistakably, he preferred to be led to a tap to fill the can himself. Jacob supposed he felt there was a risk of being given poisoned water. 'Show me.' The command was spoken in thick French.

'This way,' said Jacob, wisely offering no argument as he led both men through the hall into the kitchen. The second man, a private, held a rifle. They followed close on Jacob's heels, and in the kitchen saw a middle-aged woman sitting at the table, and a young woman standing in front of the range.

The German private stationed himself just inside the door, rifle held across his chest, eyes taking in Helene and her strong, healthy figure. The sergeant looked around, his attitude that of a man who belonged to the invincible elite of Germany. The silence increased the tension, and Helene suspected he knew it. Her body was stiff, her feelings rageful. Her mother's lips were tightly compressed. Jacob was sombre.

'*Das Wasser*,' said the German sergeant and walked to the sink. He stood the can in it, unscrewed the cap and turned on a tap.

'That is hot water,' said Helene.

'*Was das?*' asked the German.

'Hot water,' said Jacob in German.

'*Heiss?* Ah, so.' The German turned off the hot flow. He moved the can and let the cold water tap run. It gushed into the container. He glanced at the door to the scullery, Madame Aarlberg's dairy. The door was slightly ajar. Madame Aarlberg affected interest only in the running water. Helene, nerves on the brink, wondered what her father would do if the German swine decided to push that door wide open. Would he at once do what that mad idiot of an English sergeant had said he must? Declare his presence and hand him over? Helene clenched her teeth. The German sergeant shifted his glance to her, his eyes speculative beneath his helmet, his broad face dusty.

'Your daughter?' he said to Jacob in his guttural French.

'Yes,' said Jacob.

The sergeant, making a bold study of Helene's figure, let a grin show. Her eyes flashed fire.

'Not bad, this one, eh, Steiner?' he said to the man with the rifle. 'Bursting with health, eh?'

'I can show you better than that in Bavaria,' said the private.

'But not with this one's wild eyes,' said the sergeant, while the water ran and ran.

'I didn't know you were talking about her eyes,' said the private.

The sergeant laughed. He was a man basking in the sun of victory. Poland, Holland, Belgium and the British Expeditionary Force had all been crushed with ease. France was next.

He turned off the tap and screwed the container's cap back in place. He glanced at Jacob.

'Bring it,' he said.

Madame Aarlberg winced to have Jacob spoken to like that. Jacob, however, nodded in silent assent and lifted the heavy can from the sink. He carried it to the door. The man with the rifle stood aside, but followed him as he went through to the hall and the open front door. A prod from the rifle directed him to the standing truck. The inky night sky was studded with diamonds, and Jacob made out the dark figures of soldiers in the open troop-carrier. He hefted the can high and hands took it from him.

In the kitchen, the German sergeant looked around again. He saw bottles of red wine in a rack. With the easy arrogance of a superior being, he helped himself to four bottles, then smiled at Helene.

'*Danke, Fräulein,*' he said.

Helene looked through him. He left. Jacob came back. They heard the truck engine roar into life. Madame Aarlberg drew a deep breath.

'It was not too bad,' she said.

The truck turned on the forecourt and moved down the lane towards the road. Bobby reappeared.

'I don't think that was very pleasant for you,' he said.

'It was disgusting,' said Helene.

'It could have been worse,' said Madame Aarlberg, 'they only wanted water.'

'But robbed us of four bottles of wine,' said Helene.

'I suppose some conquering heroes do take liberties,' said Bobby. He looked at Helene. 'This isn't the best time of our lives, is it?'

'I have just endured the insufferable,' said Helene.

'My fault for being here,' said Bobby. He felt intensely sorry for this family. If the French Army performed no better than the British, France would suffer German occupation for God knows how long. 'I'll take a look at the road now,' he said. Only a sore head troubled him. A long rest and a substantial meal had cured him of fatigue.

Jacob was resigned now to the sergeant's determination to cross the road, if he could, and attempt the by-ways in the dark, trusting to luck and a sense of direction, in the hope of reaching the beaches while the night was still young and the Germans waiting for morning light. Possibly, just possibly, the evacuation had not yet finished. However, Jacob doubted if the sergeant could successfully negotiate unknown ways, particularly through wooded areas. He was more likely to get hopelessly lost.

'Sergeant, if you find the road clear enough to cross, I will take you to Dunkirk.'

'Jacob?' said Madame Aarlberg in alarm.

'No, not you, Papa,' said Helene, 'you have fought your war. This one is mine. If this crazy man wishes to risk himself, I must be the one to at least see he doesn't get lost.'

'No, I can't let you do that,' said Bobby firmly.

'Is it for you to decide?' said Helene tetchily. 'No. It is for my father and me. Someone must go with you. I will.'

'I object,' said Bobby.

'Ah, because I am not a man?' demanded Helene.

'What's that got to do with it?' asked Bobby. 'You look a fine strong girl to me, and as good as any man, but you're not coming with me. If we were caught, I'd just be taken prisoner. You'd get shot.'

Helene ground her teeth.

Jacob said, 'Sergeant, Helene is very capable and will know how to take care of herself.'

'Well, I'll let her come as far as the road with me and point me to the best crossing point,' said Bobby. 'But that's all.'

'If every English sergeant is as bumptious and foolish as you,' said Helene, 'no wonder the British Army was beaten so easily.'

'That's a sore point with me,' said Bobby. 'Shall we go?'

'Now? If you wish,' said Helene, and shrugged.

Bobby thanked Jacob and Madame Aarlberg warmly for their kindness, help and hospitality, which he would not forget, then said *au revoir* to them. Jacob's faint smile suggested the parting was merely temporary. He and his wife watched as the British sergeant left the house with Helene. The darkness quickly swallowed them.

Madame Aarlberg sighed.

'It doesn't seem to matter now,' she said.

'Whether he gets away or not?'

'No, taking the risk of helping him. It seems an insignificant thing compared with what we shall have to face if France is beaten. That is terrible to contemplate, Jacob.'

'I know,' said Jacob, and put an arm around her.

*   *   *

129

Helene and Bobby were silent. Behind them, the farmhouse showed no lights, the shutters of its kitchen windows being closed, and they halted for a short while to let their eyes adjust to the darkness. Then Helene began to walk towards the fields lying fallow. Bobby followed. She said nothing, but he could hear her moving, her skirt whispering around her active legs and vigorous thighs. Farm buildings loomed on either side, Helene electing to take the same route by which Jacob had brought Bobby to the farmhouse. She could have reached the road directly by way of the lane, but it would give them no cover, and who could say another German truck would not thunder up to the house at any time?

She was not disposed to take unnecessary risks. She remained silent as she led the way, although she was fretful with ragged nerves. On the one hand, she wished this man out of the way. On the other, she knew there was no sense in what he hoped to do. He would never be able to break through the arc of massive German armour which, according to the radio late this afternoon, was now sealing off Dunkirk before moving to occupy it tomorrow. It was idiotic of the man to even think he could. The Germans would be bivouacking in the fields and everywhere else, waiting for daylight. Yet to discourage him meant giving him shelter until the situation became better, if it ever could.

She stopped on the path adjacent to a hedge. Bobby halted behind her. She grimaced in the darkness. He must surely know now there was no

130

use in going farther. The sounds that came to her ears were undeniably those of men out of the vehicles that were filling the road.

Bobby, peering over her shoulder, whispered, 'That sounds like Jerries talking their heads off. Not in my favour, is it?'

'It never was, but you would not be told.' Helene's irritations surfaced. 'It is the way of the English, not to be told.'

'Yes, we're a stupid lot,' said Bobby. 'Can we get closer to the road? I'd still like to take a look.'

'You are crazy, the worst I have ever met,' breathed Helene, but turned and went on. She stopped again when they were only thirty metres from the road. It was not necessary to go further. From where they were now it was obvious the road was filled with military vehicles almost nose to tail. Dark figures stood beside many of them, their voices carrying. Men flushed with successful conquest obviously felt no need to whisper.

Bobby knew then that the Germans were not going to play about. They were going to smother Dunkirk.

'Oh, sod it,' he said in English.

'You are swearing?' said Helene. 'I am not surprised. You can see for yourself what you are up against. A risk is a risk. Suicide is stupid. But go if you must.'

'I'd go if I could,' said Bobby, 'but I can't, can I?' He had felt it would be like this, while nursing a hope that it wouldn't.

'You are suffering? Who is not?' said Helene,

131

feeling there was nothing to do but return to the farmhouse and for everyone to go to bed, even if sleep proved impossible. Mesmerized in a sickening way by the dark outlines of men and machines, she wondered what was the point of bothering about this man. She stared as he sat down against the hedge. 'Now what are you doing?' she hissed.

'Thinking,' said Bobby, his mind on Dunkirk, his only avenue of escape.

'Good. Stay there and think all night, if you wish. I am going back.'

'Thanks for everything,' said Bobby.

'God give me patience with English idiots,' breathed Helene. 'What is there to think about? You know you can't go tonight. Or are you thinking it is now or never?'

'I don't believe in now or never,' said Bobby. 'There's always some alternative.'

'Try it, then,' said Helene. 'Jump into the Nazi frying-pan and see how it will burn you alive. The swines are going to be here all night, and I am going back before they begin to make use of these fields.'

She walked away, retracing her steps. Bobby thought about what was sensible, then came to his feet and followed her. When they reached the house, Helene's parents were listening to the radio. The latest news was that France was having to write off the British Army and its air force, and face the Germans alone. Jacob was not in the least surprised by the return of Bobby, and to hear from Helene that a German armoured column was camped almost on their doorstep. Bobby suggested he should take himself off and sleep in a field.

'In a field?' said Madame Aarlberg, sad-eyed for France.

'Now he wants to risk being trodden on by jack-boots while he's asleep,' said Helene.

'The bed you used today is yours, Sergeant,' said Jacob. 'The Boche won't be looking for wandering British soldiers tonight. Some may come in the morning for things like water or wine. In the morning, we can talk again.'

'I'm owing you enough already,' said Bobby, 'but could you stretch to a bath?'

'Bath, you say?' asked Madame Aarlberg. 'There is always hot water.'

Abruptly, Helene said, 'I am going up to my bed.' And she disappeared without saying good night.

'She is not herself,' said Madame Aarlberg.

'Are any of us?' asked Jacob.

'I know a bath won't solve any problems, yours or mine,' said Bobby, 'but I'd be grateful if I could have one.'

'Of course,' said Madame Aarlberg.

Bobby indulged in a long soak, during which he reflected on his prospects. Prolonged reflection should have told him they were almost nil, but Sergeant Bobby Somers didn't believe in negatives. That kind of attitude was totally foreign to all members of the Somers and Adams families. He thought of Tim and Uncle Boots. He felt confident they'd stuck to being positive enough to get themselves to the beaches in time to be taken off. Along with Emma's lovelight of the moment, Jonathan Hardy, a stalwart bloke.

He'd got to get home himself, he'd got to.

He slept surprisingly well once his head touched the pillow. Jacob and his wife lay awake for some time before they managed to doze off. As for Helene, the angry one, she tossed and turned at the thought of Hitler's war machine overrunning France. She slept hardly at all.

Neither did France.

Across the troubled waters, Jonathan slept like a log. So did Tim and Boots. In the officers' quarters of a certain ATS unit, Polly slept like a woman who, by reason of giving to life more than she took out of it, deserved the bliss of slumber. Rosie slept gratefully because of the deliverance of Boots and Tim, although she worried about Bobby for a while before closing her eyes. Eloise, in her training camp, slept after a long day of hard work interspersed with moments of exhilaration. She knew Boots and Tim were safely home. Rosie had phoned the camp Commandant, and the Commandant had had the good news relayed to Private Eloise Adams, an Anglo-French volunteer recruit.

Emma would have gone happily to sleep if only her brother Bobby had arrived home in company with Tim and Jonathan. As it was, she kept waking up.

So did Lizzy and Ned.

Tommy and Vi, and Sammy and Susie, while relieved at the return of Boots and Tim, had Bobby's absence on their minds when they retired, but once asleep concern was blanked out.

Emily woke up in the middle of the night to find she was not alone in the bed. She'd had it to herself for months. Who'd invaded it tonight? Oh, Boots, of course. She turned and snuggled up. Boots was dead to the world, and Emily had her first experience of snuggling up to an unreactive human log.

Oh, well.

The port and the beaches of Dunkirk were deserted and silent. At midnight, a senior British Army officer, Major General Alexander, and a senior Royal Navy officer, Captain Tennant, had made a survey of the beaches and the harbour from a motor-boat. They satisfied themselves that not a single Allied soldier had been overlooked. All had been taken off.

They left.

The dark, night sea washed the trampled and gouged sands.

The miracle, accomplished, was over.

Sergeant Bobby Somers, however, needed another one if he was to get home himself.

Chapter Nine

Jacob opened the bedroom shutters to let in the morning light. Bobby, who had slept the night through, despite all that was on his mind, woke up.

'Sergeant Somers?' said Jacob, and Bobby saw how sombre he was.

'All right, Jacob, tell me the worst,' said Bobby.

'The Boche are entering Dunkirk.'

'That's worse than the worst,' said Bobby, grimacing.

'I have to agree,' said Jacob. 'Even if you could get through to the town, you could get no further. I regret, all your ships have gone.'

'Then I need a lifeboat,' said Bobby. 'Do you know what the road is like?'

'Noisy and busy,' said Jacob. 'When you have washed and shaved, come down to breakfast and we will talk.'

'Do you have a razor I could borrow?' Bobby, twenty plus what the blitzkreig had done to him in a few weeks of calamitous war, was rough round the edges.

'My razor is on your washstand,' said Jacob.

'You're a good old scout, Jacob,' said Bobby, slipping from the bed. He wore only his brief underpants. His body, thought Jacob, looked strong, hard and fit. British soldiers rarely ran to fat. The Tommies of the last war had been very lean, some even stringy. 'If I haven't said so before, I owe you more than I can ever repay.'

'I repeat, Sergeant, your fathers were my friends and comrades.'

'They must have had a helpful comrade in you,' said Bobby, his bandage still in place, his wound sore but bearable. 'I'll send you a picture postcard when I get back to England.'

Jacob smiled.

'I think, for the time being, it would be better if you dressed in the clothes I've put on that chair for you,' he said. 'Yes, better in case any of our workers should see you in your uniform and talk about you. Leave your uniform where it is. I will take care of it, and your rifle and helmet. For the time being, you understand.'

'Yes, understood,' said Bobby.

Helene, up early despite a wretched night, came in from the fields for breakfast. She had seen to the chickens and also made sure one of the workers was attending to the dairy herd. She looked what she still was, an angry and troubled young woman of France. She gave Bobby a brief glance, then a disgusted look, for he was wearing a blue shirt buttoned to the neck to hide his identity disc, with dark blue trousers and farm boots. The items all belonged to her father.

'Why is he dressed like that?' she asked Jacob.

'To make him look like one of our workers, Helene, until he can get away,' said Jacob.

'With his war wound staring any Germans in the face?' said Helene.

'An accident, not a war wound,' said Jacob. 'It's one of our first-aid dressings, not a military field dressing.'

Silently, Helene sat down. Bobby said good morning to her. She did not respond. Breakfast began, but it was not a happy meal. Madame Aarlberg's home-made French bread and rich butter provided its basis, but not much was consumed, although the coffee pot was raided until it ran dry. However, one disturbing factor was missing. There were no sounds of war, no sounds of heavy guns or roaring planes. But this did not ameliorate Helene's unfriendly mood. She was frankly out of sympathy with everything except the fate of France.

Madame Aarlberg hid her sadness, but Jacob's sombre look was very evident. If he too was worrying about the forthcoming German on-slaught on the heart of France, he nevertheless suddenly asked what was the best way of helping Sergeant Somers.

Not taking kindly to that, Helene said, 'We should be asking what is the best way of helping France.'

'Only the French Army can do that now,' said Jacob.

'We can help with prayers, Jacob,' said Madame Aarlberg.

'Perhaps, perhaps,' said Jacob, 'but France is in the hands of its fifth columnists, headed by Laval. Laval alone is worth fifty divisions to the Nazis, and Hitler himself will probably decorate him.'

'No, our soldiers will fight,' said Helene fiercely. 'General Gamelin won't be influenced by people like Laval.'

'Gamelin and other generals have no heart for the war, Helene,' said Jacob, 'and Laval and his kind have made France unsure of herself.'

Bobby, following the French dialogue, said, 'Are you saying France will collapse, Jacob?'

Jacob? Ah, thought Helene, now he has made my father his brother. He is a worming snake.

'France is in a defeatist mood,' said Jacob.

'No, no, I can't believe our armies won't stand up to the Germans,' said Madame Aarlberg.

'I hope I'm wrong, I hope they will,' said Jacob. 'If France falls and if Hitler then invades and conquers Britain, Europe will exist in darkness far beyond my life span. So what must we do? All of us, French, Belgian, Dutch and all others, must do everything possible to help Britain become a fortress that will successfully resist a German invasion. They still have their Navy, and they represent Europe's only hope. What I am saying, Helene, is that to help Sergeant Somers is to help Britain. More so if such help could be multiplied.'

'I'm not sure how you can have such faith in a people who have let France down so badly,' said Helene.

'It comes from knowing them in the last war,' said Jacob.

'So?' said Helene, not caring that Sergeant Somers was following the dialogue. 'It seems to me, Papa, that since the last war they've gone soft.'

'Well,' said Bobby, 'we're not a nation of puddings, not yet. Winston Churchill's tubby, of course, but he's no pudding. He growls. Puddings don't.'

'Churchill?' said Madame Aarlberg. 'What is he saying about Churchill, Helene?'

'That he's not a pudding,' said Helene tersely.

'Mercy, how could he be?' said Madame Aarlberg.

'It's this man's crazy way of talking,' said Helene.

'You did mention that Hitler's gobbling up Europe,' said Bobby. 'He's gobbled up the Czechs and Poles, and made a meal of the Norwegians, Dutch and Belgians. And he's chewed up my lot.' Bobby grimaced. 'The French are next on his menu. Then what? Any other people he fancies. That's when he'll get fatal indigestion, and it'll blow him apart.'

'We are to wait for that to happen?' said Helene, fuming. 'It is just talk, stupid talk.'

'I think it was about Hitler destroying himself,' said Madame Aarlberg. 'Ah, that is something to pray for.' She looked at Bobby. 'It was well said, *mon Sergent.*'

'Oh, just a wish and a prayer. And my friends call me Bobby.'

'We are pleased you have friends,' said Helene,

who thought that what his friends called him was trivial and irrelevant. In any case, what a stupid name.

'Let us call him Maurice Picquart,' said Jacob. 'One of our farm workers, until we can safely get him away.'

'Mother of Jesus,' breathed Helene, 'you are now suggesting he stays indefinitely?'

'Indefinitely?' said Bobby. 'That's not for me.'

'No, of course not,' said Jacob, 'only until you can escape the Boche.'

'That is dangerously indefinite,' said Helene.

'A few days, perhaps,' said Jacob, whose calm approach to events and crises rarely fell to pieces. 'I am sure, as one of our farm workers, he could use a hoe. If we could help him reach Switzerland—'

'Switzerland?' Helene was exasperated. What was the point of the whole family risking their lives to help one British soldier when Hitler had millions of men? 'Is everyone going crazy?'

'I don't fancy Switzerland,' said Bobby. He still had Dunkirk in mind. Dunkirk was close to England. 'I'll get interned among cuckoo clocks. A motorboat from Dunkirk would suit me better.'

'A motorboat?' said Helene. 'What an imbecile.' She hesitated before going on. 'Do as my father says, do some work for us for a while. We are short of workers, and I can show you many fields that need hoeing.'

'That's fair,' said Bobby. 'I'm willing for the time being. Well, until Dunkirk has settled down.'

'I'll see if I can get a French identity document

for you,' said Jacob, who felt Bobby might come to need such.

'Who will you talk to?' asked Helene.

'A friend, naturally,' said Jacob.

'Who?' persisted Helene, wanting to guard her father against taking foolish risks.

'Someone I can trust,' said Jacob. He came to his feet. 'I must talk to our farmhands.'

'To tell them you've hired a new labourer called Maurice Picquart?' said Helene.

'It's the wisest thing to do,' said Jacob, and looked at Bobby. 'You are suitably dressed for the fields, my friend, and if you will go with Helene, she will give you a hoe.'

'Yes, I'm willing,' said Bobby, who always favoured activity. It was Sunday, but no-one had spoken about church. It was impossible for the family to attend Mass in Dunkirk, and so farm work was the order of the day.

Madame Aarlberg, still without her daily help, began to clear the table. Helene, with a critical look at Bobby, thought that although the shirt and trousers were credible, his bandaged head spoke more of a war wound than of a farm accident.

'Come,' she said brusquely, then delayed a moment longer to switch on the radio. With Dunkirk in German hands and the British gone, the news dealt mainly with the immense task facing the French now that massive German armoured divisions were preparing to launch an offensive in the direction of Paris. The morale of the French Army was high, however. And so on. Helene switched the set off, then took Bobby to a large field of young sprouting flax, having planted a hoe in his hands. The sun was up, the green plants looked defiant, but a host of weeds looked menacing. There was still smoke over Dunkirk, but it was lazy and dying, and the skies were clear of German dive bombers. The road was quiet, except for the occasional passing of what she supposed were German vehicles.

'This is it?' said Bobby, studying the long rows of shooting flax and proliferating weeds.

'Yes,' said Helene. The morning sun emphasized the outdoor nature of her complexion, which was of the kind to arouse delicate little shudders in the fastidious ladies of Paris. 'We have been short of workers for many weeks.'

'We've been short of a—' Bobby checked just in time. He'd been going to say Wellington. That wouldn't have done much for this abrasive French girl. 'A Napoleon,' he said.

'You are telling me your commanders didn't know how to fight the Germans?' said Helene.

'Not much,' said Bobby. 'Well, that's the general view of the men. The infantry were put into trenches. It was going to be trench warfare all over again in the minds of our High Command.'

'My God,' breathed Helene, 'even I know tanks ride over trenches. What blockheads, what idiots, donkeys and imbeciles!'

'Don't advertise it,' said Bobby. 'It's secret infor-mation. If it gets out, the mighty might fall from a great height. Well, I'll get started.' He stripped off

143

his shirt. In his singlet, his tanned arms and shoulders caught Helene's eye. She wasn't impressed.

'You are too warm even before you have begun?' she said.

'No, not yet. But I know I will be.' Bobby took off his identity disc and stowed it in his pocket. Helene gave his singlet a disgusted look.

'That is filthy,' she said.

'Like me until I had that bath,' said Bobby. 'But I'll wash it tonight, with my pants. If I can have use of your washtub.'

'My mother will do that for you!' Helene frowned, then became brisk. 'Now, commence here. Weed each row in turn. Let me show you how to do it.' She took the hoe from him and manipulated it with quick efficiency. Turned weeds fell roots uppermost. 'Do you see?'

'Thanks,' said Bobby, who thought it friendlier not to tell her he knew what a hoe was and how it should be used. He took it and began work. She stayed a few moments to watch him. He looked strong and vigorous, handling the hoe easily and exposing roots to the sun.

'Don't dirty your bandage, and go to the house for lunch at one,' she said, then left him to it.

'What if the Jerries show up?' called Bobby.

'Who?' Helene stopped and turned.

'The Boche,' said Bobby, 'the Greater German Reich swines.'

'They won't, not today, not yet,' she said. 'They are busy in Dunkirk, and perhaps looking for

British soldiers in hiding. They will look for men like you later.'

I'll make sure they don't find me, thought Bobby. I'll do them in the eye yet.

It was Sunday, the third day of June, but Tommy and Vi, with Sammy and Susie, called on Boots instead of going to church. So did Lizzy and Ned. They all wanted to hear first-hand about Dunkirk. The day was another hot and summery one, and they all sat in the garden. Boots and Tim were relaxing. They had ten days leave before rejoining their units. The uppermost questions concerned Bobby. Wasn't it known at all where he was yesterday, the last day of the evacuation? Tim had to answer that one. He said he'd been with Bobby up to early morning, then they got separated due to Bobby's responsibilities as a sergeant. What responsibilities? Oh, rounding up members of his gun crew to bring them all together. But didn't he rejoin you afterwards? He was some way back, said Tim, and I suppose he was satisfied at knowing I was ahead of him, that he couldn't lose me. But didn't you stop and wait for him? We weren't allowed to stop, any of us, said Tim, the officers kept us moving. But when you reached Dunkirk, didn't you stop and wait for him then? The town marshals and beach marshals kept every man in line and moving forward, said Tim, which was true enough.

'Tim,' said Ned, 'was Bobby wounded in any way?'

'Not while he was with me,' said Tim, whose

slight wound had been dressed on landing. His leg was merely stiff now.

'But did you come under attack in Dunkirk?' asked Ned. 'The beaches were being strafed continually, weren't they?'

'Yes, we got our dose of that,' said Tim.

'Oh, lor', frightening,' said Vi.

'Bobby could have been hit?' said Sammy.

'You don't think about friends or yourself catching it,' said Tim.

'Boots, why aren't you saying anything?' asked Susie.

'Yes, why?' asked Lizzy.

'I can't add anything to what Tim's said,' responded Boots. 'But we all know Bobby. He'll turn up one way or another.'

'I've said that a dozen times to Ned, and he's said it a dozen times to me,' remarked Lizzy, 'but I'm beginning to get all the wrong feelings.'

'Trust Bobby,' said Tommy.

'I'll put money on him,' said Sammy.

'I'll put my last shirt,' said Tim, who was finding it difficult to hide his feeling that Bobby had caught a packet during the air attack.

Emily came out.

'Boots, Rosie's on the phone,' she said. 'Oh, and I'm making a pot of tea for everyone.'

Boots let a smile show as he got up. Tea was the eternal saviour. He went into the hall and picked up the phone.

'Rosie?'

'Oh, hello, Daddy old love, I was going to ring

last night but got squiffy instead with Polly. It was late, anyway, and I thought you'd be flopped. Was it very bad over there?'

'Not half as much for me as for a hell of a lot of others,' said Boots.

'But you made it, with Tim,' said Rosie, 'and I'm happy about that. You're incorrigible, going off at your age to cross swords with the Germans again. I'm trying to get two days leave so that I can come and talk to you.'

'And put me in a bathchair?' said Boots.

'Oh, you're not actually decrepit,' said Rosie, 'just inclined to think you're still a Boy Scout. Oh, I had a telegram from Major Armitage to let me know he's back too.' Major Charles Armitage was her natural father. She conducted a friendly relationship with him and elected not to be drawn into anything closer. 'He landed three days ago.'

'He's still a Boy Scout too, is he?' said Boots.

'Don't get clever, sweetie,' said Rosie. 'Oh, I should have asked, is Bobby back?'

'I'm afraid not,' said Boots.

'Oh.' Rosie's bright tone dropped an octave. 'I don't like what that might mean. Does Tim know what happened to him?'

'Tim lost sight of him yesterday morning,' said Boots. 'They got separated on the march to Dunkirk. But why he isn't back is a mystery at the moment, Rosie.'

Rosie went for the only solution that was acceptable.

'It can only mean he's a prisoner of war,' she said.

'He'll hate that. Bobby likes room to move.'

'Yes, I know, Rosie.'

'I was up in the clouds a moment ago,' said Rosie, 'now I'm down in the dumps.'

'Don't go too far down,' said Boots, 'Bobby's a survivor.'

'Bless you, Daddy old love, I'm so pleased you're home and walking about. Is Nana pleased too?'

'Not while I'm walking about. She thinks that at my age and in my state of health, it's too risky.'

'Are we back to bathchairs?' asked Rosie.

'No, just to square one,' said Boots.

'Yes, the Army has to start all over again, doesn't it?' said Rosie. 'That's what you mean, don't you?'

'That's what I mean,' said Boots.

'Well, I can tell you that here in our little patch, we're right behind you, old thing,' said Rosie. 'But how is the Army ever going to get back to France if the French collapse?'

'Ask me something easier, Rosie.'

'What's going to happen if air raids begin?'

'I'm going to run for cover along with everyone else,' said Boots.

'I'll be thinking of you all while I'm under an umbrella,' said Rosie. 'So long, see you as soon as I can. Regards from Polly, and can I talk to Tim for a minute or so?'

'I'll get him,' said Boots. 'So long, poppet.'

Bobby worked through the morning, the sun hot on his back. He found the quiet peaceful atmosphere of the fields strange after all that had gone

148

before. Now and again he glimpsed farmhands in the distance. Other than that, he saw no-one. Nor did he sight any German military traffic, since the road wasn't visible from the flax field. At eleven, however, he did see Madame Aarlberg, for the equable lady herself brought him a bottle of white wine and some homemade biscuits. The sun touched her with warmth, its light revealing an untanned complexion. She had never worked in the fields, only in her house and her little dairy.

Examining the work he had done, she said, 'Ah, that is very good, I think, and my husband will be pleased with you.'

'It's not very much compared to what you've all done for me,' said Bobby. He had stripped himself of his singlet and she saw perspiration filming his neck, shoulders and chest. His dark brown hair looked damp. So did his bandage. 'It's good to be working while waiting,' he said. He gulped mouthfuls of wine from the bottle, and ate a biscuit. 'Any news, *madame?*'

'The Germans have begun an advance on Paris,' she said.

'Well, I hope the French Army knocks hell out of them,' said Bobby.

'I could wish, yes, that Hitler had long ago been struck dead,' said Madame Aarlberg. 'There must be many good Germans. How did they come to accept a man like him as their leader? It is so unfair for Jacob and his kind to have to endure another war, and for so many young men like you to have to fight it.'

149

'It has to be fought,' said Bobby.

'Yes. Jacob agrees.' Madame Aarlberg looked sad. 'But it is so destructive, so wicked. You feel bitter about what happened to your army?'

Bloody mortified, thought Bobby.

'I just hope we get the chance to have another go,' he said.

'Yes,' Madame Aarlberg sighed. 'Jacob has gone to Bergues,' she said.

'He was able to go by road?' asked Bobby. 'By car?'

'The Citroen?' said Madame Aarlberg. 'That is in Dunkirk being repaired. For a month it's being repaired, and now? Ah, now it's beyond repair, perhaps. No, Jacob is walking to Bergues, but not by the road, by other ways. By other ways, it is not too far. He will be there now, and will see you later today.'

'Jacob's a fine man,' said Bobby.

'Yes,' said Madame Aarlberg, 'and not as foolish as my daughter seems to think.'

She left then to return to the farmhouse.

Polly took the bit between her teeth at midday and phoned Boots. At least, she hoped he'd be the one to answer. Alas for her hopes.

'Hello, Em'ly here, who's that this time?'

Polly made a face and said nothing. She hung up.

Rats to the woman, she thought. Why isn't she at Sunday church instead of being in my way? She's always been in my way. She's clinging to her home, I suppose, because Boots is there. I'll never understand what happened. The man belongs to me, I feel that in every fibre of my being, yet she's got him.

Yes, how the hell did it happen?

It happened, Polly, she told herself, because years ago you were in the wrong *estaminet* at the right time.

Oh, rats.

Emma, putting aside her worries about Bobby, looked delightful in her most picturesque summer dress for her visit to Jonathan, the material pre-war apricot silk from Uncle Sammy's factory stocks. The waist was pinched in, the hem just below the knees, her legs sheathed in a pair of precious silk stockings. Edward was in the hall when she was about to leave.

'Well, look at you, sis,' he said, 'you'll knock 'em for six down the Old Kent Road in that outfit.'

'I'm not planning to knock anyone for six,' said Emma.

'Ten to one you lay Jonathan out,' said Edward. 'Give him my regards.'

Emma took a bus to Walworth. Jonathan proved to be still in bed, but Jemima told her she could go up.

'But is he asleep?' asked Emma.

'If he is,' said Jemima, 'I'm sure he's ready to be woken up and to take a look at you.'

'He be smelling sweeter,' said Jane.

'Aye,' smiled Job, 'gave himself a scrub all over before he turned in last night.'

'I'll tell him you're here,' said Jennifer, and went to the foot of the stairs.

'Jonathan, Emma's coming up to see you!' she shouted.

'That girl, she could wake the dead at times,' said Jemima. 'But go on, go up, Emma.'

Emma went up and found Jonathan lying on his back, sleepy eyes blinking at the ceiling. Emma, looking down at him, drew a little breath at what his six months in France had done for him. He was deeply brown and leaner, and very much a man now. Little tingles attacked her.

'Jonathan?'

He turned his head. There was a slightly drawn look about him, and that tugged at her heart-strings. He smiled.

'Well, there you are, Emma, and a fair old Sunday treat,' he said. 'Seen you looking famous many a time, haven't seen you looking as famous as now. Heard about the BEF, did you? Gone with the wind. Remember the book and how you loaned it to me?'

'Yes, I remember,' said Emma, 'but no, the BEF hasn't gone with the wind. You're all home. Well, nearly all. But look at you, you're not even shaved.'

'Never mind about me, look at you,' said Jonathan. 'I'm fair tempted to jump out of this bed and take you round the back of the gasworks.'

'You're bluffing,' said Emma, her smile over-bright. 'Would you like a kiss when you've got rid of all those bristles?'

'Do I have to wait?' asked Jonathan.

Emma stooped, kissed his lips, then let her emotions surface.

'Jonathan, I didn't ever think I could miss anybody like I've missed you.'

'That's mutual, Emma.' Jonathan sat up, his pyjama jacket open, his chest tanned. The men of the BEF had spent hours sunbathing during the phoney war period immediately preceding the German onslaught.

'Bobby's not home yet,' said Emma, seating herself on the edge of the bed.

Jonathan felt a little sense of shock, then quickly went to work in a reassuring way.

'Well, let me tell you, Emma, I got to really know your brother in just the few days our lot fell in with his lot, and it's my belief that if any latecomers are going to turn up, he'll be one of them. He's a fighter, Emma, and won't take setbacks lying down. You can believe me.'

'Oh, that's bucked me up no end,' said Emma. 'I like you for it, Jonathan. Are you going to get up and take me for a Sunday morning walk?'

'I will, if my legs work after all that mileage to Dunkirk,' said Jonathan.

'We could try them out, couldn't we?' said Emma.

'Good idea,' said Jonathan, and slipped from the bed. They looked at each other, he in his pyjamas, she in her silk creation. 'Emma, durned if you don't be downright lovely to come home to,' he said.

'Oh, I'm pleased you said that.' Emma, all over tingles, received a kiss. The tingles melted. 'Oh, come on, then, Jonathan, let's go round the back of the gasworks when you've shaved and dressed.'

Round the back of the gasworks was a joke they shared.

Downstairs, Jemima heard them laughing.

'I think Emma's tickling Jonathan,' said Jennifer.

'Something in that,' said Job. 'I were tickled by a girl once, and it fair put my braces in a twist.'

'So what did you do, Dad?' asked Jane.

'Married her,' said Job, 'so's I could tickle her back. It fair stood her on her head. Never saw a prettier picture, did I, Jemima?'

The family laughter returned.

'Already we have this problem?' enquired Jacob's friend, a lawyer of Bergues.

'Already,' agreed Jacob. 'But I'm only asking for an identity document.'

'Is that all? I'm to arrange a forgery? I'm expected to have no respect for my honourable profession?'

'You're expected to defend your honourable profession to the death, naturally,' said Jacob, 'while using your influence to procure the necessary document for an Allied soldier, a man worth a little risk.'

'That is your interpretation of my responsibilities? Well, when France is about to die, what is a mere forgery? We shall be concerned with real worries soon. The situation here is more fluid than it will be when our towns and cities are governed by Nazi *gauleiters*. Yes, at the moment the Germans mean to subordinate everything to the necessity of taking France out of the war as quickly as possible. Afterwards, my friend, it will be different. Then, when other forged papers are required, the risks will be such that the bravest men will step with caution, and cowards like me will stay in the shadows. However, as things are, I think I can let you have the document this afternoon, even if it is Sunday.'

'Thank you,' said Jacob. 'I'll call back when?'

'Say at three. The jackboot isn't yet on my neck. But before you go and enjoy a prolonged lunch, give me details. Incidentally, since you're so close to the coast, a strong sailing boat is the obvious thing, and before the Germans have closed off every outlet. The weather is still excellent for sailing, I believe.'

'Excellent,' said Jacob.

'Even for a night trip, would you say?'

'Even for a night trip,' said Jacob.

While events and disaster were still clear in their minds, and disillusionment still an angry factor, Boots and General Sir Henry Simms spent the whole afternoon in Whitehall. It was Sunday, but the place was alive with senior Army figures trying to come to terms with what had caused such a humiliating defeat. Sir Henry attempted to secure an interview with the CIGS and to demand a complete revision of the use of tanks. He and Boots were met by blank faces at every turn, and repeatedly told to address any recommendations in writing. Sir Henry asked for an interview with the Prime Minister himself, and was told Churchill was in conference with Gort, Commander-in-Chief of the salvaged BEF, and had too much on his plate in any case.

Eventually, they left. Sir Henry took Boots to his club and there they split a bottle of whisky. By the time Boots arrived back home his mood was mellower.

Emily was cross that he had absented himself. Chinese Lady was quiet. She understood. She had once been the wife of a soldier.

Emma and Jonathan hadn't spent time round the back of any gasworks, of course. That, being a joke, remained a joke. Jemima, at Jonathan's request, had made up a Sunday picnic for them, and they had taken it to St James's Park. Eating in the open air was a pastime that had helped them to get to know each other a year ago. It helped Emma to decide Jonathan was an utterly barmy country chap planted by some kind of accident in the heart of Walworth with his family. It helped Jonathan to decide Emma was in a class of her own, a girl as cool as a cucumber but as delicious as a peach. Right now, if it hadn't been for the war, his uncertain future and his limited soldier's pay, he'd have asked her to marry him.

In St James's Park, they ate their picnic, then strolled to feed the ducks. It intrigued Emma to see that even in 1940, even in wartime, there were actually still crisply uniformed nursemaids wheeling prams or escorting their charges. And there were still tall handsome Guardsmen making eyes at the nursemaids.

'Would you like to be a Guardsman, Jonathan?' she asked.

'I'd sooner be in a meadow chewing a straw and driving the cows home,' said Jonathan. 'That's if there weren't any damn' old war, and the nearest milkmaid was called Emma Somers. A hundred to one you'd look a real country armful in a bonnet and smock, Emma.'

'Kindly explain exactly what you mean by a country armful,' said Emma.

'Well, I reckon my explanation might turn out to be a bit biased,' said Jonathan. 'Tell you what, how about if we stop one of these nursemaids and I get you to ask her? Remember how you used to ask questions of those people we bumped into at Camberwell Green? Regular knockout you were, Emma, asking about zoos and so on.'

'That was when I was ill,' said Emma.

'Ill?' said Jonathan.

'Yes, I caught a complaint from you,' said Emma, 'and when I went to the doctor about it, he told me it was nothing very much, that I'd simply gone potty, the same as you.'

'Well, whatever the complaint was, I'd say it suited you,' said Jonathan. 'It put roses in your cheeks, did you know that?'

'Those roses were my blushes of embarrassment,' said Emma, watching the ducks gliding and darting, and liking the feel of Jonathan close beside her.

157

'Ah, now you come to mention it, that were when you were a right shy and blushing young thing,' said Jonathan, 'and hardly able to say a word for yourself.'

'Stop trying to make me giggle,' said Emma.

'What's wrong with a giggle?'

'It makes me feel I'm ten years old again,' said Emma.

'I were ten years old once,' said Jonathan.

'And what happened?' asked Emma.

'I woke up one day and found I'd turned eleven,' said Jonathan.

Emma laughed.

'Jonathan, you're still barmy,' she said.

'Born like it, I suppose,' said Jonathan.

'Yes, you're a lovely country chap,' said Emma.

They moved away and sauntered, London brilliant with summer light and the park a green retreat from the atmosphere of war.

Chapter Ten

Helene had been in the fields all day, where she had eaten bread and cheese for lunch. At six o'clock, she came at a swinging walk along the edge of the flax field. It was a golden evening, the azure sky only slightly flushed in the west. She saw the English sergeant, still working. She regarded what he had done with frank surprise. Turned weeds by the hundred lay with their roots withering in the heat, and the sergeant was on the last row but one. The size of the field made his day's work invaluable. She walked up to him. Bobby straightened his back and let the hoe rest.

'Good evening, *mademoiselle*,' he said cordially. His long day in the sun had deepened his tan. His hair was moist, his bandage sweat-stained, his usefulness proven.

'I am impressed,' she conceded.

'Well, it's been a fine day for hoeing,' said Bobby. 'Back-breaking, but still better than doing nothing.'

Helene's dark blue eyes were cool, but hostility was absent for the moment. She silently acknowledged he stripped well. She did not like fat on men.

'My father passed me a little while ago,' she said. 'He wishes to see you.'

'Shall I finish first?' asked Bobby. 'There's only a row and a half left.'

'Tomorrow will do,' she said. 'And there are other fields. We have many.' She gestured, and Bobby surveyed the landscape of the extensive farm, the different fields each carpeted by green growth. Some greens seemed tipped with gold. 'We also have many weeds.'

'Oh, I'll work on them,' said Bobby. 'Until I can get away. Say in a day or so.'

'I wish you joy in a day or so,' said Helene with a touch of mockery. She began her walk to the farm-house. Bobby retrieved his shirt and singlet, and went after her. Long-striding, he caught her up.

'You've got a dairy herd here?' he said.

'We have cows, yes,' said Helene.

'Thought so,' said Bobby.

'Yes? You're trying to say I'm smelling of them?'

'Oh, it's a healthy scent,' said Bobby.

'Scent?'

'I like farm aromas,' said Bobby.

'It is something you will have to accept for your day or so,' said Helene. 'I take most smells into the kitchen with me at the end of each day. So does my father. We are very short of labour with so many men away in the Army. Someone must help with the herd and the field work.' She glanced at him. 'Put your shirt on. My mother won't want to see you like that. We are more conventional in the country than city people are.'

'Understood,' said Bobby. 'I don't want to upset your conventions.' He pulled his shirt on. 'Do you know what the latest news is?'

'How could I know when I've been out in the fields all day?' said Helene. 'Except one of our farmhands told me the midday news was that France must be prepared to make sacrifices.'

'Your Government is saying that already?' said Bobby. 'Can your father be right, then? That France is defeatist? I've been nursing hopes of a French victory.'

'You are not the only one,' said Helene, and took him into the house by way of the dairy door. From there they went through to the kitchen. Madame Aarlberg smiled approvingly as Bobby removed his dusty, earthy boots.

'Ah, such a long day you have had out there, Bobby,' she said.

Bobby? Bobby? Helene gritted her teeth. Was he to become one of the family, to stay until the Germans found him and shot them all?

'It's been a fine day,' said Bobby. 'Aside from my little problems.'

'But they are nothing compared to the problems of France,' said Helene.

'Helene, it isn't necessary to keep on and on about the problems of France, since we are all so aware of them,' said Madame Aarlberg. 'Nor is it fair to speak all the time as if the sergeant is to blame. You are hungry now in spite of your problems and ours?' she said to Bobby.

'I am, and that's a fact,' said Bobby. He had eaten

a light lunch with Helene's mother. 'What's the latest news?'

'It is all so bad I have stopped listening,' said Madame Aarlberg.

'I see,' said Bobby, and brooded over his options for a few moments. Then he straightened his back and said, 'Something smells good, *madame.*'

'Better than how I smell?' said Helene.

'It is roast beef, marinaded,' said Madame Aarlberg.

'Beef?' Bobby's mouth watered. The French liking for veal made beef unusual. But how did it taste, marinaded? What was marinaded. He decided not to ask. 'I can hardly wait. I don't know how you do it when you're up against all this bad news.'

'One must do something,' said Madame Aarlberg.

'You're right,' said Bobby. 'Could I use your bathroom again?'

'You want another bath?' said Helene.

'It's all this sweat,' said Bobby.

'Then a bath, of course,' said Madame Aarlberg, 'and my husband is upstairs. He would like to talk to you.'

Bobby went up, carrying his borrowed farm boots and his grubby singlet. Helene sat down at the kitchen table and drank a glass of wine to lay her dust.

'Perhaps I should bath too,' she said, 'perhaps I too should behave as if it is festival time. Perhaps we all should.'

'Yes?' said her mother, and inspected the progress of creamed aubergines. It was true, cooking was something to do, something to help take one's mind off the possibility of a French defeat.

'That stupid man told me I smell,' said Helene.

'It was a complaint? His nose was offended?'

'Any man whose nose is offended on a farm should live in a rose garden,' said Helene.

'What did Bobby say, then?'

'Bobby? Bobby?' Helene's disgust showed. 'Is he an old friend of yours already, Mama?'

'That is his name,' said Madame Aarlberg. 'What did he say to you?'

'That my smell was a healthy scent.'

'Scent?' Madame Aarlberg managed a little smile. 'How charming. Such a tactful man.'

'Charming?' said Helene. 'Are you crazy, Mama? Are you forgetting what the Germans are doing and where they are, on our doorstep?'

'No, my infant, I am not forgetting that,' said Madame Aarlberg, 'but he's a very unusual sergeant. Most sergeants bark and shout, don't they? But have a bath if you feel sensitive.'

'I'm not going to have a bath for the sake of his dainty nose,' said Helene, feeling she wanted to smash something because the conversation was so utterly trivial under the circumstances.

Upstairs, Jacob was in Bobby's bedroom, showing him an identity document in the name of Maurice Picquart of Bergues, a farm worker born in 1917.

163

'It's similar to British identity cards,' said Jacob, 'and is a safety measure for you. There, it shows your present address, this farm, and that you are twenty-three.'

'I'm twenty,' said Bobby.

'I think, my friend, you have put on a few years lately,' said Jacob. 'You are a resident employee, living in one of our cottages until we can get you away on some route that will take you to England. Of course—' Jacob looked as if gall and wormwood were at his throat. 'Of course, if France falls, the Boche will issue their own kind of identity papers for everyone. With photographs.'

'Jesus Christ,' said Bobby, 'could you put up with that, Jacob?'

'One must prepare for it,' said Jacob. 'We must also help you.'

'You're the salt of the earth, you and your family,' said Bobby, beginning to strip. The bath was running.

'I understand many French soldiers, and Belgian too, were taken off the beaches by your ships,' said Jacob. 'That heartens me. With the British, they will continue the fight, along with other men willing to risk a journey that will get them to England. There have to be people who will help them. You must fight on from Britain, what-ever happens here. Churchill is coming to see our Prime Minister, perhaps to persuade France not to surrender.'

'Churchill won't give in,' said Bobby. 'He's our prize bulldog.'

Jacob showed the ghost of a smile.

'So I believe,' he said, 'and perhaps you are out of the same kennels, my friend.'

When Bobby returned to his bedroom after taking his bath, he found Jacob had placed fresh underwear on the bed, with another pair of trousers and a grey jersey. He realized that what he most owed this family was freedom from the threat of what would happen to them if his presence became known to the Germans. He must leave as soon as it was practical.

Helene, in her bedroom, took off her clothes and put her nose to them. Her nose discovered nothing offensive. But, of course, when one lived every day with farm animals, one's nose didn't always pick up the truth. Furious that she was actually bothering about trifles, she flung the clothes down. However, she took off her underwear and put her strong shapely body under the bath-room shower. The shower did not always work. Sometimes it would only spray cold water, some-times only hot, and even when it did emit the right mixture it complained. It coughed, burped and set up a minor howling. It worked now, and as usual it also complained. She ignored all complaints and took her shower, then attired herself in fresh underwear and clean clothes.

The news that evening concerned the German thrust towards Paris, and the Aarlberg family sat down to dinner in a very quiet mood. Bobby made no attempt to impart false cheer. He was hardly up in the clouds himself. His situation was as depressing as it could be. Had he been willing to find the nearest Germans and give himself up, that would be that. But he was far from willing. He still had a fixed idea that escape lay through Dunkirk, although every British ship had gone.

He ate his meal with his mind on the necessity of getting away, but nevertheless raised Madame Aarlberg's spirits a little when he accepted her offer of a second helping of the marinaded beef.

'It is better, perhaps, than my English?' she said.

'You all speak it very well,' said Bobby, although nearly every conversation had been in French, as now.

'French, of course, is a more elegant language,' said Helene.

'French grammar's a bit bloody, though,' said Bobby. In English.

'Excuse me?' said Helene sharply.

'Sorry,' said Bobby. 'Listen, about my getting to Dunkirk tomorrow, say—'

'Crazy,' said Helene.

'It's my best bet,' said Bobby.

'Yes, for a look at an empty sea,' said Helene.

'With your new papers, Sergeant,' said Jacob, 'Switzerland is possible by train. But you have said no to that. You are thinking your best way is across the Channel?'

Madame Aarlberg looked dubious. Helene looked fed-up.

'Oh, let him go to Dunkirk, Papa, let him see what his obstinacy will do for him,' she said.

'There may still be a chance for him,' said Jacob,

166

'before the Germans mine the beaches and the approaches.'

'Why would they put mines down?' asked Helene.

'Because the British Army has escaped and they still have their Navy,' said Jacob. 'The Germans have always worried about the Royal Navy, and they'll mine the beaches and approaches to cripple any invasion attempt.'

'Invasion?' Helene was totally disbelieving. 'An invasion by the British? After running for their lives? When?'

'Not next week,' said Bobby. 'Or even next month. But some time.'

'Some time is never,' said Helene caustically.

'We'll see,' said Bobby.

'Sergeant,' said Jacob, 'we should think about getting you to a beach and a boat before the Germans completely close off the coast.'

'Not my boat,' said Helene. Her little *canot*, a six-metre dinghy, was her one joy outside the farm, and during the summer she used it regularly on Sundays. 'I am sorry, but Sergeant Somers is not taking my boat, even if it could be found. It isn't suitable for crossing the Channel, in any case, just for inshore sailing only.'

'I am thinking of any boat that might be available,' said Jacob. 'If they aren't all smashed up. Can you sail a boat, Sergeant?'

'I've helped to sail one off the coast of Devon,' said Bobby, thinking of family holidays at Salcombe.

'Helping is not sailing,' said Helene, 'especially by yourself. In a boat on the Channel waters you would be an infant.'

Bobby did not take that too seriously.

'I'd be willing to give myself fifteen minutes to grow up,' he said.

Helene poured scorn on that.

'A few hundred metres out in the Channel, and in the dark, and you would capsize the boat and sink with it,' she said. 'If you want to drown yourself, don't ask us to help you. In French law it's an offence to assist a person to commit suicide.'

'You are speaking of the sergeant drowning himself?' said Madame Aarlberg. 'I'm sure he's too resourceful to let that happen.'

'Ah, he has praised your cooking, and so you are flattering him,' said Helene. 'You are a weak woman, Mama.'

'Oh, my weakness is quite dear to me, Helene,' said Madame Aarlberg, and Bobby looked as if he was getting quite fond of Jacob's tranquil-natured wife.

'I still think Dunkirk and a boat are my best chance,' he said.

'Crazy people don't recognize they are mad,' said Helene, who thought that if the idiot would only disappear, the family could discuss something truly important, such as how to help France. 'You have lost the war,' she said, 'and should give yourself up.'

'Not if I can help it,' said Bobby. 'I'm not obliging Hitler by trotting off to a prison camp.'

168

'Oh, you think that mad dictator is sitting in Berlin waiting to hear how you are obliging him?' said Helene.

'Shall we listen to some news?' suggested Jacob, still thinking about a boat for Bobby while wondering if any of the little pleasure yachts could possibly have survived. The weather was still exceptionally fine.

Helene got up and switched on the radio. After only a few minutes, at a nod from her father, she switched it off. What was the point of listening to words of obviously false optimism, words that told them nothing except that the French were defending gallantly? One knew what that meant. The German advance was continuing. What one wanted to hear was that the French Army had gone onto the offensive and won a decisive victory.

Bobby, aware that he could say little to cheer up this family, came to his feet and set about clearing the table and washing the dishes. Jacob elected to help him. Helene sat and brooded, while her mother returned comestibles to the larder.

'Boots,' said Chinese Lady firmly, 'I don't want to interfere with your recupering—'

'My what?' said Boots. They were all in the garden, he and Tim together with Emily, Chinese Lady and Mr Finch, the evening warm and balmy. 'Oh, I see, yes, my recuperating.'

'Yes, that's what I said. I know you and Tim both need a lot of it, but you'll have to go up to the War Office some time and ask about Bobby.'

'Maisie,' said Mr Finch, 'I don't think—'

'Yes, you can go with him, Edwin,' said Chinese Lady. 'With your Government job and Boots now being an officer, they'll let you in for you to ask about Bobby. They must know something about men that haven't come back. We've got to think of Lizzy and Ned and their worries, so you and Boots ought to go up to the War Office. Say tomorrow. They start work at the War Office on Mondays, I suppose?'

'They're supposed to,' said Tim, who had quickly come to terms with the peaceful atmosphere of home after the raging elements of the blitzkreig. 'That's if they're not still playing golf.'

'Golf?' said Chinese Lady. Golf was almost like a foreign word to her. 'Golf? I hope they know there's a war on.'

'If they don't, Mum, Boots will inform them,' said Emily. 'He's good at informin' people, like Sammy is.'

'Lists of—' Mr Finch decided not to mention casualties. 'Lists of men not accounted for won't be issued yet, Maisie. It'll take time.'

'I don't see why it should,' said Chinese Lady. 'They've got all the names of everyone the ships brought home, haven't they? Well, the names they haven't got are the ones they didn't bring. Boots, ask if Bobby's name is among them, or if—' Chinese Lady checked, then became firm again. 'Yes, or if he was brought back to go into hospital.'

'We're facing up to that, are we, old lady?' said

Boots, thinking his mother the only one willing to mention the possibility.

'Yes, Boots, we have to,' she said. 'We all know it, but no-one wanted to say so in front of Lizzy and Ned. Bobby could be wounded a bit serious, and we ought to find out.'

'Maisie, if he is in hospital, Lizzy and Ned will be notified,' said Mr Finch.

'We can't wait for that,' said Chinese Lady. 'You and Boots had best go up to the War Office, and if Bobby is in hospital, ask which one.'

'Dad,' said Tim, 'Grandma might have hit on something.'

'So she might,' said Boots.

'There you are, then, lovey,' said Emily, 'you can do some askin'.'

'Yes, especially you bein' a major,' said Chinese Lady, 'though how someone in this fam'ly came to be an officer at all still makes me wonder what's goin' to come of it. I was never brought up in sight of officers, only corporals and sergeants. Your grandfather Daniel Adams was a corporal, Tim, and I never once heard him complain about not bein' an officer. Still, I'm sure we'll all get used to Boots bein' one.'

'And Rosie,' said Tim.

'Yes, bless us all, our Rosie, would you believe,' said Emily.

Chinese Lady frowned.

'It's not what I like to believe,' she said, 'I don't hold with lady soldiers or lady officer soldiers. It's not natural, and I've said so more than once. If the

Lord had ordered women to be soldiers, He wouldn't have given them – well, never mind that.' She wasn't going to say 'bosoms' out loud. 'Polly Simms, well, she was an ambulance driver in the Great War, which I do hold with. I don't know what got into her that she's turned herself into a woman soldier, I wouldn't have minded her drivin' an ambulance again, and Rosie as well.'

'Ambulances and their drivers sometimes come under fire, old lady,' said Boots.

'Well, I call that disgraceful and criminal,' said Chinese Lady.

'I agree, Maisie,' said Mr Finch.

'Bit of a liberty, shelling ambulances,' said Tim, well aware that the Germans had strafed long columns of civilian refugees.

'Yes, and another thing that's not natural is most of my grandchildren bein' sent into the country away from their parents,' said Chinese Lady. 'Tommy and Vi don't think anything of their home with no children around, nor do Sammy and Susie, with only little Paula there. And a grandparent ought to be able to enjoy the pleasure of havin' grandchildren call.'

'Shall you ask the War Office about that as well, Edwin?' asked Boots.

'I thought you might like to,' said Mr Finch.

'Passed to you, old man,' said Boots, 'you're the grandparent.'

'Is that husband of yours bein' serious, Em'ly?' asked Chinese Lady.

'About your grandchildren, Mum? He'd better

be,' said Emily, but refrained from making further comments. She felt, along with so many other people, that children evacuated with their schools to the country should stay there. It was in the air now, the possibility of German bombing raids, especially after the British Army had escaped the trap. That would have made the Germans swear their heads off in rage. Well, that was what Emily thought.

'It's not natural,' said Sammy, at home with Susie. Paula, just five, was in bed, and Sammy thought their handsome house a lot too quiet.

'You sound like your mum,' said Susie, who was stitching a tear in one of Paula's frocks. Shortage of materials meant conservation of existing garments. 'What's not natural?'

'A fam'ly house with only half a fam'ly presently residin',' said Sammy.

'I know how you feel, Sammy, even if you did say once that livin' in a full house was like livin' in Bedlam.'

'Well, if I did say that,' said Sammy, 'I was off me rocker. When there's four kids around, what's wrong with a nice bit of Bedlam? It's only natural. Bein' without three of them is so quiet it's more unnatural than an elephant laying an egg. Give me four kids and a bit of Bedlam anytime.'

'You're like Boots,' said Susie.

'Is that a compliment, might I ask?'

'And you're like Tommy as well,' said Susie, 'you're all fam'ly men. It's always surprised me that Em'ly—' She stopped and inspected her stitching.

'That she only gave Boots one child?' offered Sammy.

'Oh, I expect there was a good reason,' said Susie, 'and anyway, Boots made up for it by takin' on Rosie and then producin' Eloise.'

'Like out of a French hat?' said Sammy.

'I was never more pleased for Boots,' said Susie, 'he was born to be a dad.'

'And I was born to be a father to me business,' said Sammy.

'You were born for me, Sammy, and our children,' said Susie.

Sammy pondered.

'I can't stand all this quiet,' he said, 'let's catch the news. It's time.'

'Yes, all right, Sammy, there might be something about the men that's missing,' said Susie. 'Like Bobby.'

The BBC Home Service came forth with the news on the dot of every hour.

They listened. Almost everyone in the country with a wireless set was listening. The disaster of defeat took second place to the triumph of the evacuation.

But nothing was said about the men who hadn't made it.

'We're in trouble,' said Mr Benjamin Goodman to his wife Rachel.

'We were,' said Rachel, 'we're not now. They've

all been brought home, we've still got our whole Army.'

'But we've lost every gun, every tank,' said Benjamin.

'Benjamin,' said Rachel, 'is that making you think about applying again for an entrance visa to America?'

'My life,' said Benjamin, 'am I hearing my own wife trying to shoot me in the back? We're in trouble, and I should think of leaving? No, I'm going out, to the ARP post.'

'Why?' asked Rachel. 'Are we expecting an air raid?'

'No,' said Benjamin, 'I'm expecting to be elected Chief Warden.'

'Husband, you're a good man,' smiled Rachel. As soon as he'd gone, she made a phone call. Susie answered.

'It's Rachel, Susie love.'

'Oh, yes, Mr Goodman's married wife,' said Susie, taking off Sammy.

'And a family friend, Susie.'

'I know,' said Susie, who still had moments when the little green-eyed god shot his arrows into her. Well, Rachel Goodman was still a lushly beautiful woman who had been Sammy's only girl friend when he was young.

Rachel, who had really phoned to tell Sammy that Benjamin had put aside any idea of applying for an entry visa into the United States, said, 'I should be uncaring not to ask if Boots is back?'

'He's back, so is Tim,' said Susie, 'but Bobby isn't. We feel he's been taken prisoner.'

'I am sorry, Susie, sorry, but glad for Emily that Boots and Tim were saved. Such a splendid thing, so magnificent, the evacuation. I am proud, Susie.'

Susie softened.

'Sammy says we shall have to fight now to the bitter end.'

'We will, Susie, all of us, every man and every woman. The Germans have Hitler, but we have Churchill. Who are the more fortunate? We are. My daughters are in the country, but there or here, I would not at such a time put them in the care of any leader except Churchill. Thank you for letting me know about Boots and Tim. Such a relief that they are back, and I shall pray for Bobby. My regards to Sammy. Goodbye, Susie.'

'Goodbye, Rachel.'

Chapter Eleven

The next morning, Bobby accompanied Helene to the fields again. There were no workers visible on this side of the farm. Jacob didn't think it would be wise for his men to come into contact with his guest. He had advised them there was a new farmhand, but he knew it would not take them long to discover he wasn't French if they were given the chance to talk to him. Meanwhile, Jacob intended to find out what the situation in Dunkirk was like.

The early morning news had offered no information on the occupied town, and nothing hopeful in respect of the German push towards Paris. As for the road to Dunkirk, Jacob had found it busy with German traffic. Bobby felt the fates were working against him, and there wasn't much in the way of encouragement he could get out of Jacob's daughter either.

However, on the way to the flax field, she suddenly said, 'I must apologize for being bad-tempered last night.'

'I didn't think you bad-tempered,' said Bobby. 'Just naturally worked up about your country. Who wouldn't be?'

'All the same, I apologize,' said Helene, and that

was all until they reached the field. Then she asked him to finish hoeing the flax, and when that was done to begin on the next field, a huge area of sugar beet.

'Right,' said Bobby, and stripped off his shirt and the vest Jacob had loaned him. Helene regarded his chest and torso with about as much interest as she reserved for a coal scuttle.

'I am now going to rub shoulders with the cows,' she said, and off she went.

Bobby, despite his problems, let a little grin surface.

The United Kingdom was still in a state of euphoria over the rescue of the Army, which featured in news all over the world. There were, of course, people in Britain who weren't euphoric, people like Lizzy and Ned and other parents who were fretting about their missing sons, as well as wives worrying about their missing husbands.

Prime Minister Churchill made a typically appo-site speech in the House of Commons that afternoon. He eschewed a triumphant posture in favour of being rugged and challenging. He said the country could not assign to deliverance the attributes of a victory, that wars were not won by evacuations. True, a certain victory had been achieved by the RAF in preventing the much stronger *Luftwaffe* from raiding and bombing the South Coast landing ports. Confidence could be gained from that.

'Although large tracts of Europe and many old

and famous states have fallen or may fall into the grip of the Gestapo and all the odious apparatus of Nazi rule, we shall not flag or fail. We shall defend our island, whatever the cost may be. We shall fight on the beaches, we shall fight on the landing grounds, we shall fight in the fields and in the streets, we shall fight in the hills, we shall never surrender.'

Sammy Adams remarked to his wife that that was all very well, but fighting in the streets could cause horrendous damage to his shops and factories. Susie asked him if that was a serious comment. Sammy said he couldn't think of anything more serious than a lot of aggravating Nazis blowing the roofs off his shops and factories. Susie said she understood his concern, but hoped he wasn't losing his sense of proportion. Sammy said he didn't mind losing that as long as the fighting was confined to the fields, say. Susie said that might be hard on things like cows and sheep. Sammy said well, we'd be in the fight together, us and the cows and sheep.

Susie laughed. Sammy grinned.

'That's it, keep your pecker up, Susie,' he said.

'You're a great help,' said Susie.

During the morning, Helene had twice appeared to inspect Bobby's progress, and to make comments that were brief but not uncomplimentary. Each time, she took herself off the moment it seemed as if a conversation might develop. She appeared again at lunchtime, bringing him bread, cheese and a bottle of white wine. She hoped he wouldn't mind eating out here, she said, as her mother, without any domestic help, was too busy with housework to entertain him. Bobby said not on any account did he expect to be entertained, that it was more than enough to be given board and lodging. Helene responded to that by telling him, in abrupt fashion, that the French were falling back from the German advance on Paris.

'Sorry about that,' said Bobby.

'So you should be,' said Helene. 'France is standing alone while the British Army is safely back home sunning itself.'

'Sorry about that, too,' said Bobby.

'You don't look sorry,' said Helene, 'or ashamed, either.'

'Balls of fire,' said Bobby, 'what would you like me to do, then, cover myself in sackcloth and ashes?'

'Your bandage needs changing again,' said Helene, and walked off. She paused to look back. 'Don't go into the house,' she called, 'there's a visitor.'

'Very good, Sergeant-Major, I hear you,' said Bobby.

'You're an idiot,' she said, and went on her way.

The visitor was Henri Barnard, a neighbouring farmer who had come to talk about the German offensive. Henri Barnard, thirty, was an admirer of Helene, an admirer with hopes, but neither the war nor Helene herself made things easy for him. Indeed, although she had said hello to him she vanished immediately, apparently into thin air, an extraordinary feat for such a fine-figured, strong and robust young woman. However, Jacob was his usual friendly self and they discussed the situation over a bottle of wine and some biscuits and cheese. Henri was inclined to be optimistic, Jacob was sober and practical. He asked Henri if he knew what conditions were like in Dunkirk. A mess, said Henri. Everything close to the harbour and beaches looked devastated, and the little marina used by weekend amateur yachtsmen was badly damaged. However, that was only what he had heard, said Henri. He didn't intend to go and look for himself. The place was swarming with Germans.

'But France will survive, Jacob.'

'I hope so, Henri.'

'The uninvited guests are leaving us alone at the moment.'

'Yes, at the moment,' said Jacob.

Helene did not come in from her work that evening until dinner was just about to be served. She said a brusque hello, washed her hands at the sink, brought herself and her farmyard aroma to the table, sat down and began to eat while listening to the radio giving out news of how French armies were standing up to the German Panzer divisions. Having had their impenetrable Maginot Line by-passed where it ended at the Belgian border, the shocked French had been at sixes and sevens in their hasty attempts to create an alternative bulwark of defence. Communiqués and bulletins extolled the gallantry of their hard-pressed soldiers. Gallantry sounded a suspiciously vulnerable factor to Jacob.

'I should like someone to turn the radio off,' said Madame Aarlberg. 'One can only endure small amounts of what comes out of it now.'

Helene got up and rendered it silent. Sitting down again, she glanced at Bobby. Jacob had looked at his wound, pronounced it healing, and applied a fresh dressing.

'Did you have another bath?' she asked.

'I took a shower,' said Bobby.

'Did it work?' asked Helene.

'It worked fine,' said Bobby, 'except for a few hiccups.'

'I congratulate you,' said Helene.

'For taking a shower?' asked Bobby.

'For smelling of soap,' said Helene.

Bobby roared with laughter. Jacob smiled and so did his wife. Helene, however, regarded Bobby as if he was in need of a doctor. He asked if anyone knew what the road was like. Full of German traffic, said Jacob.

'Be patient,' he said.

'My patience is having a bad time,' said Bobby.

'But your wound is better?' said Madame Aarlberg.

'It's healing nicely,' said Jacob. 'His trouble, Estelle, is that he's prepared to put his head into the lions' den. I am trying to discourage this. It will be best, Sergeant, should you succeed in getting to Dunkirk, to know in advance what conditions there are like, and if it will offer you the means to get to England. I hope to find out for you. It's not to be expected you will simply be able to board a fishing-boat that will take you.'

'Just a sailing-boat and a compass,' said Bobby.

'I admire such simplicity,' said Jacob, 'but admit to doubts.'

'Well, I'll have a go,' said Bobby, 'just as soon as the Germans get out of my way.'

'He's mad,' said Helene.

'I like a little madness in some men,' said Madame Aarlberg.

Helene sat outside the house later on, making use of an old bench seat and taking in the vista of fields glowing with warm colour beneath the evening sun. Bobby ventured out to join her.

'Is there room for one more?' he asked, thinking she looked quite relaxed for once, while he himself was beset by the restlessness he kept hidden.

'If you wish to sit, I am not going to prevent you,' she said.

'What are you thinking about?' asked Bobby, seating himself.

'I'm not thinking, I'm waiting,' said Helene.

'For a friend?' asked Bobby.

'No, for the Germans,' she said. 'They'll come, you will see, and then they'll order our lives and tell us what to grow.'

'But you haven't lost the war yet,' said Bobby.

'We have lost it here in this corner of France,' said Helene. 'Ah, how I would like to fight them.'

'I share that feeling,' said Bobby.

'You had your chance, you and your Army,' said Helene, 'and you failed.'

'We've got to pick ourselves up and have another go,' said Bobby, and did his best then to cajole her into a friendlier mood.

She was not in the least responsive.

'How can you be as fit as a fiddle?' asked Polly. She was on the phone to her father in Dulwich.

'I'm graced with fine health and an excellent constitution,' said Sir Henry.

'Let's face it, old thing' said Polly, 'at your age something dire could be edging up on you. I want you to retire.'

'Retire? At this moment in the affairs of the nation?'

'Glad you agree,' said Polly. 'Do some pottering about. Or try going along with this new call from the Government, try digging for victory. Grow some cucumbers.'

'Damned if I'm interested in cucumbers,' said Sir Henry, 'I've got other things on my mind, like the essentials of successful tank warfare, and if I'm going to get the appointment I want, command of a corps.'

'Stay home and put your feet up,' said Polly. 'By the way, you haven't said how Boots is.'

'You haven't asked.'

'I'll ask why you took him with you to see the brasshats on Sunday. Isn't Lieutenant-General Montrose your deputy?'

'George Montrose is at home with his family in Scotland,' said Sir Henry.

'You favour Boots, don't you, old thing?' said Polly.

'Boots has a way of thinking things out,' said Sir Henry.

'I don't favour him for that myself,' said Polly, 'he never thinks anything out to my advantage. Tell him to phone me, you've got our company's number.'

'I'll mention it to him in passing,' said Sir Henry. 'Polly, isn't it time you gave up the impossible?'

'Oh, it's time all right, but I can't, can I, and it's a curse, but I'm stuck with it and have been for more years than I care to remember. God, I'm growing old while I still feel like an unrequited maiden. I'm taking a few days leave tomorrow, and if you want to please me, which you should considering my devotion to you, arrange for Boots to call some time while I'm home.'

'Good God,' said Sir Henry, 'I'm to—'

'Yes, be a sport,' said Polly, 'tally-ho and damn all the fences.'

'I'm not unsympathetic,' said Sir Henry, 'and I think Boots will hold his own, in any case. But it's a damned shame, you know.'

'What is?' asked Polly.

'That you and Boots failed to meet during the last war,' said Sir Henry. 'I've thought for years that the two of you were made for each other.'

'Despite the differences?' said Polly.

'Damn the differences,' said Sir Henry.

'And the misguided hand of fate,' said Polly. 'But thanks, old thing, for being on my side.'

Eloise also used a phone that evening, making use of a public call box outside the ATS training camp to speak to her family, and more particularly to Boots. She had phoned on Sunday morning to talk to him and Tim. This time she wanted him to know how exciting it had been at Ramsgate during the days of the evacuation. Boots asked if she hadn't found it harrowing, watching the arrival of a defeated army.

'No, no, of course not, Papa, they were so cheerful,' she said. 'Perhaps some were a little upset—'

'A little upset?' said Boots.

'Not very happy underneath,' said Eloise.

'I see, a little upset and not very happy,' said Boots.

'But it was wonderful, the atmosphere, with people cheering them,' said Eloise. 'Perhaps some were a little more upset than others, especially officers. Oh, I met one officer who was as suffering as a bear with toothache, and growled like one. One could tell he hated being beaten.'

'I didn't like it too much myself,' said Boots.

'Oh, you'll soon recover, Papa, I am always amazed at how vital you are for your age,' said Eloise.

'For my age, yes, I see,' said Boots. 'I think you and Rosie both intend to put me out to grass before the year's out.'

'No, no, of course not, Papa, you have a long time to go before you're as old as that,' said Eloise, and went on to tell him about Captain Lucas and all he had made her do for him. 'Heavens, how he was swearing on the phone, but he was very exciting in his anger. He commanded me to give him my name and the address of my training company, and said he was going to have me posted to his regiment for admin duties when it's been made up to full strength again.'

'You impressed him, did you?'

'Yes, I was most efficient, and of course, as you know, I'm not unimpressive,' said Eloise with blithe candour.

'Indeed you're not,' said Boots, 'and I presume Captain Lucas isn't unimpressive himself?'

'He's a bear, Papa, and not in the least handsome, and I should think he walks over people who annoy him. But I shouldn't mind being a help to him.'

'I see,' said Boots, 'he was impressed with your efficiency, and you were impressed with his angry growling.'

'How clever you are,' said Eloise, 'that is exactly it.'

'Women never cease to surprise me,' said Boots.

'Yes, we shall show you how well we will help you to win the war,' said Eloise. 'How sad I am for my poor France, the news is terrible, but I am standing with Great Britain now, and Hitler will see in the end just how great we are. Many kisses to everyone at home, Papa.'

'Love to you, my chicken,' said Boots.

Chapter Twelve

Bobby was at work on another field of sugar beet the following morning. The farm, still conveying an extraordinary atmosphere of peace and quiet, seemed astonishingly detached from the war being fought for the heart of France. The weather was constant in its June radiance, sunlight dappling the fields, dancing on hedgerows and softening the harsh lines of farm buildings.

At twenty-minutes-to-one Helene appeared, coming from the direction of the farmhouse and carrying a straw bag. Her eyes were on Bobby, and she silently acknowledged he worked well and industriously, like a man who enjoyed activity in the open air. Although she was against having him on the farm, at least he was proving useful. The farm labourers knew he was around. They had seen him from afar. But they asked no awkward questions. Her father had spoken to them, and they respected him enough to accept that whoever the new worker was, it was not their business to suggest his presence was questionable.

Bobby straightened up at the approach of Jacob's daughter. Her stride was easy and swinging. She had long legs for a French girl. He had come to the conclusion that French girls, generally, had shorter legs than English girls and thicker ankles.

In the heat, he wiped his forehead with his wrist, smudging his bandage. Helene came up to him. She looked at the work he had done.

'Any comments?' asked Bobby, stripped to the waist as usual.

'One rarely sees farm workers half-undressed,' she said. 'They know it's wiser to protect themselves from the sun, not to invite it to scorch them. However, you haven't done too badly in your work, no, it is quite good. I've brought lunch.'

'Well, that's kind of you,' said Bobby, knowing he must choose his words. He suspected she was existing on the brink, ready to fly at him if he said the wrong thing. He disliked quarrelling with young women. He preferred them amenable, not argumentative. It was Grandma Finch's belief that men had their place and women had theirs, and that this was ordained by the Lord, which meant there was no justification for arguing about it. Bobby was an admirer of Grandma Finch.

'My mother is still very busy,' said Helene, 'and asks you to forgive her again for not giving you lunch in the house.'

'I don't have a single complaint,' said Bobby. 'I'm grateful to be fed. If you'll leave the bag over there, by the wall, I'll get down to it in a few minutes.'

'I'm not leaving it,' said Helene, 'it's lunch for both of us.'

'Is it?' said Bobby. 'Does that make it a picnic?'

Helene let fly.

'What is the matter with you? Who can think in terms of a picnic? You are a clown if you think I can when Nazi jackboots are trampling the fields of France.'

'I appreciate your agonies,' said Bobby, 'but after all, there must be any amount of French house-wives still taking in the morning milk from their doorsteps, and men going about their normal jobs. And you and me sharing lunch for two.'

'That is not the point, and you know it,' said Helene.

'Sorry if I missed it,' said Bobby. 'By the way, I gave myself a little time off to go and take a look at the road. It's still noisy with German military traffic. Where the hell are they going? Dunkirk must be jam-packed.'

'They're going through Dunkirk to join the German forces advancing on Paris from the north,' said Helene. 'Other German armies are trying to break through from the north-east.'

Bobby said soberly, 'I know how you feel, and I didn't mean to make jokes, only to point out that as we can't do much about what's going on else-where, we could have a friendly lunch together.'

'We can have lunch, yes,' said Helene, straight-faced. She noted his smudged bandage and the firm lines of his chin and mouth. His bare chest, shining with sweat, looked as if the sun had drenched it with moist light. She herself looked cool in an open-necked beige shirt and dark brown skirt. Her hair could have looked more stylish, and she could have tied it with something more attractive than a black bootlace, but why should she bother?

'I'm ready to eat,' said Bobby.

'Yes, one must do that, one must eat,' said Helene, 'and housewives must still take in their morning milk.'

'Well, let's sit, shall we?' said Bobby, who considered the best way of getting along with difficult females was to humour them and let their awkwardness wear itself out. In any case, he had no wish to pick a fight with Helene. Far from it. He had, in fact, taken quite a fancy to her, and he found her challenging touch-me-not attitude exciting rather than off-putting.

They sat with their backs against the stone wall, from where the fields could be seen as sunlit carpets of green. The sky was cloudless, the horizons clear of all smoke. There was not a German in sight, but they both knew how deceptive that was. Bobby still kept his restless feelings in check. Jacob wanted him to wait until they had news of the situation in Dunkirk. And night would be the best time to go, in any case.

Helene had placed the straw bag on the ground between them. It created a barrier. She extracted a French loaf split in two, filled with cold meat and divided in half. She gave one half to Bobby, then produced several good-sized spring onions and a bottle of white wine. She dipped into the bag again and brought out two enamel mugs. She handed the bottle to Bobby, who drew the loosened cork and filled the mugs she held out. She gave him one.

'You would prefer to drink from a glass?' she asked in her exacting way.

'Out here I've been drinking straight from the bottle,' said Bobby.

'Yes, in the fields glasses get broken, and all we French peasants drink straight from the bottle, of course.'

'I didn't know you and your parents were peasants,' said Bobby, enjoying the coolness of the wine. 'I thought you were a nice middle-class farming family, very kind and hospitable to a stranger like me.'

Helene performed a little fidgety shrug.

'You mean we're middle-class peasants, of course,' she said.

'No, I don't,' said Bobby, 'but if you are, then I'm a lower middle-class English peasant myself. Our family's come up a step from the working-class ranks. Of course, everyone's descended from peasant stock. Agriculture existed a long time before industry, and helped people to become longer-living than town dwellers.'

'That is so?' said Helene.

'Well, isn't it?' said Bobby, and bit into his bread and meat.

'Is it? How boring,' said Helene, and sank her strong white teeth into her own crusty bread.

'There's nothing boring about the fact that people who work on the land are healthier than people who work in factories,' said Bobby. 'Look at you, for instance.'

'Excuse me?' said Helene, bridling.

'You're a first-class example of health and strength,' said Bobby.

'Do you mean I have big muscles?'

Bobby took a look at her. She sat in profile to him, and in profile her features were very pleasant, her figure worth a second look.

'I don't see any muscles,' he said.

'Good. It's not my ambition to grow bulging muscles.' Helene munched a spring onion. 'You can stop looking.'

Bobby, regarding the vista again, said, 'One could almost forget the war out here.'

'You could, I could not,' said Helene, and watched as his teeth took the head off a spring onion. He found its flavour sharp and strong, much more so than the English variety. It changed his expression. 'What is wrong?' she asked.

'The thing bit me,' said Bobby.

Helene actually laughed.

'It's only a spring onion,' she said.

'It still bit me,' said Bobby, 'but I'll be ready for the next one.'

'Food should be friendly, of course,' said Helene.

'Your mother's is very friendly,' said Bobby, discounting the enmity of garlic.

'Ah, my mother,' said Helene, wishing the Nazis would disappear from the face of the earth and leave people to enjoy a peaceful life, whatever its perversities. 'She has captivated you? Is it her warm heart you adore, or her food?'

'Full marks for her cooking,' said Bobby, enjoying the simple lunch and the wine. Helene, drinking from her mug, made a covert study of him. Yes, he did look a resolute young man, resolute enough to take a chance in a sailing-boat.

'Why, when you are so desperate to get back to England, do you sit here talking in a ridiculous way?' she asked.

'What's ridiculous about admiring your mother's warm heart and her excellent cooking?' countered Bobby. He refilled both mugs. 'I admire both your parents, and can't thank them enough for their help and kindness. I'm on edge about my situation, believe me, I am, but there's no point in kicking the horse or smashing the piano. Better to sit and talk—' He stopped as he glimpsed movement out of the corner of his eye. He turned his head. He saw three German soldiers, leisurely strolling about sixty yards away. 'Bloody hell,' he said.

Helene, seeing them too, stiffened. They halted to look around. One made a gesture in the direction of the farmhouse.

'They have come, the first of them, as we knew they would,' she said in a matter-of-fact way. 'You had better run.'

'I don't think so,' said Bobby, 'it's the guilty who run, and that makes the hounds give chase. Innocent people should go and have a chat. I'll do that, while you go and warn your mother.'

He was giving her orders?

'I will please myself what I do,' she said. The

three German soldiers were strolling again. Bobby finished his food and drained his mug.

'Let's go and talk to them before they arrive and talk to us,' he said.

Helene stared at him.

'You are going to offer yourself for inspection?' she said. 'You are crazy.'

'This is your family's farm,' said Bobby, rising to his feet, 'and you naturally want to know what they're doing here, so should we sit here looking as if we don't care? We should care, and they know that. So let's go and talk to them.'

'I will go. You will stay here.' Helene rose. 'You can't risk having to answer questions, and I can't risk having to lie for you.'

'That's true, you can't,' said Bobby, 'and it's the last thing I'd ask of you.'

'So stay here,' said Helene. Bobby grimaced. 'What are you making a face about? You don't like taking orders from a woman, is that it?' She was on target there. Bobby, in fact, didn't think it was natural for a woman to give orders, but simply to play up and play the game as per the unwritten rules. 'Well, we are two of a kind,' said Helene, 'I don't like taking orders from a man. But this time you must do as I say. I will go by myself to ask these Nazi pigs what they're doing here.' She began to walk with determined strides towards the Germans who had stopped once more, this time to take in a broad sweep of farmland. Bobby, left to himself and his thoughts, let a grin show, despite the intruding

Germans. It could be a life's work for some man, getting the better of Helene Aarlberg. Well, that kind of work would be far from boring.

He watched her in her swift advance on the Germans. Helene's hatred of Hitler and his Nazis burned as she approached the three men in the field-grey of the *Wehrmacht*, the regular German Army. They turned, a captain, a lieutenant and a sergeant. They were armed, the officers with holstered revolvers, the sergeant with a rifle.

Arriving, Helene addressed them clearly and slowly to make sure she was understood if any of them spoke French.

'Excuse me, but what are you doing here?'

The captain smiled, showing very good teeth in a tanned face. If Helene was on edge at her first encounter with the enemy, he was now well-used to such happenings.

'Permit me to enquire who is addressing us?' he asked in good if guttural French.

'I am Helene Aarlberg. What are you doing on my parents' land?'

'Nothing very much, *mademoiselle*, as you can see.' The captain regarded her without any sign of offence at her brusqueness. 'I regret not being able to tell you more at the moment.' He looked over her shoulder at the standing figure of Bobby. 'Who is that half-dressed gentleman?' he asked with a smile.

'Who do you think?' said Helene. 'One of our workers, of course.'

'Calm yourself, *mademoiselle*, we aren't here to set fire to your farm or shoot your workers. This is a large farm?'

'It's large compared to small,' said Helene, entirely distrustful of his politeness. 'I have a right to know why you are here.'

'All in good time,' said the captain. He might have pointed out her rights were limited to those allowed by Germany, the occupying power in this conquered department of France, but asked instead, 'How large is the house?'

'What is large to you?' asked Helene.

'Bedrooms, how many?'

'Several.'

'How many?' He was pleasantly persistent.

'Six,' said Helene, and the lieutenant made a note on a small pad.

'Other rooms?'

'Six or seven. Or eight. It depends on what you see as rooms. If you wish to meet my parents—'

'I have no orders yet to meet anyone. This is merely a preliminary survey. Thank you for your help. That's all, *mademoiselle*.' The captain smiled again. 'My apologies if we disturbed your private moments with one of your workers.'

Helene flushed with anger.

'You are mistaken in your assumption,' she said, and turned on her heel and left before she committed the error of losing her temper.

Her rageful mood was a visible thing to Bobby as he watched her return. It was in her quick, furious movements and the rapid swish of her skirt.

'Were they unpleasant?' he asked when she reached him.

'Insulting,' said Helene, eyes snapping. 'It was your fault, you idiot. Must you stand about half-undressed?'

'Pardon?' said Bobby.

'It gave that officer the disgusting idea you'd have had your trousers off as well if his arrival with the others hadn't interrupted you!'

'Well, I don't think much of his manners,' said Bobby, 'but I'm hardly in a position to go and knock his head off. He actually said that, did he?'

'He didn't need to, I could see the way his mind was working,' said Helene bitingly.

'Don't get alarmed,' said Bobby, 'my trousers are staying on.'

'That is a funny joke, you think?' flared Helene.

'No, a serious promise,' said Bobby, taking note of the fact that the Germans were leaving. 'What else happened?'

'He refused to give me any information, but asked about the size of the farm and the house.'

'Christ,' said Bobby, 'I hope that doesn't mean bad news for you and your parents.'

'There has been no good news since your Prime Minister and ours gave Czechoslovakia to Hitler in 1938,' said Helene.

'That wasn't their best day's work,' said Bobby.

'I must find my father and talk to him,' said Helene.

'Ask him what my chances of getting away are like now,' said Bobby.

'Is that an order?' Helene was cutting.

'Just a request,' said Bobby.

'Why do you make such requests?' she asked.

'Because I like you,' said Bobby.

'Like me?' Helene stared at him.

'I've a lot of admiration for a girl who can stand up for herself against three uniformed jack-booters,' said Bobby.

'I don't want you to like me,' said Helene, 'and I don't need your admiration.'

'Sorry about that,' said Bobby, 'but I can't help myself, and it's not actually forbidden to like you, is it?'

'You're mad,' said Helene, and went striding away in the direction of the farmhouse.

What a character, thought Bobby, what a fascinating specimen of French fire and flame. Game as they come. The kind of girl a bloke could climb a mountain with, as long as she wasn't in a temper. In a temper she might knock him off balance when they were halfway up. He went back to work with the hoe, wondering if this waiting time was in his favour and if he was right to put his trust in Jacob. One could wait a little too long in circumstances like these.

Helene found her father in the house. He and her mother had company. Neighbour Henri Barnard had called again. The arrival of Helene visibly pleased him. Told of the intrusion of the three German Army men, Madame Aarlberg expressed resignation of the inevitable, and Henri said although it was what they could all expect, it was not what any of them were going to like. Jacob was of the opinion it was an example of things to come, particularly as the latest news suggested the French armies were being forced to effect strategic with-drawals. The question of what to do about the British sergeant was becoming more pressing, but the family did not want to discuss it in front of their neighbour. Henri was a good neighbour and a reliable friend, but discretion was the wiser course at the moment.

Henri Barnard at thirty looked a fine figure of a man, although he was stout rather than merely large. He had dark red hair with a widow's peak. This, combined with a strong pointed nose and bright button-like eyes, gave him the appearance of an avuncular fox at rest as he sat in the comfort of a yielding armchair, hands folded over his stomach.

'Myself,' he said, 'I refuse to accept defeat until it happens, and even if it does happen, we shouldn't consign ourselves to darkness. France won't simply lie down, no, no. The British have suffered a terrible defeat, but are now broadcasting defiance. There are rumours that a number of their soldiers who failed to reach Dunkirk have escaped capture, that they're in hiding and refusing to give themselves up. I don't doubt some of them are hoping to find a way of crossing the Channel.'

'Those are rumours?' enquired Jacob.

'So I believe,' said Henri, eyeing Helene fondly. She was pacing about. 'If these men can still show defiance, so can France if the worst happens. From a reliable source, the news is that there are still boats at Dunkirk, the boats of our amateur yachtsmen, which could possibly be used by any Allied soldiers willing to risk the Channel at night.'

'Are there sailing-boats that escaped German bombs, then?' asked Jacob.

'Incredibly, yes,' said Henri, 'some of the small ones east and west of the harbour. I'm willing, as a patriot, to let a couple of Allied soldiers take mine.' Like Helene, he had a sailing-boat, but larger than hers. He knew she was fiercely patriotic, and he wanted her to know he was not less so. He had hopes of marrying her, the age difference of no importance, for Helene was much more of a woman than a girl. Helene, alas, was proving elusive.

'It's no good offering a boat to any man unless he can sail it with the right kind of expertise,' she said, 'and it's no good at all offering any boat that may be damaged or sunk. Do you know what the condition of yours is like?'

'No, I don't have that information,' said Henri, 'only that some boats are still properly moored and afloat. If this weather holds and the Germans delay closing the harbour and beaches off with barbed wire, chances to cross the Channel are available to escaping soldiers.'

Madame Aarlberg wondered if whispers concerning the presence of Sergeant Somers were circulating, and if one had reached Henri's ear.

'They'd also have the chance to drown themselves,' said Helene. 'Even in good weather, you can't treat the Channel like a pond. You wouldn't attempt it in your yacht, and I certainly wouldn't in my small boat. They're not built for it, Henri, and craft large enough to cross will have been taken.'

'I agree, it would be a great risk for a small boat,' said Henri. 'But all of us willing to give assistance to escaping soldiers should let each other know of our inclinations.'

'You are right, Henri,' said Jacob, but still said nothing about Sergeant Somers.

'I'll see what I can do about securing more exact details,' said Henri. 'I've a few friends in Dunkirk.'

'So have we,' said Madame Aarlberg, 'but they're not being allowed to move freely. Marie, my daily help, managed to telephone this morning to say everyone is restricted.'

'Well, I should like to know if my boat is undamaged,' said Henri. 'I wonder if the radio will give us some better news now of the fighting?'

Helene switched on the living-room radio, then hitched her skirt and sat down. Henri could not help casting an admiring glance at her legs, which he was sure would look superb when sheathed in silk.

The news was not long in coming. It dealt with concentrated German assaults on French positions. The French were holding firm, their line straightening out. Another strategic withdrawal? The newsreader didn't say so.

'I feel a sense of doom,' said Madame Aarlberg.

'Come, Estelle, we shouldn't get too depressed too soon,' said Henri. 'Helene, if you aren't too busy to walk to my farm with me, I can show you—'

'I regret I really am much too busy, Henri,' said Helene. 'You know how it is, and I must get back to work. So must you, Papa. Henri, please excuse me.'

When she had gone, Henri said, 'I'm having a hard time trying to find favour with her.'

'Oh, Helene has a way of discouraging everyone,' said Madame Aarlberg, 'but not everyone should give up.'

Jacob, who liked Henri but did not think him right for Helene, said, 'A man willing to change direction, Henri, might find the way less stony.'

'You're recommending me to look elsewhere?' said Henri in surprise.

'Oh, there are many pleasant plums on a French tree, Henri,' said Madame Aarlberg.

Boots, in response to a phone call from Sir Henry, arrived at his Dulwich house at two-thirty. The butler showed him into the well-appointed study, a spacious room which, with its wall-to-wall book shelving, was a library as well as a workplace.

'Major Adams to see you, Sir Henry.'

'Good,' said Sir Henry, rising from his desk, which was littered with papers. He shook hands with Boots, and the butler departed, closing the door quietly behind him.

'You spoke on the phone of a draft letter to the CIGS,' said Boots.

'Yes, an outline of suggested tactics,' said Sir Henry.

'Regarding tank warfare, Sir Henry?' said Boots.

'What else?' said Sir Henry. 'It's the single bee buzzing in my bonnet. I'd like you to read it and to make marginal notes. I'm drafting a similar letter to the Prime Minister.'

'I'm still a learner in respect of tanks,' said Boots.

'You were once, you aren't now,' said Sir Henry, 'so don't be so damned modest. Further, you know all there is to know about how the Germans use theirs, and that's enough to give you the right kind of approach to this letter. No, I don't want you to read it now. I want you to take it away with you and go through it carefully. Let me have it back in two days time. It's here.' Sir Henry crossed to a table in the middle of the room, a table also littered with papers, as well as several military manuals. He took up three sheets of foolscap paper, neatly clipped together. He folded them and placed them in a buff envelope. He handed the envelope to Boots, who slipped it into the side pocket of his jacket. 'Not asking too much of your leave, am I, Boots?'

'It might be asking too much of my short time on your staff,' said Boots.

'Must point out the value of a fresh and un-cluttered mind,' said Sir Henry briskly, 'especially in respect of the reading of this draft. The exercise won't do you any harm at all. By the way, Polly's home on leave until Sunday. Like to say hello to her before you go? She's in the garden.'

'I can always find time to say hello to Polly,' said Boots, and Sir Henry thought how typical of the man. His relationship with Polly was an awkward

one, but he never allowed himself to be discon-
certed or embarrassed.

'You know the way, Boots.'

When Boots emerged from open French
windows to step onto the paved patio, he saw a
garden table in the middle of the perfectly shaved
lawn. There were two chairs and an umbrella, but
no sign of Polly. He glanced around the garden, at
its flowerbeds, its shrubberies and its greenhouse,
but there was still no sign of her.

'Hello, old sport, looking for me?' She materialized beside him, having silently followed him out.
She was wearing a turquoise blue creation into
which she seemed to have poured herself. As usual,
several of her years appeared not to have caught up
with her, and her smile was a little self-mocking, as
if she considered herself absurd in her long pursuit
of him. Her grey eyes held a hint of blue, her clean-
cut lips faintly touched with carmine. Boots, caught
off guard, felt a wrench that this elegant, endearing
woman had had nothing from him in all the years
he had known her.

'Polly?'

'I'm not asking for anything, what's the use?'
murmured Polly. 'But it's so good to see you, dear
old love.'

Boots did what he had always tried to avoid. For
the first time since he had come to know her, he
lost his head. He kissed her, warmly, positively and
with great feeling. Her surprised mouth leapt into
delight. It clung and parted, and she pushed her
tongue against his. Her arms wound around him

and she pressed close in pure bliss. She felt herself twenty-one again in the vital surge of healthy blood and incurable ardour. Rapturous thought rushed because of his own ardour. Oh, ye gods, he does love me, I know it now.

There were minutes of sheer happiness before Boots unlocked her arms and stood off.

'Something fell on me,' he said.

'No, it didn't,' said Polly faintly.

'I forgot the rules,' said Boots.

'They're not my rules, I've never made any,' said Polly.

'I've had to make some of my own,' said Boots.

'You can make another hundred,' said Polly, 'but it won't help you. I know what those kind of kisses mean. You love me, and I'm sure of that at last. Do you know what that does for me?'

'I don't think I can answer that,' said Boots.

'It puts me in my own kind of heaven,' said Polly.

'That's a little fanciful, isn't it?' said Boots.

'I don't care if it's as fanciful as Jupiter descending from Olympus in a golden cloud,' said Polly. 'Don't you understand even now just how I feel about you?'

'Frankly,' said Boots, 'that's never made sense to me.'

'You old darling,' said Polly, 'you're fishing for compliments, and you're trying to remind me I'm upper class. Rats to that. You've tried it before, and it won't work. Where's Emily?'

'At the office, doing her job as general manager,' said Boots.

'She's what?' Polly was incredulous. In Emily's place, with Boots back from Dunkirk, she knew she would never have given priority to her job. 'Emily's actually at work?'

'She's had some time off, but the firm's short of staff,' said Boots. 'Labour's at a premium.'

'Dear me, I am sad,' said Polly drily. 'Well, you can spend the afternoon with me, old sport. Stepmama's up in town, doing a Red Cross stint, and my father's busy drawing diagrams of tank deployment. We shan't be interrupted, we'll have some tea, forget the war and you can tell me how you'd make love to me if you threw all the rules away.'

'Is that a good idea?' asked Boots, frankly thinking her as captivating as she had ever been.

'Exciting, don't you think, lover?'

'Too much for my imagination,' said Boots.

'Oh, I'll help,' said Polly, 'my own imagination knows no limits. But you will stay for a couple of hours, won't you?'

'Could I say no when my time's my own?'

'I ought to hate you for being another woman's husband,' said Polly, 'but I can't. That's damned forgiving of me, isn't it?'

'It's you, Polly.'

She touched his hand.

'I'll order tea, darling.'

That evening, in the Aarlberg kitchen, dinner was consumed in fits and starts, due to bursts of encouraging news. The great German assault along the whole of the French front from the coast to Sedan had shaken the French during the first days, but now it seemed as if they were more than holding their own. The only really serious withdrawal had been to Soissons, a hundred kilometres north-east of Paris, and there, it was reported, General Gamelin intended to bring up reserves and take the offensive at last.

Madame Aarlberg showed a smile or two as she served coffee. Helene seemed brighter. Jacob's expression indicated he was reserving judgement. Bobby had made no comments himself. He simply hoped the French had learned from British mistakes, and were concentrating their armour, not using it piecemeal.

He again asked about his chances of reaching Dunkirk. Jacob said they were not forgetting him.

'The longer I stay here, the more difficult those chances get, surely,' said Bobby, 'and it won't make things easier for you.'

'Be sensible,' said Helene. 'We don't wish to send you on your way with just a prayer, we wish to have a plan.'

'I've got my own plan,' said Bobby, 'which is to get to Dunkirk and find something that'll float. There must be something. I don't like staying on here, I don't like it for your sakes, especially now the Germans have started to call. I'm putting you at real risk. I've got to get away soon, or I'll be a problem to myself as well as to you.'

'I'm sorry you find us unappealing,' said Helene.

'Unappealing?' said Bobby. 'I don't recall saying that.'

'You said you don't like staying here.'

'I'll get cross with you if you talk like that,' said Bobby.

Jacob cleared his throat. Madame Aarlberg hid a smile. Helene sat up.

'Excuse me?' she said challengingly.

'I'll get cross if—'

'I heard you,' said Helene.

'I'm glad you did,' said Bobby. 'You know very well what I meant. It was nothing to do with my personal opinion of you and your parents.'

'What are you like when you get cross?' asked Helene.

'I bite,' said Bobby.

'Ah, such a pity you didn't get cross with the Germans and bite them instead of running,' said Helene.

'Helene, you are disgraceful,' said her mother.

'Very well, I apologize,' said Helene, 'but all his talk of finding a boat is crazy.'

'It's all I've got, a chance of finding something that floats,' said Bobby. 'I'd even risk a raft, if I could find a sail for it.'

Helene gave him a pitying look. He gave her a smile. His self-confidence, she thought, was stupid complacency. He would never make it. He would drown himself.

She frowned. He was full of himself, like all the English, but no, he did not deserve to drown.

'What is the charge?' asked the ATS Commandant.

'Insolence, ma'am,' said Lieutenant Raleigh.

'Details?' said the Commandant, a brisk, no-nonsense woman.

'I asked Private Adams why she had left the camp without permission, ma'am. She said to make a phone call. I said in future she must get permission. Private Adams replied in French. I asked her what it meant, ma'am. She refused to say. I warned her she would be charged with insolence. She said—' Lieutenant Raleigh paused for a moment, as if to carefully collect herself. Eloise, at attention, kept her face in order. Lieutenant Raleigh delivered the remembered words. 'She said, "Please do so, if that is your silly wish." I then advised her she would be charged with insolence, ma'am.'

'Disgraceful,' said the Commandant. 'What have to you say for yourself, Private Adams?'

'Oh, I'm penitent, of course, ma'am,' said Eloise.

'What was it you said in French to Lieutenant Raleigh?'

'I said, "The fussy little dog of my aunt has been sent to the top of the Eiffel Tower."'

'And you thought that amusing?' asked the Commandant. 'No, you need not answer that. I think seven days confined to barracks, Private Adams, will suffice, with a warning to conduct yourself acceptably in future.'

'Thank you, ma'am,' said Eloise, and wondered a moment later what Captain Lucas would have thought of the incident. She thought he would either laugh or say he was disappointed in her.

Somehow, she felt he would laugh.

But, really, having to ask permission just to walk a little way to the public phone box, how petty. One thing she was sure of. Captain Lucas would throw petty women into a river.

Chapter Thirteen

It was twelve-thirty the following day, and the news was not too bad at all. The French were holding the Germans, and their counter-offensive was about to begin. Helene, wanting to believe, believed. Madame Aarlberg, entering the kitchen, found her daughter preparing a lunch of bread and cheese, with salad.

'Why are you doing that, Helene?'

'Oh, as you're so busy, Mama, I thought I'd take the sergeant's lunch out to him again.'

'But he can come in for it today,' said Madame Aarlberg. 'There's asparagus quiche in the oven. The English don't like too many cold lunches, so your father says.'

'That crazy man hasn't complained yet,' said Helene, mixing and dressing the salad. 'I'll include a portion of the quiche, shall I? Yes, very well, Mama.'

'Well, he deserves a little extra,' said Madame Aarlberg, 'he works very hard for us.'

'He likes the work,' said Helene, 'and we need him to like it. Some fields are monstrously overgrown. It's time Papa went after our labourers.

213

They're idling and have no conscience about it. I think I'll eat my own lunch out there with the sergeant. It will save time.'

'Will it?' asked Madame Aarlberg, eyeing her daughter with interest. It was not very often that Helene was seen preparing food. All her working priorities related to the farm, not the kitchen. 'I hope you don't intend to quarrel with Bobby.'

'Of course not,' said Helene, 'I am past being provoked by his liking for the trivial.'

'How very tolerant of you,' said Madame Aarlberg.

A field of onions was under Bobby's active hoe, the weeds in rampant profusion. In the distance, on the east side of the farm, he saw some of Jacob's farmhands at work in fields thickly green. Cows, looking like nursery toys, dotted a field of pasture. Above, the sky was an unbroken blue. Many miles to the south the battle for France was being fought.

Bobby applied the hoe mechanically, his mind on Dunkirk and the chances of escape. Was it crazy to hope a sailing-boat would be available? Wouldn't the Germans there have cleared the harbour and the breakwaters of anything that could float? He thought of Helene. He was always thinking of that young woman.

She arrived then, out of the blue, as it were.

'Are you ready to eat?' she asked. She was carrying a cane basket.

He straightened up. Helene silently acknowledged how healthy and vigorous he looked, and very much in command of himself. He smiled at her.

'You're a welcome sight,' he said, 'and so is that basket.'

'The basket more so, of course,' she said.

'Equally, I'd say, if my lunch is in it,' he said.

'It contains lunch for both of us,' she said. 'It's a help to my busy mother.' She found a place on the edge of the field, in the shade of a hedge. They seated themselves and she unpacked the basket. Bobby poured the wine and she distributed the food. There were plates and cutlery today because of the dressed salad and the quiche.

'That looks good,' said Bobby. 'Is the news good too?'

'France is now ready to counter-attack,' said Helene.

'Jesus,' said Bobby, 'if that's a fact, there's hope for all of us. Is it a fact?'

'It's what I heard on the radio,' said Helene, not knowing that the French offensive was more a matter of wishful thinking than any fact.

'That's put me in the mood for a celebration,' said Bobby.

'My own mood has been terrible lately,' said Helene. 'I'm sorry if I've been unkind to you.'

'No hard feelings,' said Bobby, 'you've put up with me like an angel.'

'I have not,' said Helene, 'and it's absurd to say I

have. But you are full of absurdities, such as thinking you could cross the Channel in a small sailing-boat.'

'You've said that once too often,' said Bobby.

'What do you mean?' she asked challengingly.

'It's got my blood up,' said Bobby. 'But don't let's get into another argument. Eat your lunch, there's a good girl.'

Helene sat up, her back stiff.

'What did you say?' she asked.

'Be a good girl and eat your lunch,' said Bobby.

'Then say nothing more,' breathed Helene. 'Do not speak to me. I won't be patronized.'

Bobby, enjoying the quiche, said, 'After all this time we ought to be able to do better than that, Helene, we ought—'

'Don't call me Helene. I am Helene only to my friends.'

'Don't be like that,' said Bobby. 'You ought to consider me one of your friends by now – hello, who's that, a French cowboy?'

Helene turned her head. In the distance was a man riding a horse.

'That is a neighbour of ours, Henri Barnard,' she said, 'and I think he's on his way to our house again, perhaps with more news about conditions in Dunkirk.'

'Is he a farmer too?' asked Bobby.

'Yes.' Helene was brusque. 'He would like to marry me.'

'That doesn't surprise me,' said Bobby. The

horseman disappeared behind undulating terrain. 'Good for him, I'd say.'

'Oh?' Helene sniffed. 'What about what is good for me?'

'Wouldn't it be good for you to be a farmer's wife?' asked Bobby. 'I think you'd like it, wouldn't you?'

'That doesn't mean I would like to be Henri Barnard's wife,' said Helene. 'You could see, couldn't you, even from this distance, that he's fat?'

'Large, I thought,' said Bobby.

'He's a kind man and a very good friend,' said Helene, 'but fat and old.'

'He didn't look old from here,' said Bobby.

'He's thirty, perhaps more,' said Helene.

'That's old?' said Bobby.

'Yes,' said Helene.

'Well, I don't think I'm fat and old,' said Bobby.

'So?' said Helene.

'You wouldn't fancy me, I suppose?' ventured Bobby.

'Excuse me?' Helene looked puzzled. 'Fancy you?'

'As a husband,' said Bobby, offering a smile as well as a proposal.

Helene stared at him, thinking she had never met, nor ever would meet, such a crazy man.

'You?' she said, with a touch of mockery.

'Not right now, of course,' said Bobby. 'I've got to get back to my regiment somehow and rejoin the war. But after the war—'

'You?' she said again.

'Just a thought,' said Bobby.

'You?' she said yet again. 'As a husband? That is not even a poor joke.'

'No joke,' said Bobby, 'and after all, we might make a good team.'

'A good team?' Helene gave him a pitying look.

'Yes, you've got character and I've got a liking for making life adventurous,' said Bobby.

'You've got a liking for making silly jokes,' said Helene, 'and would make a very silly husband. Do you think this is the time for such an absurd conversation, when the war is so desperate? In any case, I'm not in need of a husband, and even if I were, I would not choose any man from your country. I'm sorry, but I would not, especially after—' She made a dismissive gesture. 'No, I am sorry, but never.'

'Fair enough,' said Bobby, 'and I'm not offended. I know you like being frank and speaking your mind. I admire that. By the way, I think I'll make a run for Dunkirk tonight.'

'Then you're an idiot,' said Helene. She ate food angrily. 'How many times do I have to tell you that even if you found a boat, it would be madness to attempt the Channel? Because you are stupid, do you think the Germans are too? They will have guards everywhere. Why can't you be sensible? Now that you have a French identity paper, you could stay on here as one of our workers.'

Bobby gave her a searching look, and she wondered why she had said that.

'Are you making jokes now?' he asked.

218

'I am making sense, which you are not,' she said. 'You could stay here until the war in France has been decided, one way or another. Then things will settle down one way or another until it becomes obvious what is best for you to do.'

Mother of God, she thought, what am I saying?

'I can't wait as long as that,' said Bobby, 'and besides, I've got a responsibility to try to get back to England and my regiment.'

'Very well,' she snapped, 'go whenever you like, get yourself shot and killed. How true it is that when an obstinate man means to do something suicidal, no-one can make him see how stupid he is.'

'It's not my intention to commit suicide,' said Bobby.

'Who cares? I do not.' Helene felt angry, irritable and provoked. The day was another beautiful one, the farm a splendid panorama of many colours. The war was terrible, but the farm would always remain constant in its appeal and productivity. What was wrong with him staying here and taking time to make the kind of plans that would guarantee his escape? Her father was bound in time to help him find the right way, the right plan, with the assistance of friends. For this sergeant to believe he could do it all by himself, when the Germans were still so active in this region, irritated her excessively.

As soon as the meal was finished, she repacked the basket and left, her mood making her departure a silent one.

'Many thanks for the lunch,' called Bobby, 'and

would you tell your mother the quiche was first-class?'

Helene said nothing to that.

Nor did the current news make her any happier, for it was all about the French forces effecting more strategic movements, which meant, of course, that the counter-attack had run into trouble. Further, her mother said Henri Barnard had called again to say a holding company of German troops had taken up quarters on a permanent basis in and around Dunkirk.

'That will put our sergeant's nose out of joint,' said Helene.

'He is safe here,' said Madame Aarlberg.

'He doesn't care for being safe here,' said Helene, 'he intends to leave tonight.'

'Does he know how dangerous it will be?'

'What is that to a man as stupid as he is?' said Helene.

'Is that you speaking, my infant, or your temper?' asked her mother.

'I don't wish to discuss it,' said Helene.

'I don't think Bobby is stupid, Helene, just brave enough to take risks.'

'I don't wish to talk about such a madman,' said Helene, and stalked out.

Sammy was at the firm's Shoreditch factory, talking to Tommy about an officially requested increase in the production of Army and RAF uniforms. Tommy said the increase could be managed in view of the fact that the manufacture of civilian garments was on a limited basis. Output was governed by supplies of dress material, and all such supplies were rationed.

'By the way,' said Tommy, 'you know we're losing Freddy to the Army, do you?'

'I know,' said Sammy, 'and it's hard luck on Cassie. We'll have to find a replacement.'

'I'll take Bert on,' said Tommy, 'he'll be as good as anyone you can find. He knows the factory and its systems frontways and backwards.' Bert Roper was the maintenance man, a loyal stalwart and the husband of Gertie, chargehand to the seamstresses and machinists. 'And he'll find his own replacement, you can bet on that.'

'Leave it to you, Tommy,' said Sammy, 'I'm sad of heart about Freddy. Cassie's goin' to have to grit her teeth. She's never been separated from Freddy since she was a ten-year-old.'

'Cassie'll stick it out,' said Tommy.

'Where's Freddy now?' asked Sammy.

'At our other fact'ry, givin' the manager a shake-up,' said Tommy.

'Is that a good idea, assistant manager here readin' the fact'ry riot act to the manager there?' asked Sammy.

'He's readin' it on my behalf,' said Tommy. 'Their production's down.'

'Sack the bloke,' said Sammy.

'He'll be all right once he's heard Freddy out,' said Tommy. 'Freddy's not all soft centre, he can read out loud like a brass trumpet with an iron mouthpiece.'

'Leave it to you,' said Sammy.

'You a bit off colour?' said Tommy.

'Well, since you ask, so I am,' said Sammy, 'I don't like to see the business takin' second place to bleedin' Adolf Hitler.' That was strong for Sammy these days. He was entirely the reputable businessman, with contacts now in the Air Ministry and the War Office. 'The sooner he gets run over by a railway train, the better I'll like it. I mean, our kids away from home, Tommy. It ain't bloody natural.'

'Don't I know it?' said Tommy. 'But we've got to leave them there. I'm suffering feelings about German bombers.'

'You're not the only one,' said Sammy. 'Well, let's have a look at these Army fatigue uniforms you're turnin' out.'

'Gertie's looked, Freddy's looked and I've looked,' said Tommy, 'and the first batch are up to specification.'

'Funny thing,' said Sammy, 'but once upon a time you couldn't have said that word and I couldn't have spelled it. Shows what listenin' to Boots can do for a bloke. Well, I'm glad about all this collective lookin', but I'm still goin' to take a look on my own account.'

'Help yourself,' said Tommy. That was Sammy all over. He was never satisfied with any new development until he had inspected the result with his own eagle eye. He delegated, but was always watchful of what came of it. 'You've still got positive thoughts about movin' production to Luton, Sammy?'

'Like you pointed out a few minutes ago,' said

Sammy, as they entered the workshop, 'there might be German bombers in the offing.'

Tim had gone out for the day with Nick Harrison's sister Fanny, on leave from the WRAF. They were long-standing friends and good company for each other.

Emily, taking the day off because she felt she owed it to Boots, was in Hyde Park with him, together with Susie and Susie's little girl Paula. It had been Boots's idea, the trip to London's premier park, and his idea too to include Susie and Paula. They'd brought a picnic, and that over, Boots had taken a stroll with little Paula. Susie was sitting on the grass, Emily lying flat out beside her, head pillowed on her handbag, letting the sun bathe her in warmth.

The park was colourful with summer, London a hive of wartime activity, bustling with people, traffic, and men and women of the Services, their uniforms lending an additional note of excitement to an atmosphere still redolent of the wonders of the Dunkirk evacuation. Silvery barrage balloons floated over the river and the docks, and over the Houses of Parliament and other buildings sacred to this capital of the Empire.

Susie saw Boots and Paula returning from their wandering saunter, the bubbly young girl delighted at being the object of his attentions, Boots delighted with her existence. Susie thought it was typical of him to opt for an outing of enjoyable simplicity, and to include her and Paula. He loved

223

kids, and Susie found it easy to believe that after the hell of defeat and retreat, the innocence and enchantment of the five-year-old girl represented a little bit of heaven to him.

She watched them, Paula hand in hand with him, doing the occasional little skip and hop, Boots talking to her and she giggling and laughing. She let go his hand then and skipped ahead, almost running into an ultra-smart Wren officer. The Wren officer stopped, Paula looked up at her, and the woman said something. Up came Boots, and he said something too, and the Wren officer laughed. Then they were chatting, Paula between them, Boots in a new uniform, one of two delivered to him this morning by special messenger from London tailors whose clientele included Army officers. Susie smiled, sure that the Wren officer was going to do her best to prolong the conversation. Boots still had an effect on women.

'Wake up, Em'ly,' she murmured, 'Boots has just been discovered by a lady sailor.'

Emily sat up, took a look at the scene and said, 'That husband of mine, when's he goin' to behave like an old married man?'

'D'you think that Wren officer sees him as old?' asked Susie.

'He's over forty,' said Emily.

'Count your blessings,' said Susie, 'he's just given her the push.'

The Wren officer was on her way, and Paula was hand in hand with Boots again.

'Well, that saved me goin' over and knockin' her

three-cornered hat off,' said Emily, and laughed.

Susie thought the whole atmosphere of the radiant day exciting but strangely haunting.

Finishing her day's labours just before six, Helene was suddenly aware of the presence of more German military men. They were in a field on the other side of a stone wall that separated the Aarlberg farm from Henri Barnard's. Four officers. They were talking to Henri. From a slightly elevated point, Helene observed the quartet with eyes of hatred. As far as the German people were concerned, she'd never had any quarrel with them until they began to worship Hitler and fascism. She despised such worship for what it made of Hitler, a dictatorial monster of supposed omnipotence.

To her, the four officers were acolytes of the monster. Their stiff upright figures seemed to diminish Henri's largeness. She turned her back on them and began the long walk to the house, choosing a route that would enable her to pick up Sergeant Somers. He always worked until she appeared. She suspected he kept going because he needed to be active. Activity held his frustrations at bay, she supposed.

She wondered if she had been unnecessarily unkind to him. But it was hardly believable, his proposal and the way he had made it, as if it was all in his day's work. Marry him, after he and all the other British soldiers had been made to run like rabbits from the German tanks and guns? The impertinence of it, the arrogance. No wonder the English had a reputation for considering themselves the salt of the earth.

She walked in her angry way again, her stride eating up the ground. Not far from the onion fields, she negotiated a gate by swinging herself over it, as she often did when her mood demanded physical action. As she landed, a man laughed, stepped forward from behind the hedge, wound an arm around her waist and launched her into another swing. Her skirt flew high. Another man laughed. The arm released her, and another took its place. Again she was lifted from her feet and swung. Further release came, and two German corporals, hugely amused, grinned as she straightened herself. Her dark blue eyes became icy. The Germans clicked their heels and bowed to her.

'*Wo sind wir jetzt?*' asked one of the other. Where are we now?

'With this French *Fräulein*,' said the other.

Helene, freezing them with a look, attempted to walk on, but an arm encircled her waist from behind and squeezed her. She turned and smacked the man's face, hard. It outraged him, this assault on a uniformed representative of Germany's might, and seconds later Helene was on the ground, the man astride her waist, hands pinning her wrists, her skirt and slip up around her hips, her legs kicking. The other man stood looking at her legs, a delighted smile on his face. Helene let her arms and wrists go limp. The German's grip relaxed, she wrenched her hands free and struck him across his mouth.

'*Canaille!* she hissed.

The German, lips bruised, stared down at her, expression one of surprised admiration for her spirit.

'What should be done with you?' he asked.

Bobby arrived then, at a rush. He had seen everything from the moment Helene swung herself over the gate, and he had begun an immediate sprint. Helene saw him as he came to a halt, and she was almost shocked at the fury on his face. The standing German looked at him, and the German astride her lifted his head. Both became men of uncertainty, for all their sense of Aryan superiority. It was the uncertainty of men discovered in the act of making a plaything of a woman.

Bobby held himself in check.

'Get up, *Mademoiselle* Aarlberg,' he said in French, and he took two steps forward to extend a helping hand to her. 'Get up, if you please.'

Helene eased her body free of the straddling German, who made no move to stop her, and she came to her feet. The German rose and looked at his fellow NCO, who shrugged. They were both equipped with holstered machine-pistols, but made no attempt to draw them. France was not yet beaten, and they were not yet the owners of Paris and the masters of Europe. Bobby gave them a look that positively alarmed Helene. She thought he was actually preparing to knock both men down, one after the other. He would be arrested and shot.

'No,' she said, 'come away.'

One German made a gesture. It told them to go,

to get lost, and it re-established him and the other NCO as the people in command.

For some seconds, Bobby gave no ground. Then he turned and walked away, taking Helene with him, his hand on her arm. He was silent for a little while. Then, releasing her arm, he said, 'Are you hurt?'

'No,' she said, 'I'm humiliated, not hurt. The other swine was looking at my legs.'

'I apologize for them,' said Bobby.

'Why should you do that, why should you apologize for German pigs?' asked Helene, face flushed.

'Because when a woman suffers that kind of thing from a man, it shames most other men,' said Bobby.

'My God,' said Helene, 'for one terrible moment I thought you were going to strike them.'

'Well, I did have a rush of blood,' said Bobby, 'but it cooled down in time to save me from losing my head. Are you sure you're not hurt?'

'Yes, I am quite sure,' said Helene, 'and thank you.' She bit her lip. 'I must tell you I shan't accuse you again of being a man who runs from Nazis, and I'm sorry I ever said you were. But—'

'Think nothing of it,' said Bobby, 'it was understandable.'

The farmhouse came in sight, and Helene said, 'Please say nothing to my parents about those Germans. It will upset my father and distress my mother.'

Bobby nodded.

'If that's what you want,' he said, 'I won't say a word, not one.'

'And I think you've changed your mind about going to Dunkirk tonight, haven't you?' said Helene.

'No, I haven't changed my mind,' said Bobby. 'I feel that if I don't go tonight, Dunkirk will be padlocked from tomorrow onwards.'

Helene let fly.

'Then you're still a fool, an imbecile, a madman! Go, then, go!'

And she whipped on ahead of him in her temper.

Chapter Fourteen

Helene entered the kitchen in a rush. Her mother looked at her, seeing the flush on her face. She is angry again, of course. It was not a good time for her, or for any of the young people of France, for they could see that what ought to be the best years of their lives turning into their worst years.

'Now what is wrong, Helene?'

'Everything,' said Helene. 'That idiot, Sergeant Somers, is definitely going to commit suicide tonight. He has made up his mind to get to Dunkirk and look for a boat.'

'But isn't that what you would like?' asked Madame Aarlberg.

'Mama, what do you think I am? A supporter of a silly suicide attempt by that obstinate man? Here he is.'

Bobby came in.

'Good evening, *madame*,' he said.

'Helene tells me you mean to get to Dunkirk tonight,' said Madame Aarlberg.

'Yes, I have to go, I've been here long enough,' said Bobby, 'and I'll risk what's in front of me.'

Helene breathed an unladylike imprecation, and went upstairs to her room. Her exit from the kitchen was of a fuming kind, and she emphasized what a rage she was in by slamming the door shut behind her.

'Helene, I'm afraid,' said Madame Aarlberg, 'is exceptionally angry.'

'Sorry about that, I think it's something to do with my lack of sense,' said Bobby. 'Might I use the bath again?'

'Of course,' said Madame Aarlberg.

'Wait, what's the latest news?'

'Battles are raging,' said Madame Aarlberg, and sighed. 'I'm afraid the good news is being over-taken by more bad news, Bobby.'

'Believe me, I feel for you and your country,' said Bobby.

'I know you do. Go and have your bath, and we will try to get through the evening without too much unhappiness.'

The evening meal was eaten with the radio silent, much as if the family hoped that by leaving it switched off the news would somehow take a turn for the better. Helene was also silent, saying rarely a word, and she refused altogether to even look at Bobby. However, his imminent departure had to be mentioned, and when Madame Aarlberg served coffee, Jacob said that if his mind was made up, he would need assistance. Bobby said far better for him to rely on himself, that too much had already been done for him.

Helene muttered.

'Bobby, we must give you some help to make

sure you reach Dunkirk,' said Madame Aarlberg.

'If I could have the loan of another pair of socks from Jacob,' said Bobby, 'that will be enough.'

'In a moment, in a very little moment, I'm going to scream,' breathed Helene. 'A pair of socks, he says, a pair of socks. Well, give him a pair, Papa, and show him the way to the nearest asylum for idiots with clean socks but no heads.'

They heard the back door of the little dairy open then, and the sound of a voice.

'I may enter?' It was Henri Barnard.

Jacob glanced at Bobby. Bobby nodded and silently slipped out, taking his coffee with him. Jacob rose to his feet and got rid of Bobby's plate, cutlery and wine glass.

'Come, Henri,' he called, and Henri Barnard entered from the little dairy, the converted scullery.

'Ah, my apologies, you are still at dinner,' he said.

'No, we've finished except for the coffee,' said Jacob. 'Sit down, Henri, and have a cup.'

'Thank you, Jacob, I will,' said Henri, and seated himself in the chair Bobby had been using. Helene got up, fetched a cup and saucer, and Madame Aarlberg poured the coffee. Henri took a mouthful, then regarded the family ruefully. 'I've had damned German officers on my farm, looking the place over. They advised me they might requisition use of my house. No request was made. None. They simply said they might or might not want it. But I can't say they weren't polite. They were very polite, but also like blocks of wood, you understand.'

'I saw them with you,' said Helene.

'Why should they need a house here?' asked Jacob. 'Some of them spoke to Helene yesterday about our own place, but like you, Henri, we are well outside Dunkirk.'

'I don't want them taking my house over,' said Henri. 'I recommended yours as the better farm and better house, Jacob.'

'Henri, you did not!' protested Madame Aarlberg.

'No, no, of course not,' said Henri.

'I am hearing too many unsuitable jokes lately,' said Helene. 'Does no-one care about France?'

'I care, Helene, with all my heart,' said Henri, 'but don't wish to give the impression I've accepted the possibility of defeat. By the way, as I told you earlier today, Estelle, there are still some small undamaged boats to the west of the harbour. Mine is there, and so is yours, Helene. My informant was positive.'

'It's hardly believable,' said Henri.

'West of the harbour, Henri?' said Jacob.

'That's so,' said Henri, button-like eyes bright. 'Do you have someone in mind?'

'One never knows what might be wanted,' said Jacob.

'We're concerning ourselves only with possibilities?' said Henri.

'One never knows,' said Helene.

'Well, friends of escaping Allied soldiers should

233

be prepared to render assistance,' said Henri. 'Dunkirk is garrisoned by the Germans now. By the way, Helene, my real reason for calling now is to ask if you would play hostess for me at dinner tomorrow evening. My brother and his wife will be my guests. Would you be so kind?'

'I protest,' said Helene. 'How can anyone think of giving a dinner party when France is so much on the rack?'

'Perhaps it could count as a gesture of brave defiance,' murmured Madame Aarlberg.

'It's playing a fiddle while Rome is burning,' said Helene, 'and I'm not in the mood to join in or to dress up. I'm sorry, but you must do without me, Henri. Let your housekeeper stand in.'

Henri sighed, finished his coffee and came to his feet.

'If you should change your mind, Helene, let me know,' he said. 'One should show these Nazis we are still undefeated. Oh, and should a possibility become a certainty, Jacob, remember I'm willing for my boat to be used.'

'I'll remember,' said Jacob, and saw him out.

'I think Henri has guessed,' said Madame Aarlberg when Jacob returned.

'Did he mention our new worker?' asked Helene.

'He said he'd heard of him, and asked who he was.' Jacob rubbed his chin. 'I told him he was a recent and welcome addition. He smiled and offered the use of his boat again. We must think about that, and how to get our sergeant to it.'

'Are you crazy too, Papa?' asked Helene.

'Helene, do you wish Bobby to stay on here now?' asked her mother.

'I keep telling you, I simply don't wish to help him commit suicide. Either the Germans will shoot him or he'll drown himself.'

'What he really needs is a companion, an expert,' said Jacob. 'One might have thought Henri in his patriotism would have volunteered not only his boat but his services. But he has his farm, of course, and the responsibilities of running it.'

'Henri is too set in his ways to exchange his farm for exile in England,' said Madame Aarlberg.

'All the same,' said Jacob, 'Sergeant Somers would have a better chance if given the assistance of an experienced yachtsman.'

'But Henri isn't experienced in crossing the Channel,' said Helene, in new exasperation. 'No owner of an inshore sailing-boat is. So what will you do, Papa, go and tell the crazy one he can take his chance?'

'I think—' Jacob checked at the noise of a car pulling up on the gravelled forecourt. It was followed by silence as the engine was cut off, and then the sound of car doors opening and shutting.

'Germans?' said Madame Aarlberg quietly.

'Perhaps,' said Jacob. 'Helene, go and make sure the sergeant stays out of the way.'

Helene sped from the kitchen. She found Bobby sitting on the top stair. She ran up, warned him and he disappeared into his bedroom. A knock on the front door was answered by Jacob, and he was confronted in the warm evening light by a tall, correct-looking German major and a poker-faced lieutenant. On the forecourt stood an open Mercedes car flying a Nazi pennant, a German soldier sitting at the wheel.

'Good evening, *m'sieur*, my apologies for disturbing you.' The French was exemplary. 'I am Major Kreik, and my colleague is Lieutenant Dorff. You are?'

'Jacob Aarlberg.'

'May we have a few minutes of your time, M'sieur Aarlberg?'

'Very well.' Jacob's calmness matched the German's politeness. 'Enter.' He took the two officers into the living-room. Almost at once, as if determined to give him any necessary support, his wife and daughter appeared. Major Kreik glanced at them. Lieutenant Dorff hardly bothered. He considered France and its people decadent. Helene recognized him as the lieutenant who had taken notes yesterday. 'My wife and daughter,' said Jacob. Major Kreik took his cap off and executed a little bow, though without clicking his heels. He was an Army officer of the old school, not an ss man.

'*Madame? Mademoiselle?*' His manners were faultless. 'I'm sorry to interrupt your evening, and I acknowledge that events can't be to your liking. War has no kind facets. However, there are certain arrangements to be made. You are the owner of this farm, M'sieur Aarlberg?'

'With my wife.' Jacob was still calm, Madame Aarlberg hoping for a peaceful outcome, and Helene praying, because of her parents, that the visit was nothing to do with the fact that they were sheltering a British sergeant.

'I am correct in addressing myself to both of you, then,' said Major Kreik. 'First, please be kind enough to conduct us over the house.'

Helene stiffened.

'May I ask why?' enquired Jacob.

'You may, *m'sieur*. If the house is suitable, we shall require use of it, and as you are subject to the authority of an occupying power, as set out in the Geneva Convention, you must allow this. An official requisition order will arrive in your hands. Please proceed.'

So that was it, thought Helene. That was why German officers had been nosing around. The house was to be taken over by Hitler's plunderers and while France was still fighting. Helene gritted her teeth in silent rage, then thought of the man upstairs. Sergeant Somers. Mother of God.

'I cannot bear this,' she said.

'Unfortunately, *mademoiselle*—'

'I don't wish to be part of it,' she said. She turned and swept from the room.

Jacob guessed her motive, so did her mother. Adopting an air of dignified resignation, Jacob began a tour of the house, showing the Germans the ground floor, every room, every cupboard and the door to the cellar. Their inspection of everything was brief but keenly observant. He eventually led the way upstairs. On the way up, Major Kreik commented on the spaciousness of the house.

'I'm to infer you're finding it suitable so far?' said Jacob drily.

'You will be advised in due course,' said wooden-faced Lieutenant Dorff.

Jacob opened bedroom doors, one after the other. The Germans did not enter any of them, they merely made a brief examination from each doorway. Jacob showed nothing of his relief when the bedroom being used by Bobby was seen as empty of everything except furniture. The bed was covered by an overlay.

In Helene's room, her presence leapt to the eye. She was lying on her bed, reading. She turned her head.

'Spare me the suggestion that I may be thrown out,' she said.

'The fortunes of war can be hard on the losers, *mademoiselle*, as Germany found out in 1918,' said Major Kreik. 'Accept my apologies for disturbing you.'

'Please go away,' said Helene, and the Germans withdrew, Major Kreik the epitome of politeness, Lieutenant Dorff much less inclined to humour the hostile young Frenchwoman, although he said nothing.

The tour and inspection did not take very long. Major Kreik asked very few questions. Back again in the living-room, Jacob turned to the Germans.

'You've decided?' he said.

'A moment, *m'sieur*,' said Major Kreik. He removed his gloves, laid them aside with his cap and cane, and drew a map from his pocket. He opened it up and placed it on the polished surface of a mahogany table.

Upstairs, Helene was off her bed and down on one knee beside it.

'Stay where you are, do you hear me?' she whispered.

From under the bed, Bobby whispered, 'I hear you, Helene.'

'Count yourself fortunate the Boche swine aren't here looking for men like you. I am going down to see exactly what they're saying to my parents. You are not to show yourself.'

'I'm quite comfortable,' whispered Bobby.

'Ah, always you talk like an idiot,' hissed Helene, and left. Going downstairs she met her mother and they entered the living-room together, where they found Major Kreik had an open map spread flat on the table. It was a large-scale map of the area, printed in German. Having drawn Jacob's attention to it, he now began to explain the full purpose of his visit.

'I am in command of the 33rd Flieger Abwehr Battery.' An anti-aircraft battery. 'My headquarters are to be sited here.' He placed a finger on the map. Jacob leaned and looked.

'I see,' he said, 'on our farm.'

Helene's expression threatened an outburst, and her mother touched her arm in a gesture of restraint.

'Only part of the area, that between your house and the road, *m'sieur*,' said Major Kreik. 'I regret, but that is how it will be. We require use of land on either side of your approach lane. Accommodation will be built for the men. I further regret, *m'sieur,* that you will have to vacate your house, which will be used by my officers and myself. If you have a cottage available, no doubt you and your family could move there.'

'There's a cottage standing empty at the moment,' said Jacob, his restraint admirable, 'and there will only be my wife and myself. My daughter is moving to St Omer to take up work as a lawyer's clerk.'

Ah, thought Helene, I am to be sent safely out of the way of Germans who will be all over the place? We shall see.

'The cottage will comfortably accommodate you, M'sieur Aarlberg?' enquired Major Kreik, and Lieutenant Dorff looked down his wooden nose at such extreme politeness.

'It won't be as accommodating as the house,' said Madame Aarlberg.

'When are we to leave?' asked Helene. 'Before breakfast tomorrow or after?'

Major Kreik regarded her not without sympathy.

'Not for a week, *mademoiselle,*' he said. He refolded the map and put it back in his pocket. He took up his cap, cane and gloves. 'My apologies again for disturbing all of you.' He moved to the door, Lieutenant Dorff following. He turned, his expression quite pleasant. 'Ah, one small thing, M'sieur Aarlberg. Some individual British soldiers have fallen into our hands during the last few days. There may be others here and there. You must notify the German Military Headquarters in Dunkirk immediately in the event of any of them appearing on your farm. This applies to all Allied soldiers who have not given themselves up. You understand?'

'I do,' said Jacob. 'I hope in turn you'll understand that such action on my part won't commend me to my neighbours or my conscience.'

'I understand perfectly. Unfortunately, it is necessary. However,' said Major Kreik with the slightest of smiles, 'your person, your conscience and your family are now under the protection of the Fuehrer and the Greater German Reich. Goodbye, *m'sieur, madame, mademoiselle*, and thank you for your co-operation.'

He and Lieutenant Dorff left. Jacob saw them out, closing the front door quietly on them. Rejoining his wife and daughter, who had returned to the kitchen, he heard the sound of the Mercedes starting up and driving away.

They looked at each other.

'In a week,' said Helene fiercely, 'their jackboots will be pounding every floor in our house. But of course I'm not going to St Omer, Papa.'

'I think your mother and I would prefer you not to remain here,' said Jacob. 'Ah, where is the elusive sergeant?'

'Hiding,' said Helene tersely.

'But where?' asked her mother.

'Under my bed, with his rifle and helmet,' said Helene. 'And his uniform is in the bed. There was no time to get him out of the house. Well, now I will go up and bring him down.' Up she went. Entering her bedroom she said, 'You can show yourself now.'

Bobby eased himself into view and climbed to his feet. His uncut hair looked untidy, his bandage in need of a change.

'That was a close shave,' he said, 'but thanks for getting me tucked out of the way. What were they after?'

'This house and part of our farm,' said Helene, eyes hot.

'You're not serious, are you?' said Bobby.

'Of course. Would I joke about Nazis and their taking ways? But it might have been worse, they might have found you and then shot all of us.'

'Christ,' said Bobby, 'I'll leave as soon as it's dark.'

'Don't you understand anything?' said Helene. 'Our phone isn't working, the Nazis are all over Europe, our French armies are losing their battles, and your country is an island that will be bombed into the sea. It can do nothing, nothing, to stop Hitler and his mad ambitions. To go back there is ridiculous. Why can't you stay?'

'Because there's still a war to fight,' said Bobby, 'and because I don't believe nothing can be done. And because staying would make life too dangerous for you and your parents. We both know that.'

Helene drew a long breath.

'Very well, I will take you,' she said.

'Take me where?' said Bobby.

'To Dunkirk.'

'You won't,' said Bobby.

'I've said I will.'

'And I've said you won't.'

Helene fumed.

'Who are you to say what I will or won't do? You know very well you can't manage on your own, and I know I can't let you find a boat in which to drown yourself. I have to go with you.'

'Do you mean across the Channel?' asked Bobby.

'Of course,' said Helene.

'I won't let you,' said Bobby.

'It's no use arguing,' said Helene, 'if your mind is made up, so is mine.'

'God Almighty,' said Bobby, 'what a headache you are. The risks are mine alone. Damn it all, if anything happened to you, how the hell could I face your parents again?'

'Shouting will do you no good, nor swearing, nor bullying,' said Helene.

'Anyone who tried to bully you would have to run for his life,' said Bobby. 'And who's shouting?'

'You are ready to,' said Helene.

'You're not coming,' said Bobby, 'is that clear?'

'It might be clear to you, it isn't to me,' said Helene, and suddenly temper ran from her, and she spoke calmly. 'Two will be better than one. You know it, but won't admit it. It's because I'm a woman—'

'A girl,' said Bobby.

'That is what you think. You think too that because you're the one wearing trousers I'm inferior to you. You're mistaken, I'm as good as you are, and at sailing much better. You will never get across the Channel without me, and because you're not too bad as an English sergeant, after all, I'm not going to let you drown yourself. I've said that to you a hundred times lately. Now, do you wish to give up stupid argument?'

'Jesus Christ, I'm speechless,' said Bobby, who had never had any girl talk to him like that before.

'A welcome change,' said Helene. It was done, she had made her decision, and she knew it was the right one. Her father had implied that in the event of the defeat of France, anyone who wanted to help Britain carry on the fight should go there. And it was depressingly obvious by now that the French Army was no match for this colossal German fighting machine. 'I'm sorry if I said your country could do nothing. My father believes it could and must, that a new Allied army must be built there, and that it must accept volunteers from Europe to help in one way or another. I will volunteer. My chance and your chance will come if we can find Henri Barnard's boat, which is larger than mine. His is a yacht, mine is only a sailing dinghy. We need to take certain things with us, like a torch and a compass.' Helene was speaking quickly and firmly to discourage interruptions. 'A company of German soldiers is garrisoning Dunkirk, so we must take care when we get there and not go blundering about.'

'I've got a reputation for not blundering about,' said Bobby.

'Good,' said Helene. 'Perhaps we shall find

244

things in our favour, perhaps not. Perhaps the Nazis have put every undamaged boat out of action. We shall see. Henri's boat is moored near mine. We'll leave here as soon as it's dark, and take the route my father showed you on that map. It keeps us off roads and brings us quite close to the west side of the harbour. But it will all be a matter of luck. There are bound to be German patrols and slipway sentries. We must take spare clothes in a waterproof bag, because we shall have to swim to the boat.'

'Save my soul,' said Bobby, 'do you know what you're saying? That I'm to take you away from your parents and lead you into God knows what?'

'I think this is what my father has come to expect of me, more so now that we are to have German soldiers around us,' said Helene. 'That is why he has mentioned a boat more than once.'

'But it could mean you losing all contact with your family for years,' said Bobby. 'No, I can't agree, and it's too dangerous, in any case.'

'More for you than me,' said Helene, 'and whether you agree or not, I've decided. We shall leave together tonight. All you need to do now is pray for the Channel to be kind to us, if we can get to the boat. You can put up with my company, can't you?'

'Put up with it?' Bobby shook his head at her. 'Would I have – no, I won't mention that again. I realize it was a bit ridiculous, after only a few days, so let's forget it. But before I agree to let you come with me, we'll have to talk to your parents.'

* * *

Madame Aarlberg was sad and uncertain about all the implications, and apprehensive of the dangers. Jacob, however, had felt almost from the beginning that it was a boat and Helene's sailing expertise that represented the British sergeant's best chance of a return to England. It also represented Helene's best chance of escaping the torments of German occupation. Young, healthy and proud, she would not suffer that lightly. Nor would she take kindly to unpleasantness. Jacob considered Hitler's fanatical hordes, drunk with power and conquest, capable of doing what they liked and taking what they wanted. He knew he and his wife would miss their daughter excessively, but the island of Britain was the place for her. He was sure it was the place for all young people who could get there. His every hope was presently vested in Britain and Churchill.

Yes, Helene had always held the key that would open the door for Sergeant Somers, but she alone had the right to decide, and without being subjected to persuasion. Now, having decided, she was refusing to draw back, despite her mother's uncertainties. Her mother, in any case, had also known exactly how the sergeant could best be helped, just as she knew that to live under the Nazi jackboot would drive Helene mad.

Jacob warned her to take nothing for granted the moment she and the sergeant set out. Bobby was still inclined to argue, for he knew he was responsible for bringing about a venture which, if successful, would deprive two exceptionally kind

246

people of their daughter for the duration of the war. He resolutely put aside thoughts of what failure might mean.

'I'm afraid this is all my fault,' he said.

'That, my friend, isn't true,' said Jacob. 'We are all at the mercy of circumstances, in peace as well as war. In war, of course, circumstances are simply more difficult to overcome.'

'The feelings of people also mean much,' said Madame Aarlberg, wondering how Helene would get on in what might soon become the beleaguered island of Britain. She would know no-one except Bobby, and Bobby would surely be with his regiment. But perhaps his family would help to take care of her. However strong and independent Helene was, everyone needed to see familiar faces and hear familiar voices once in a while.

'Jacob,' said Bobby, 'how will you manage when the Germans take over your farmhouse?'

'We'll be living in one of the cottages,' said Jacob, 'and will manage better than if we had to share the house with them.'

'Well, if France goes down, I hope you'll find life bearable,' said Bobby.

Helene switched on the radio. A few minutes listening were enough to confirm that the German Panzer divisions were continuing to push the French armies back and to break through in places.

'It doesn't get better,' said Jacob, and the radio was switched off.

Bobby felt for the family. Helene returned to the subject in hand, saying that if they found it impossible to reach the relevant jetty, they would have to come back to the farm and think of some other way of getting to England. Bobby didn't think that a good idea, and said it would be better to lie low and wait for an opportunity to contact some French fishermen. He supposed Dunkirk did have its quota of fishermen?

'Thousands,' said Helene, 'and they're all waiting for a man like you so that they can take him across the Channel. Naturally, all their trawlers have escaped German bombs.'

'Well, there's one thing I must insist on,' said Bobby. 'We've got to face the possibility of being caught. So I must wear my uniform, and if we run into a patrol, Helene must say she's brought me in so that I can give myself up, that she persuaded me to. In fact, she must say that immediately. In uniform, I won't be shot, and Helene, in handing me over, will look as if she's on their side, which is how she must look.'

'I must look like a French Nazi? Never,' said Helene.

'You must do as I say about this,' said Bobby.

'Helene has a will of her own, I'm afraid,' said Madame Aarlberg.

'I know,' said Bobby, 'I've bumped into it several times.'

'How can you ask me to hand you over?' demanded Helene, incensed.

'If you're stopped, Helene, what else could you do?' asked Jacob.

'You wish the Nazis to decorate me?' said Helene.

'Bobby is being sensible,' said her mother.

'Being sensible will make me look like the most perfidious woman in France,' said Helene, and ground her teeth because there seemed to be no alternative.

A little later, Bobby went up to change and to give the family time to talk privately together.

Chapter Fifteen

At dusk, Bobby was ready to leave. Helene called down that she would only be a few minutes. Jacob shook hands with the man into whose care he was relinquishing his daughter.

'My wife and I are aware of the obvious risks, my friend,' he said, 'and are sure you'll avoid the unnecessary ones. If Dunkirk proves too difficult, return here.'

'I hope nothing's going to be so difficult that I'll have to land myself on you again,' said Bobby. Now that a move was going to be made at last, his adrenalin was flowing. His dressing had been removed, and his uncovered wound was healing. 'You know and I know how much I owe to you and your wife.'

'We could not have done less, Bobby,' said Madame Aarlberg, 'and it has been a pleasure for Jacob and me to come to know you. I have much faith in you and feel sure you will reach England in some way. What will happen to Helene there?'

'I'll take her home and she'll live with my family,' said Bobby. 'I'll be given immediate leave and keep an eye on her until I rejoin my regiment. She can stay with my family for as long as she likes, but I don't suppose she'll sit counting her fingers. Not that young lady. Rely on me to keep in touch with her, and to help her in any way I can. And my parents will take very good care of her, believe me.'

'Thank you, Bobby,' said Madame Aarlberg, 'I'm sure that of all things she'll want you to keep in touch with her. She has an aunt in Switzerland, by the way, and perhaps we shall hear from her through her aunt. I am glad Jacob brought you here. You have been no trouble, only a very good farm worker.'

'I won't forget you,' said Bobby, 'nor you, Jacob.' He shook hands with them both and received a warm kiss on his cheek from Jacob's equable and hospitable wife.

Helene appeared then, dressed in jersey, skirt, black stockings and rubber boots, a velvet beret on her head. Bobby said a final goodbye to her parents, and since Madame Aarlberg was moist-eyed, he went out through the back door to let Helene say her own goodbyes. She joined him after a few minutes, and they began a silent walk in the deepening dusk.

Bobby had left his rifle and tin hat with Jacob, who had them securely hidden. Bobby said he'd come back for them one day. He carried an oilskin bag that contained spare underclothes for both of them, and a blouse and skirt for Helene, with a nightdress. To attempt a Channel crossing after dark in a small yacht was enough by itself to contend with. To do so in garments soaked by the sea would rapidly reduce their resistance to the elements. If they were stopped and questions were asked about the contents of the bag, Helene was to say she expected to stay in Dunkirk overnight. All the spare underwear was wrapped in the night-dress.

Tucked under her beret was a small compass, and she carried a torch, a credible item for a woman bringing a British soldier to the German authorities by night. Inside his battledress, Bobby had a small bottle of cognac, but for obvious reasons they had no food with them.

The road was quiet and they crossed it at leisure. The night was warm and only a light breeze fanned their faces. Helene led the way then, taking the cross-country route that would bring them to the outskirts of Dunkirk. With her knowledge of the terrain, the night was no great hazard to her, eyes already adjusted to the darkness. She broke the sensitive silence when, after fifteen minutes, they entered the first wooded stretch.

'Did you feel the breeze?' she asked.

'Yes.' Bobby was close behind her. 'That's going to be a help.'

'Yes, as long as it doesn't mean a gale will arrive. The Channel can be wicked.' Trees closed in on them, but she did not lose the path. Her keyed-up state sharpened her sense of direction, and she did not want to use the torch unless it became necess-ary. If the night was quiet, it was a quiet that induced one's imagination to paint unwelcome pictures. 'When we get aboard, you must do as I say. You must promise that.'

'I know, when sailing, there has to be a skipper,' said Bobby. 'You're the skipper tonight.' They were conversing in whispers, as if suspecting the Germans in Dunkirk had ears planted in nearby birds' nests. 'It's a damned dark wood.'

'Of course. But we're on the path and we shall only be walking for an hour or so.'

'Good,' said Bobby, and Helene said nothing more. He went along with her silence, being quite sure she was feeling the wrench of parting from her parents.

They came out of the wood in a little while, and Helene veered to cut across a dark meadow. Above them the inky sky was sprayed with bright stars.

'Where are you?' whispered Helene.

'Right behind you,' said Bobby.

'My nerves are on edge,' she said.

'Then we're two of a kind at the moment,' said Bobby, 'and I don't think there's a cure under the circumstances.'

'No jokes, if you please,' said Helene, and wondered what on earth had happened to make her decide she wanted to go to England with such an absurd man. What could she do in England except run for cover with everyone else when the German bombs came raining down?

She kept going, seeking and finding paths that were either open to the night or enclosed by the trees of little woods. She and Bobby were both alert, both conscious that the night belonged to

Germany, not to France. Once they heard the noise of vehicles on a distant road, but they encountered no people, no patrols. Helene did not expect to encounter people. Few took this route to Dunkirk at night. And none, probably, since the Germans had taken the port.

Still, the darkness was full of obstacles that were unseen until one was almost on top of them. Helene did not want the venture to fail at this stage, before they had even reached Dunkirk, and she picked her way very cautiously at times. Bobby stayed behind her. He felt that was where he should be, guarding her back. She was a fine, courageous young woman, and very capable, but all the same he was responsible for her safety.

'How much farther?' he whispered eventually.

'We are almost there. It's time to start praying.'

'You pray,' said Bobby, 'I'll say the amens.'

'That is not amusing.'

On she went, Bobby close on her heels and keeping a tight grip on the rope handle of the oilskin bag. It was not long then before they found they had left silence behind them. They were on the outskirts of the port, west of the harbour, and murmurs of life were perceptible. They thought of traffic, of patrols, and of Germans awake and vigilant. There was a road to cross, the coastal road. They halted a little way from it. They were out in the open, darkness their only shield. There were no lights except those of the masked headlamps of a vehicle or two. They waited, Bobby beside Helene at this point. After two minutes they moved cautiously forward. Helene's boots were rubber-soled. So were Bobby's. They were boots given by Jacob, Bobby having left his Army boots to be disposed of.

They came to another halt, an abrupt one, as a German truck came out of the darkness. It rumbled heavily by, going east. They waited again, listening for other traffic. Hearing none, they advanced. Bobby took a quick look up and down the road, put his hand on Helene's arm, and they ran together, swiftly and silently, like fast-moving shadows. They kept going, sprinting into sheltering darkness at the sound of another vehicle approaching at speed, its unmasked headlamps glaring. They flattened themselves on the ground, and the vehicle, a German Army car, rushed by like a blurred montage of glass and steel.

'Quickly now,' whispered Helene, but Bobby put a hand on her shoulder, restraining her.

'Not yet,' he said, 'listen and wait.'

'I am giving the orders, it was agreed,' she said.

'Wait,' said Bobby.

Ah, thought Helene, he thinks that with three stripes he can command me. But she waited. Bobby, his head turned, searched the darkness and listened. He was determined to avoid all possible contact with French civilians or German military. The way ahead seemed quiet. Helene fidgeted.

'Now,' she said.

'Right,' said Bobby, and they came to their feet. Again Helene led the way. The warm night air was touched with freshness, the freshness of the sea away to their right. Helene moved on knowing feet, her eyes peering and straining, her heartbeats erratic. Bobby followed with the oilskin bag. Houses stood black and silent, many damaged and gaping. As for inhabitants, it seemed that not a single one was abroad. Of course. Dunkirk was probably under curfew. He caught the smell of the sea, and his ears twitched a moment later. He seized Helene by her arm and pulled her into the deep shadow at the side of a house. From there she heard what he had heard, the sound of marching men, the steady tramp of boots. 'A patrol,' he whispered.

'Yes,' she breathed. They were close together, hips touching. His free arm slipped around her, and she supposed it to be the protective gesture of a man who considered women the weaker vessels. Although she always felt quite capable of looking after herself, she had a feeling then that in a tight corner close companionship strengthened one's courage.

They tensed as a German soldier left the line of steady march to flash a torch at gaps between buildings. The arm around Helene's shoulders tightened, and they squeezed themselves flat against the side of the house. The light from the torch stabbed and probed. Helene stopped breathing, and Bobby thought ruddy hell, what comes next? It hardly looked as if he'd come to give himself up. If that light found them, God save the Navy.

The torch clicked, the light went out, and the

German rejoined his comrades. The patrol marched on. Bobby's arm relaxed and fell away. Helene turned, drew in air and expelled it. They stood there, waiting until the sounds of tramping boots died away.

'OK?' said Bobby.

'Yes.'

'Good girl,' he said, and she experienced a little spasm of hysteria. She suppressed it. Good girl? That was a pat on the head.

They came out of the deep shadows and went on, Bobby again on her heels. She walked quickly, nerves driving her. She turned right at an inter-section, and led the way down to a road running alongside the waterfront. It was a road that had been littered with debris, but was clear now. Clear of debris and of any night owls. Dunkirk was indeed under curfew, and those inhabitants who had not fled from the *Luftwaffe*'s assaults were denied freedom of movement after dark. To Helene and Bobby, the town was menacing, every murmur a threat, every shadowed nook and cranny a place from which German eyes peered. In staying behind Helene, Bobby knew that a single moving figure would not be spotted as easily as two.

A noise ahead made them pull up. Helene darted to her left, Bobby following, their eyes very much used to the darkness now. Debris, cleared from the road, formed hills of rubble coated with sand and dust, and they went down on their knees behind a man-made heap. A truck full of German soldiers came rumbling along the waterfront road from the centre of the town. They were singing with the rich-voiced vigour of men whose well-being owed much to a surfeit of wine and the certainty of total victory. Helene and Bobby, invisible, kept their silence as the dark bulk of the truck loomed up and passed them. Helene wondered how long the people of war-torn Europe would have to listen to German songs of triumph.

They waited. Progress had been all stops and starts since they'd reached the outskirts of the town. Quietness came again, and they went on. The coolness of the sea air invading the warmth of the night touched their faces.

The old road, running parallel with the beaches, might have been treacherously ankle-breaking, but its broken surface had been repaired, its craters filled in. Having crossed it, Helene went on for a hundred metres or so, then turned right. She moved forward slowly, close to a wall, Bobby behind her, then came to a stop. Bobby had the feeling they were at the top of a hard-surfaced descent. A slipway?

In the lightest of whispers, Helene communicated information.

'Our jetty is down there. It will be guarded, I think.'

'Bound to be,' breathed Bobby.

More waiting and listening, Bobby with a hand on Helene's right arm, lightly pressing it. Is that to reassure me, encourage me or merely to tell me to be cautious? What a fusspot. No, that is wrong, no-one can say he's a fusspot. Old-fashioned? Yes, old-fashioned, with funny ideas about men leading and women following. He's dying to take charge. He would be, he's a sergeant.

Yes, someone was down there by the wooden jetty. No, on the jetty itself. The sound of movement became the crisp noise of boots on planking. Bobby strained his eyes. Although they were well adjusted to the night, the intense blackness that was the void over the sea defied vision for long moments. Then he and Helene took in the dark figure of a helmeted German soldier on the jetty, his rifle slung. He had his back to them and was moving forward to the end of the jetty. A beam of light sprang from his hand. It swung from side to side, playing over a picture of boats lashed together around the jetty. The bright circle of light revealed most were waterlogged wrecks, and all were only small craft.

The beam travelled and lengthened, illuminating more small craft tied to mooring posts. Several of these were damaged. Helene gripped Bobby's hand tightly, communicating a message, and he supposed she had spotted her own boat. She had, and she could discern no damage. With the light of the torch still playing, she looked for Henri's boat. It should have been near hers. It wasn't. Larger than hers, she suspected at once that it had probably become the property of some German officer. That meant she and Bobby would have to use her boat. Henri's would have been better. It was an eight metre yacht, small but very good. Hers was a clinker-built six metre *canot*, a dinghy, dangerously small on open waters. She and Bobby would have to pray harder for the weather to hold. Bobby. What an odd name for a hard-muscled sergeant.

The light went out. The sentry stood musing. Bobby drew Helene back a few yards until it was safe to whisper.

'You saw your friend's boat?'

'No. It isn't there. We shall have to use mine. It's moored twenty-five metres out from the jetty. We can swim to it, yes, but only under the nose of the sentry.'

'It'll be a damn' long nose, you can be sure. Can we enter the water farther down?'

'It would have to be well away from the sentry, and too far from the boat. From the jetty, I could swim blindfold to it.'

'That's it, then, from the jetty,' said Bobby.

'Yes, that's best, if we could manage it.'

'Good girl.'

That again? Did he think he'd taken her father's place?

'We must do more waiting,' she said.

'And watch for our chance,' said Bobby.

They moved forward, halting halfway down the slipway to stand with their backs against the wall. For the moment, there were only themselves and the sentry, now slowly prowling about down there by the sea. He was probably as bored as they were tense. His torch, clipped to his belt, was perhaps used to alleviate his boredom from time to time. Bobby reflected on the possibility of having to kill him. In his pocket was something he had carried with him since his Scouting days, his old clasp knife, still as serviceable as when it had left a Sheffield factory years ago.

He was at war with Germans. He had played his part with his battery in the shelling of Germans, although never from any favourable position, such was the strength and rapid movement of their armour. Even so, it was just possible he had helped to kill a German or two. It didn't affect a bloke too much when he was remote from his target. Here was a German, however, whom he could only kill at close quarters and in a calculating way. How quickly would the man die? Bloody quick, he hoped. But the risk of a noisy dying had to be taken.

Or he might be able to draw the man away from the jetty, and give Helene and himself a chance to enter the water unobserved.

Helene stared as her mad sergeant put aside the oilskin bag and went down on his hands and knees. She wanted to ask him what he was doing, but felt they were too close to the sentry to even whisper the question.

Bobby moved about, searching for pebbles. He found several in the shallow gulley of the slipway, and put them in his pocket. He came upright and rejoined Helene against the wall. It occurred to him then that if they could see the sentry, he would be able to see them. He need only fix his gaze for a few seconds. He had finished prowling about and was standing at the end of the jetty again, his back to them. He drew a packet of cigarettes from his pocket, extracted one and put it between his lips. Bobby, knowing he wouldn't move while lighting it, whispered in Helene's ear.

'Now.'

They moved fast as the German struck a match. Praying that their feet would not strike anything but sand, they darted into the lee of the timber-built jetty and sank to their knees. That put them out of sight of the sentry whichever way he turned. He did turn. They heard him. Then there was silence, like that of a man listening. He had caught perhaps a whisper of suspicious noise. If he had, he made no move except to strike another match. Bobby thought the advantage was now theirs, in that they knew where he was, while he did not even know they existed.

Their knees were couched in sand, the oilskin bag at rest. Bobby gave Helene a little nudge, and she eased herself slowly and carefully under the jetty, amid its bulky timbers. Bobby wormed his way forward, turned and brought the bag in between uprights. It brushed one upright, and Helene thought the little frictional whisper loud enough to alert the sentry above them. But he only drew in a lungful of cigarette smoke and coughed happily.

The slipway and jetty comprised an outlet to the sea for yachting enthusiasts. The sentry alone stood between Helene and her boat. She and Bobby could enter the water from beneath the jetty, but could not be sure they would not be heard. If they attracted the light of the torch, that would be it. Finish. Some attempt had to be made, however, and they must prepare themselves. Cramped beneath the jetty, they began the awkward task of removing their outer clothes. They could not afford to make the slightest noise. The sea was silent, the sands silent, conditions so calm within the wide sweep of the harbour that the tide scarcely rippled as it lapped around the forward timbers of the jetty and the lashed boats.

It was laborious work, undressing. Bobby had to remove his uniform, shirt and boots, Helene her jersey, skirt and boots. She had never had a more trying time. She had to lie flat and lift herself in order to push her skirt down. Her audacious sergeant lent a hand by pulling it off for her. However, in the end there they were, still undiscovered, crouching in their underclothes. The sentry, by his addiction to tramping about, talking to himself out loud or lightly whistling a song, had unknowingly helped. The sounds he made covered any little sounds they made themselves. He's a very obliging bloke, thought Bobby.

They were huddled on their knees, the oilskin bag between them. Helene opened up its wide neck, and Bobby pushed their garments inside it one by one, together with their boots, Helene's beret, handbag, compass and torch, and the gift of Jacob's cognac. Helene pulled on the rope drawstring and closed the bag. She and Bobby were glimmering figures in their white underwear, she in her waist slip and bra, he in his vest and pants. He peered at impeding timbers, looking for a gap. He made out an opening just wide enough for them to squeeze through. Lashed boats blocked any entry into the water on either side of the jetty, but at the front there was room between two craft. The sentry, however, was close to the edge. They could hear him above them, talking to himself. He'd be able from that point to pick up sight and sound of two people entering the water.

Bobby, the pebbles to hand, thought about the next move. Ease himself out from under the jetty, stay hidden and toss the pebbles as far up the slipway as he could? No, not very clever. It would distract the sentry, yes, and make him move, but it would also let him know someone was about. He'd make use of his torch, and its beam would forage around. Almost certainly, after examining the slipway, he'd poke about around the jetty and turn the light on the sea and the moored boats. No, forget the pebbles. At this stage, Bobby didn't want the man to investigate the jetty or light up the boats. His clasp knife was in his hand. He had to start thinking again about killing the German.

He touched Helene's hand and pressed it. In return, she lightly patted his shoulder. His gesture was a reassurance, hers mocking.

There was silence now, a silence that was suddenly broken. A man was calling.

'*Wie geht es Ihnen, Hans?*' How are you, Hans?

264

'*Ach, Walther, was möchten Sie?*' Walther, what do you want?

Bobby had no idea what this exchange in German meant. He only knew he and Helene were lucky this second man hadn't appeared earlier. There had to be a second man in the vicinity. A lone sentry without a nearby back-up was the exception, not the rule. Helene and Bobby kept very still and silent as they heard the man at the entrance to the slipway call again. They were both able to get the meaning of one word. '*Zigaretten.*' Cigarettes. That was well up to scratch, thought Bobby. For sentries the world over, the forbidden cigarette was a must during hours of monotony.

Booted feet strode along the jetty as the sentry walked to meet his comrade, and the moment he was off the jetty and on the slipway, Bobby breathed a whisper to Helene.

'Go.'

The chance had arrived. Helene pushed forward on her knees between beams, and her knees quickly encountered sopping sand that felt like mud. Bobby was behind her, pushing the oilskin bag in front of him. She entered the water, and its coldness bit at her flesh. She slipped under and dug her feet into sand to thrust herself clear of jetty and boats. Bobby pushed his head into the looped drawstring of the bag and surged forward. As he entered the water the bag, buoyant, floated under his chin and chest. He clasped it and propelled himself on by use of his muscular legs. In front of him, Helene swam evenly, using the breaststroke, not the noisy crawl. He could just make her out amid the black water. They were committed now to a distance of about thirty yards. That was hardly taxing. It was one's nerves that were wearing. He heard the two Germans talking, and he thought about that torch and its powerful beam. One man laughed. The other said something, and the torch clicked on.

Helene and Bobby felt its light, even though it was pointing away from them. Helene slipped beneath the surface again. Bobby was unable to fully immerse himself because of the buoyant bag. But he kept going. He had no option. Helene's head came up, a vague shape in the darkness, but he saw it. He could still feel that light, and was sure it was going to pinpoint him.

It went out.

Helene, reaching her boat, swam round to its blind side, and Bobby caught up with her. They trod water together while she helped him to free himself from the bag. Still treading water he lifted it and rolled it over the side of the boat, into which it fell with a little rustling sound. That made them hold their breath for a few moments while they listened once more. From where they were now they could see neither the jetty nor the men. But they heard them still talking. Well, Alleluia, thought Bobby, we're winning. What a girl, what a game one.

Helene moved and found the mooring rope. She released it, and the boat swung gently. Bobby, gliding through the water, reached the stern and put both hands to it. The wooden dinghy, sails stowed, eased slowly forward. He knew, and Helene knew, that it was too risky to climb aboard there. Helene had discussed with him exactly what they should do. He began to push, and she let her body swing into line with his. They pushed together and the boat began to glide. How black the sea and sky were, but it was all too easy to imagine the Germans could not miss seeing the moving dinghy and bare heads and arms. The men's voices carried so clearly that they sounded only a few yards away.

Bobby and Helene pushed, their legs thrusting under water, but they did not hurry their movements. The urgency that consumed them had to be controlled. Silence was everything. The sea rippled and pulled around their bodies, but its surface was calm and the boat glided soundlessly. The jetty was receding, but there was still the threat of that powerful torch. Its light could still reach them. Their backs suffered cold, sensitive prickles. The boat swung. Helene righted it, heading it due west, she hoped. She was fully aware of the calm harbour waters and of the even pull of a tide outgoing and in their favour. Her wet face felt a sweet warm breeze.

Still without haste in their determination to take no chances in distancing themselves unseen from the waterfront, they used their legs to keep the boat gliding slowly on, Helene righting its course from time to time. She thought of the Channel and its perversities, and how much they would have to rely on conditions remaining favourable. Whether or not her boat could make the crossing was in the hands of Providence. A heavy swell and a blustery wind, and they would be in for a fight. What am I doing here, she asked herself, am I as crazy as he is?

The tide had the boat now, making the work easier for them. Well behind them, a light flashed on. Hell, thought Bobby, and waited for the beam to reach them or to discover a boat was missing, and for a shout to go up. It probed about in the darkness behind them, but they were out of range, thank the Lord and his angels. Could Jacob's daughter be counted as one of them? At this moment, she could.

Out went the light. Relief surged through Helene, and Bobby gave her another of his little paternal pats. I'll hit him, she thought, but exhilaration at realizing they were free of German eyes prevailed over all other feelings. They must be a hundred and fifty metres from the jetty by now. There was a stronger flow of water, a pulling flow. It took the boat on, and they used their hands to keep a tight hold of it, the line of their bodies steering it, keeping it on course for the open sea. They continued in this way for a little longer, and then Bobby spoke at last.

'Now, my infant?' he said, imitating her mother.

'I am nobody's infant,' breathed Helene, 'but yes, now.' Bobby swam round to the port side, Helene to starboard, and he held the moving boat as steady as possible while she heaved herself upwards. Over the gunnel she went in supple, agile fashion, her soaked slip up around her waist, her bare thighs glimmering wetly, her black stockings shedding rivulets. The boat was swinging, Bobby hanging on to it. She found the oars, placed them in the rowlocks, feeling her way. The oars dipped into the water and she used them to keep the boat steady while Bobby clambered in with a great to-do of arms and legs. 'Clumsy,' whispered Helene, as he landed in the rocking boat like a floundering fish.

'Don't mention it,' said Bobby, righting himself. 'I'll be frank,' he said in English, 'you're not just a farmer's daughter, you're a ruddy marvel.'

'Holy Mother, you're still making jokes,' she breathed. 'Take the oars and keep the boat steady or it will run away with us on the tide.' She made room for him on the seat, with the modest craft rocking and pulling. Bobby took the oars, dipped them and steadied the boat. Helene did a sudden hasty cover-up job, pulling her wet slip down. Bobby could not help a fleeting grin. At a time like this, not many French girls would have made a first priority of covering up their pants. But there it was, Jacob's daughter did spend a few seconds doing exactly that, although in the darkness everything about her was only a pale glimmer.

Her modesty taken care of, Helene reached under the stern seat and groped for the anchor. It was there, a fisherman's anchor. She let it sink soundlessly into the water, and the rope uncoiled fast. The yacht became steady in the harbour waters.

'Sails?' said Bobby.

'Of course.'

They went to work. The stowed sails were pulled out, and they applied themselves to the task of fixing and hoisting them, Bobby's summer holidays at Salcombe with his family and Boots's family having given him a knowledge of the basics when it came to messing about in boats. Helene whispered he was not doing too badly, and might even be quite useful. Bobby let that go. He had his mind on the harbour and the possibility that they might still be detected. He accepted Helene's occasional instructions as they worked together on the sails.

The work kept them from feeling cold, and if the darkness made things difficult for them, they triumphed in the end, mainsail and jib in position. Both sails flapped as the breeze caught them, and the yacht dragged protestingly at its anchor. Bobby ducked his head as the boom swung.

'Take care,' whispered Helene, 'it's all too easy to fall overboard.'

'Thanks for telling me.' Bobby wondered how far their whispers carried on such a calm night. 'God, it's dark out here and back there. Let's get changed and then head for the white cliffs of Dover.'

The night was warm, but they were cold now in their wet underwear, and the change into dry garments had to be made while they were still at anchor.

'You first,' whispered Helene. She was at the tiller.

'Your privilege.'

'Yours. Do as I say.'

'That's an order, I suppose.' Bobby grinned. What a Turk. She was still fighting him, determined not to let him get the upper hand. She didn't seem to realize that men were men, and women were women. He opened up the bag and rummaged for garments, and for a towel they had also packed. With the white sails creating a little light, he was faintly visible to her. She expected him to turn his back, but he proceeded as he was, seated centrally and facing her. He did not seem at all concerned that he might embarrass her. Bobby actually did not think Frenchwomen suffered embarrassment. He'd seen old photographs of French housewives watching naked Tommies bathing in a river during the last war. He stripped off his wet vest and pants, and vigorously towelled himself. His body glowed from the friction.

Helene muttered and averted her eyes. The sails flapped, the boat rolled a little, and her eyes went back to him. If she was not precisely embarrassed, she did experience little burning feelings. She watched as he pulled on the dry pants supplied by her father. He was neither awkward nor self-conscious, his actions all seemed easy and natural. She understood, of course, that the circumstances hardly called for coyness. He pulled on a dry

271

singlet, quick in his movements, for he knew Helene must be cold, while he felt magically warmer as he dressed himself in his uniform.

'Now you, Helene,' he whispered. 'Change places.'

They effected the change, and Bobby took control of the mainsail and the tiller.

'Yes, like that,' she murmured, 'to stop too much drag on the anchor.'

'Right. You go ahead.'

She was French, yes, but not brazen. She sat with her back to him.

'Turn your head,' she said.

'Hell's bells,' breathed Bobby, casting a glance back into the darkness that masked the port, 'what a time for a French girl to start feeling shy. Get changed. I'll watch the sails, nothing else.'

'Don't talk,' she said.

'Get on with it,' said Bobby.

Resigning herself, Helene took everything off at speed, then towelled herself. Bobby thought she had a very fine back and a good firm waist. All too aware of him, Helene suffered a multitude of goosepimples, and rushed herself into clean underwear, and into her jersey and skirt. Immediately the comfort and warmth of dry clothes gave her an almost sensuous pleasure. Her beret she left off, so that her damp hair could run in the wind.

'I'm ready now,' she whispered.

'Congratulations, we're both pleased with you, me and God,' murmured Bobby.

'Idiot,' said Helene.

'Up anchor, skipper?'

'Yes. Now we can go. As for God, pray for Him to go with us.'

'Amen,' said Bobby.

Chapter Sixteen

'It's late,' said Sally Cooper, wife of Horace Cooper, 'and we don't want to stay up all night arguin'.'

'I have to point out it's not an argument,' said Horace, a stalwart husband and dad, 'not now it's settled.'

'But supposin' you don't get accepted, after all,' said Sally, 'you'll be here on your own.'

'Not for long,' said Horace, 'I'll get called up in the usual way before the year's out.'

Horace's promising cricket career with Surrey had been nipped in the bud by the war. However, his captain had advised him that his years with Surrey qualified him for admission to the Army as a PT instructor with the immediate rank of sergeant. Horace had a preference for joining the RAF and being trained as a pilot. Sally was against all the risks of that for a husband and father, and worked on him until her arguments prevailed. Horace had subsequently filled in an official application at an Army recruiting centre, and was now waiting for a reply. Meanwhile, following a conversation with Freddy and Cassie, Cassie's dad had been in touch with his sister in the country, and she'd written to say that neighbours of hers would gladly offer to take Sally and her children, two boys, for the duration. That meant Sally and Cassie, sisters-in-law and long-standing friends, could be close country neighbours and a comfort to each other while Freddy and Horace served their time in the Army.

Sally simply didn't think she ought to go until Horace was called up one way or the other. However, Horace was putting his foot down, which was no easier for him to do with Sally than it was for Freddy with Cassie. Sally and Cassie, having grown up in Walworth, had profited by being observant of the obvious, which was that married life went along on a much less disorganized basis if the wife had the last word. Occasionally, of course, a wife did concede, and Sally, after reflecting, conceded now. She knew Freddy and Horace would feel happier if she and Cassie, and their children, were far away from London in the event of air raids.

'All right, Horace, perhaps you're right, only it'll grieve me a bit, our house standing empty. It was never meant to stand empty, it was built for fam'lies like ours.'

'We've friends who'll keep an eye on it for us,' said Horace. 'It's a family house right enough, and you've given it something extra.'

'What something extra?' asked Sally.

'A touch of the Sally Browns,' said Horace. 'That's worth a lot to any house, that is, a touch of the Sally Browns.'

'Let's go to bed, so's you can treat me to a touch of the Horace Coopers,' said Sally in the manner of a wife who knew when to be nice to her better half.

In bed with husband Ned, Lizzy Somers said, 'I think we'll have to resign ourselves to Bobby bein' a prisoner of war.'

'I think we will,' said Ned quietly.

'When can we expect to hear official?' asked Lizzy.

'It'll take time, Eliza. The Red Cross people help to gather information, which they pass on. They're allowed into prisoner of war camps.'

'I hope we don't have to wait too long,' said Lizzy.

'We'll see,' said Ned.

'Bobby's goin' to hate bein' penned up,' said Lizzy.

'If I know Bobby,' said Ned, 'he's probably digging his first escape tunnel right now.'

Not on any account was Ned going to do other than go along with Lizzy's self-induced belief that Bobby had suffered nothing worse than being taken prisoner, even though that was bad enough.

The boat was skimming over the dark sea, the breeze lively, stiffening the sails. They were far out in the Channel now, the boat open to the elements, the sea coming at it in a light rippling swell. But it was causing no problems, and was, in fact, as friendly a sea as Helene could have hoped for. The conditions were fine for sailing as she steered the boat due west, with Bobby periodically checking the compass by the light of the torch. His other

276

responsibility was to do whatever was required of him.

He looked at the sails, curving stiffly to the wind, and felt the craft running well.

'I think we're going to make it,' he said.

'Chickens should not be counted before they hatch,' said Helene. She peered at the black waters, then searched the indigo sky for the North Star. 'I've never sailed at night before, and feel blind.'

Bobby switched on the torch to check the compass again.

'Well, you're still on course,' he said, 'and that can't be bad for a blind skipper. I think you're going to earn medals. By the way, what's the name of your boat?'

'*Fifi.*'

'*Fifi?*'

'You don't like it?' said Helene, her firm grip on the tiller keeping the rudder straight.

'Love it,' said Bobby, 'makes me think of French can-can dancers.'

'Tell me,' said Helene, hair blowing and whipping, 'don't you feel a little scared at what we're doing, riding the Channel at night?'

'At the moment,' said Bobby, 'I'm enjoying the ride. It might not be much like going up and down off the beach at Salcombe in Devon, but that was only holiday sailing. This is the real thing.'

'This,' said Helene, 'is very real, especially for a six metre boat. You must feel a little scared. It's going to take hours to reach your coast.'

'The wind's in our favour, isn't it?' said Bobby.

'It's not against us,' said Helene.

'Nothing to be scared about, then,' said Bobby, a vigorous optimist. 'I stopped living on my nerves as soon as we set sail and I saw how you handled *Fifi*. Listen, you're not scared yourself, are you?'

'I am pent up,' said Helene.

'Well, we can't have that,' said Bobby. 'How about a song, say a sea shanty, like "Life On The Ocean Wave"?'

A gust of wind buffeted the sails, and Bobby steadied the main.

'If you begin to sing,' said Helene, 'I shall kick you overboard.'

'That's not very friendly,' said Bobby. 'Look, the only thing that's bothering me is that the nearer we get to England the farther you get from France and your home. But believe me, my parents will give you a home and all my relatives will make sure you aren't lonely.'

'Thank you,' said Helene. The surging strength of the Channel was making itself felt, and so was its greediness. Its waters were always hungry. It was Neptune's insatiable cousin, and a strong wind could make it dangerously predatory. It could really blow in the Channel and turn a surging sea into a ferocious one. At the moment they were riding what was only a mild swell, and if conditions continued to be kind, they might actually reach Dover without incident. How far was Dover from Dunkirk? Seventy kilometres? Yes. They would be sailing all night. It was a relief to discover the English sergeant was so reliable. He knew how to be the right kind of help. She could not now fault his determination to get home and to rejoin the fight against Hitler, and it made her pray that the boat and the weather would not fail them. There was a new life for her in England. How much would she see of him? She knew no-one in England. She would have to rely on his family to help her adjust to everything that was foreign to her. She was to make up her own mind about what she wanted to do as a contribution to the war effort, and much would depend on the outcome of the battles going on between France and Germany. She wondered what was happening now. Were the French armies still having the worst of things? It would be sickening if they were beaten as badly as the British had been. Was her father right, did France and its generals have no real heart for the war?

'Where are we, in the Atlantic?' asked Bobby.

'Atlantic?'

'There's water everywhere,' said Bobby, but cheerfully.

'Compass,' said Helene, 'compass.'

'Aye, aye, skipper.' Bobby steadied himself against the slight rolling, switched on the torch and checked the compass. 'Two points to starboard,' he said. Helene adjusted, and on the boat ran. 'That's it, there's a good old girl, steady as you go now,' he said.

'What did you call me?' asked Helene.

'I was talking to *Fifi*,' said Bobby, 'but all praise includes you, of course.'

'Thank you,' said Helene drily, but she smiled. The wind blew a little then, in a series of gusts. The boat rolled, straightened and scudded.

'Shall we splice the mainbrace?' suggested Bobby.

'Excuse me?' said Helene.

'It means pass the rum round. We've got cognac. Let's have a mouthful. It'll keep us warm and keep us going.' Bobby produced the bottle that was tucked inside his battledress, uncapped it and passed it to Helene. He took control of the mainsail while she took a few sips. Warmth spread to induce a sense of well-being. Bobby helped himself to a generous mouthful. *Fifi* ploughed gamely on in the swell.

'Will I like your country?' asked Helene.

'I hope you will,' said Bobby, 'but you'll be up against food rationing, and the absence of French veal. Also, there's not much garlic about. And I'm not sure you'll like our coffee, although the tea's always first-class.'

'You are terrifying me,' said Helene. The bow dipped and rose, and up came spray. 'I shall manage. I'll miss my home and parents, of course, but nothing is more important than standing up to the Nazis and beating them in the end.' A gust of wind hit the boat again and flung her hair over her face. A little frown arrived. She did not like these gusts. But she said brightly, 'It was on the radio that many French soldiers were taken off the beaches with the British.'

'Well, that'll be interesting for you,' said Bobby.

'On the other hand, when I promised your parents I'd make sure you weren't lonely, that didn't mean I was to let you run around looking for spare French soldiers.'

'What is wrong with French soldiers?' asked Helene.

'Nothing, I hope,' said Bobby, wondering if there was anything darker than a sea at night. 'But I have to look after your welfare. I owe it to your parents, and to you. You're quite a nice girl when you're not beating my brains out.'

For all her pent-up nerves and for what the night might throw at them, a little laugh escaped her.

'Oh, perhaps you aren't too bad yourself, even if you are mad,' she said.

'Does that mean we've now got a chance of being friends?' asked Bobby.

'If we're not friends already, what am I doing here?' asked Helene.

'Good question,' said Bobby.

'See what you have done as a friend?' said Helene. 'You have made me as crazy as you are.'

'But we're going well,' said Bobby.

The boat heeled to a rising wind. The sea heaved, *Fifi* rolled and spray showered. Helene bit her lip. A rising wind was the last thing she wanted. It would whip up the Channel waters and create havoc.

The night was far advanced, and exactly where they were Helene did not know. She only knew they were in trouble, trouble that was heart-breaking because she and Bobby were going to survive only by a miracle. For the weather to have changed so drastically was cruel, although the possibility that the elements would turn against them had always been on her mind.

The change had been wickedly sudden. The helpful breeze had given way to a gusting, blowing wind, and the mild swell of the sea had become high and heavy. The thudding waves alone were a menace to her small craft, threatening to overwhelm it and drown it. Fierce gusts were an additional hazard. She was desperately worried, and Bobby was desperately baling. He had been doing that for half an hour, while with shortened sails she had been fighting the dangerous turbulence of wind and sea. They had last checked the compass an hour ago, just before the wind had begun to blow and bluster. They had still been on course then. Conditions now made further checks impossible. But the course hardly mattered. They were fighting for their lives. The boat lifted, smacked down, rolled and shuddered, and the heaving sea flung huge bursts of spray over them. They were both soaked, both wearing the rubber lifebelts she always kept stowed in the locker.

Bobby worked away, baling savagely. He felt horribly guilty about what he had let Helene in for. He alone was responsible for her being here, and she was having hell's own job keeping the dinghy afloat. Several times he had had to stop bailing to lend her a hand. The rudder was sickeningly wayward, and even shortened sail screamed to go its own abandoned way. The biting impact of cold spray took his breath and the showering sea poured into the boat.

Sod it, he told himself, it's only water. Get rid of it, man.

Only water. It swirled, slopped and chased about, continuously fed. He dipped the canvas bucket, filled it and emptied it, repeatedly. A heavy running wave made a solid hit on the port side. The boat rolled madly, and Helene slid on her seat. Bobby, on his knees was flung on his side. The boat shuddered, but swung up and righted itself. Brutally, the wind battered it, and the craft staggered.

'Pig of a sea,' gasped Helene in the teeth of the gale. Her arms were aching, her body racked with strain, her feet and ankles in water.

'Hold on, hold tight,' shouted Bobby. The boat swung crazily to a blast of wind and a pounding wave. Sea poured over the side. The mast was leaning, bending and creaking, the sails shrieking, the seas rising higher. Helene, pale, her teeth clenched, fought and prayed, but she knew if they continued to ship water so fast, they would founder in a matter of minutes.

Fifi yawed and spun. Bobby baled like a madman. His head came up then, and his back stiffened. Above the noise of the wind, the sea and the sails, his ears picked up a powerful humming sound, a sound that grew rapidly into a vibrating violence.

'Jesus Christ, Helene,' he shouted, 'I think there's a German E-boat out there!'

'An E-boat?' gasped Helene, an anguished young woman at this moment. 'What is that?'

'German torpedo-boat! They're sharks! They'll eat us alive!'

'But they will see us, they must!' Helene wanted to survive, she wanted both of them to survive, even if it meant being in German hands until the war was over. She heard the sea monster then.

It came at them from out of the wind-lashed night, a dark grey shape of horrendous power and speed, cutting the heaving waters apart so viciously that the friction created a phosphorescent edge from bow to stern. It was this that enabled Helene and Bobby to discern the raider of the sea. It was indeed like a shark, a huge creature of wet shining ferocity. Helene, appalled, wrenched on the tiller. *Fifi* careered and shipped gallons. Bobby, hanging on to the mast, used one hand to drag the torch from out of his battledress and to switch it on. The light, such as it was, showed itself to the oncoming raider, now only split seconds away. Terrifying disaster loomed, and Bobby flung himself at Helene in the instinctive hope that if they went down he would have hold of her and they could fight the sea together. *Fifi* whirled about, the boom lashing itself into a frenzy. But the great grey shark, carving the sea apart, veered away.

'Christ, the wash!' shouted Bobby, an arm locked around Helene as they were thrown off balance by the crazily spinning dinghy. The torpedo boat was roaring past them. Its powerful wash hit them, lifted their helpless craft and tossed it like a cork. It keeled over and plummeted down. Helene and Bobby, split apart, hurtled from it, and Helene catapulted into the sea. Her capsizing boat smashed down only inches from her, and the sea smothered her. Wildly, frantically, she clawed her way to the surface, her lifebelt providing the propulsion that brought her head clear. The heavy sea, disturbed by the huge wash and whipped by the wind, smacked into her face and took her breath. Desperately, she sucked in air and shouted.

'Bobby! Are you there? Where are you? Bobby!' It was the first time she had used his name.'

Under the tossing, tugging water, cold and vilely uncharitable, an arm swept around her. Above the surface came Bobby's head, and he shook it to clear his eyes. He coughed up salty sea. The raging swell carried them about. Bobby coughed again and shouted something completely crazy.

'First time we've met like this.'

'Oh, my God, don't,' she gasped, and flung her arms around him, knowing that if they hung on to each other they stood a better chance of surviving. Together they trod the heaving sea.

'Hold on,' shouted Bobby, 'I think they saw us.'

'Do you think I'm going to let go?' gasped Helene. 'Never.'

A thudding wave flung them about, and Bobby's shoulder smacked against the capsized yacht. *Fifi* was actually floating, keel uppermost, and the keel was dancing, swaying and heaving. The sea surged and pulled, but Helene grabbed and Bobby grabbed, and they held on to the upturned dinghy.

A great light blazed. The torpedo-boat was executing a wide circle, its brilliant white beam piercing the darkness. It dazzled and blinded them.

'There we are,' said Bobby, 'they did see us.'

'Do you mind that they're Germans?' gasped Helene.

'I mind more about you,' said Bobby. The blaze of light went out, and a smaller one came on as the torpedo boat, engines idling, glided slowly towards them. The light played on them. A voice bellowed.

'Ahoy there! Ahoy!'

'God Almighty, it's one of ours!' shouted Bobby. 'It's a British MTB!'

'Ahoy there!' The small light bathed them, and the torpedo-boat was close, nudging through the swell, its sharp bow pushing water aside.

'Well, come on!' bawled Bobby. 'Don't hang about! It's perishing out here!'

Helene let go of the heaving boat, and with the high running waves pounding at them, she flung one arm around Bobby and held on for dear life.

'Oh, you crazy man,' she gasped, 'see now what a mad way this was to try to get to England?'

'Hope you like fried fish and chips,' said Bobby.

The torpedo-boat, riding the swell, nestled gently alongside *Fifi* and the survivors.

The crew of the MTB made a great fuss of them after listening to their story. Wrapped in blankets after stripping off their wet clothes, they were given hot toddies of rum and coffee to drink while waiting for their garments to be dried. They were landed at Portsmouth eventually, where they endured a prolonged interrogation, together at first, then separately. There was a blitz on concerning the entry of aliens, the chaotic nature of events at Dunkirk having provided enemy agents with German-inspired opportunities to be taken off the beaches disguised as Dutch, Belgian, French or Polish soldiers. Some having been unmasked, the Government justifiably assumed Britain might be importing a fifth column, hence the setting-up of interrogation units at ports of entry before the Dunkirk evacuation had been completed. This had resulted in the apprehension of more than one enemy agent.

Nevertheless, Helene did not take too kindly to a prolonged questioning. She was in need of a sympathetic reception, a bed, and a chance to sleep the day through. Along with all that, she was utterly determined not to be separated from Bobby, which was something to wonder at.

'Why are you asking all these stupid questions?' She delivered herself in angry French to a French-speaking officer. 'Do you think me a German? Do I look like a German, or speak like one? Sergeant Somers has told you how my father brought him to our farm. It is no use to keep asking me about a passport or an identity document. Everything was lost when my handbag was lost, when the boat was lost. I have already told you that. I have come here to help you fight the Nazis, not to blow up your factories. If you think me a German, perhaps you think Sergeant Somers is a German too.'

'We're checking, we have certain formalities to—'

'Checking? On Sergeant Somers? You are mad. He is a soldier you should be proud of.'

'All this can't be helped. You must bear with us.'

In the end, they called on the services of a French officer, one of a number who had chosen escape to Britain. He put several intelligent and searching questions to Helene. She answered them in a way that convinced him she was who she said she was. And when Bobby's identity and description had been verified and his damp AB64 accepted as authentic and not forged, he and Helene were cleared for entry. Bobby was freshly kitted out at a nearby depot, and the local Red Cross supplied Helene with clothes and underwear. Both were given railway warrants and emergency ration coupons, and Bobby received money against outstanding pay. Helene was requested to report to the French Embassy in London for the issue of a passport, and Bobby was told he had ten days leave, during which time he would receive instructions regarding where to rejoin his unit. They were then given breakfast. If they were still in need of sleep, they were borne along by the elation of having reached England safe and sound.

'Something's obvious,' said Lieutenant Woodruffe, RN, liaison officer of the Combined Services, Portsmouth. He also had charge of public relations. 'Who's looking after them at the moment?'

'Petty Officer Clewes,' said a shore-based, middle-aged Navy Commander.

'He'll escort them to the railway station when they've finished breakfast,' said Captain Rogers, an Army man.

'I suggest we hold them for a while,' said Lieutenant Woodruffe. 'There's a hell of a story here for the Press and radio. It'll give another boost to public morale. Think of it, Sergeant Somers and this French girl braving the Channel at night in that small craft. I'd only brave the Hyde Park Serpentine in one that size myself. Think of the dramatic intervention of one of our MTB's. It's a story the whole country will want to hear about. Permission, gentlemen, to call up the local newshounds and the BBC, and to hold the couple here for interviews with the reporters.'

'By God, get cracking, Lieutenant,' said the Commander. 'Churchill himself will want to know about this.'

Chapter Seventeen

'I notice,' said Chinese Lady over the breakfast table, 'that nothing's been done about Bobby.'

'Are you looking at me, Maisie?' asked Mr Finch.

'You and Boots were supposed to ask the War Office what had happened to Bobby,' said Chinese Lady.

'I thought we'd all accepted he'd been taken prisoner,' said Mr Finch.

'It's all we could do,' said Tim.

'Yes, we've got to accept that, Mum,' said Emily.

'We did say he might be seriously wounded,' said Chinese Lady.

'Lizzy and Ned will be notified,' said Boots.

'Well, it seems to me that notifying's a long time comin',' said Chinese Lady, who had never liked bureaucratic dilly-dallying.

Emily, finishing her second cup of tea, said, 'I'd best get off to the office now.'

Chinese Lady regarded her daughter-in-law with slight disapproval.

'It's Saturday, Em'ly,' she said.

'Yes, I'll be back before one,' said Emily.

Chinese Lady wasn't impressed. With Boots

and Tim home on leave, she considered Emily ought to be a wife and mother first, not a general manager. She didn't approve of women general managers, anyway, or women soldiers, and she'd made that quite clear more than once. Still, Sammy did say Emily was doing a good job, and that the war wouldn't make it easy to get a replacement. That was the trouble with war, it turned a lot of things upside-down.

She frowned a little as Emily said she'd see everyone later, then went off to her work.

Boots, noticing the frown, said, 'Don't take it to heart, old lady, Emily's got something to offer the family firm. Her experience.'

'Well, as long as you don't mind,' said Chinese Lady, which meant, of course, that he should mind.

'Rosie's coming home today,' said Tim, 'on week-end leave.'

Boots, thoughtful up to that point, brightened.

'So she is,' he said. 'We'll get a four going at tennis this afternoon, Tim. Phone Emma and see if she'll join you, me and Rosie.'

'We'll be lucky,' said Tim, 'Emma's spending all her spare time with Jonathan.'

'Understandable,' said Mr Finch.

'Bless that girl,' said Chinese Lady, 'I don't know that even Susie was born more naturally ladylike than Emma.'

'Try Polly, then, Tim,' said Boots, 'she's on leave till Sunday.'

'Is she?' said Tim, and Chinese Lady glanced at Boots.

'I saw her when I was with her father yesterday afternoon,' he said.

'OK, I'll phone her now,' said Tim, which he did, and Polly assured him she was delighted to be asked.

'Don't mention it,' said Tim. 'Oh, have you got any decent tennis balls, Aunt Polly?'

'A boxful, Tim old scout,' said Polly. 'All I have are yours. So pleased you and your father made it from Dunkirk. By the way, still no news of Bobby?'

'I think the Jerries put him in the bag,' said Tim, who'd spent days trying to convince himself this was the case.

'Well, I'm sorry, really sorry,' said Polly.

'But we can't sit moping,' said Tim.

'No, we can't, can we, Tim old lad, so let's play some tennis, even if it does look as if we've got no sense of occasion. Ruskin Park, three o'clock?'

'See you, Aunt Polly. Wear your tennis dress, not your uniform, or I'll have to salute you.'

Polly laughed.

Mr Finch meanwhile had turned on a news broadcast, and he and Boots were listening to what they considered was obvious, that the German advance on Paris was proceeding to plan, and that French resistance was crumbling.

'Not good, Boots,' said Mr Finch.

'I'd like to disagree with you,' said Boots, 'but I can't. If France is beaten, where do we go from there?'

'We have a powerful Navy,' said Mr Finch, 'but should have doubled it, along with our submarine fleet, to enable us to strangle Hitler's Europe.'

'How do you feel personally about Hitler's Germany?' asked Boots.

'I feel nothing for that kind of Germany, Boots. It's a nation of mesmerized robots under the heel of vicious thuggery. This is my country, and has been for many years. I have never had to wrestle with my conscience.'

'Glad to hear it,' said Boots, 'conscience can be troublesome.' And he thought of his long moments in the sunshine with Polly. 'Listen, would you like to come into the study with me and go through the draft of a letter Sir Henry intends to send to the CIGS? I've made notes. Let's see if you agree with them.'

'If it's something purely military, am I qualified?' smiled Mr Finch.

'As much as I am,' said Boots. 'Sir Henry has an inflated idea of my own qualifications.'

Bobby was fuming. He simply wanted to get home. But he and Helene were surrounded on three sides by the eager beavers of the Press, and also threatened by the imminent arrival of someone from the BBC. To Bobby, after he and Helene between them had outlined the events leading to their successful boarding of the boat, many of the subsequent questions taxed his patience.

Exactly what size was the boat, Miss Aarlberg?
Six metres.
That's very small, isn't it?
It was suitable only for the harbour waters.

It was actually your own boat?

Yes.

The bombing of the port and the beaches hadn't damaged it at all?

No.

Did you consider the dangers?

Yes.

Where did you learn to speak English?

At school in France and at home with my father.

Speaking for the Daily Express, *Sergeant Somers, I think you said you had to slip out from the jetty under the noses of German sentries. Exactly how did you do this?*

Jumped into the water while they were having a cup of tea.

They were drinking tea, the Germans? Can you confirm that, Miss Aarlberg?

It is a joke.

You two heroes can make jokes about such a risky and dangerous enterprise, Miss Aarlberg?

Sergeant Somers is always making jokes. But we are not heroes, we are both crazy, and lucky to be alive.

The people of this country will think you both heroic.

I shall be astonished, then.

What were your feelings when you were trying to get clear of the harbour, Sergeant Somers?

I was wetting myself, what do you think?

Titters ran round the interview room.

Who was in charge of the boat?

The skipper, Miss Aarlberg, this young lady here.

How far from the English coast were you when you ran into trouble?

Too far to swim for it.

What were your feelings when you realized you were going to sink, Miss Aarlberg?

I wished myself home in bed.

Did you actually see the MTB, *Sergeant Somers?*

For a couple of seconds. We thought it was a German E-*boat.*

It was coming straight at you?

Straight at my nose.

What were your feelings then?

Bloody awful. It's the only nose I've got.

Can you give us your own account of that, Miss Aarlberg?

Yes. It's another joke, a terrible one.

The fact was that you saw death staring you in the face?

Yes.

According to what we've been told, the MTB *changed course at the last moment, and it was its wash that capsized your boat. Can you confirm that, Miss Aarlberg?*

Yes.

But you were picked up. How did the MTB *manage to spot you?*

We had a torch. Sergeant Somers switched it on and showed its light. I was amazed at his cool head when everything was so desperate and the shark was coming at us.

The shark?

Yes, the sea monster that was going to eat us up. Please to ask Sergeant Somers was it true.

You pictured the MTB *as a shark, Sergeant Somers?*

Too ruddy right I did. D'you mind if we go now?

Reporters clamoured to ask more questions.

How did you feel when you realized the MTB *had seen you and was going to take you aboard, Miss Aarlberg?*

I told Sergeant Somers what a mad crazy thing we had done in trying to get to England in such a small boat.

When did you tell him this?

When we were clinging to the upturned boat, and the sea monster was turning to pick us up.

And what did Sergeant Somers say to that?

He made another joke. He said he hoped I would like fried fish and chips.

The reporters burst into laughter.

He actually said that while you were still in the water, Miss Aarlberg?

Yes. Why is everyone laughing when all this crazy man's jokes are so terrible?

Are all your jokes terrible, Sergeant Somers?

I've been misunderstood. I'm a sergeant, and I don't make jokes, just serious comments.

What were your feelings when the MTB landed you and Miss Aarlberg safely here?

I thought just the job, now I can go home to bed.

Will you be taking Miss Aarlberg with you?

Don't ask questions like that. I'll be taking her home with me, to a bed of her own. Her family looked after me, my family will look after her.

What's your exact relationship with the young lady, Sergeant Somers?

Friendly.

What do you think of Sergeant Somers, Miss Aarlberg?

I told you, he is crazy and makes terrible jokes.

Two representatives of the BBC arrived then, complete with transmitting equipment. Much to Bobby's disgust and Helene's amazement, the BBC bloke with a microphone required them to put their story to the whole nation by way of the wireless news scheduled for eleven o'clock, which was in fifteen minutes time. Bobby pointed out they were both whacked, that they had a train to catch to London, and would accordingly be pleased if any further talking could be postponed for a year. Besides, he said, he needed a phone to let his family know he'd landed. Lieutenant Woodruffe intervened and said that if his family had the wireless turned on, they'd hear the broadcast. In any event, he would take him to a phone immediately the BBC interview was over. I hope, he said, that you and Miss Aarlberg realize that what you accomplished was something the whole nation should know about.

'Sod that,' said Bobby, 'my maternal grandmother will chew my ears off if she sees my name in a newspaper. She's always believed that anyone who gets his or her name mentioned in a newspaper is on a slippery slope to perdition.'

'I think I'd like to meet your maternal grandmother,' smiled Lieutenant Woodruffe, at which point the BBC bloke began to get bossy in a nice kind way. Most of the Press men had disappeared to get their reports through to local or national papers. Bobby and Helene looked at each other, eyes heavy with tiredness.

'Well, I do not mind too much,' said Helene.

'It won't take long,' said the BBC bloke, 'we'll be linking up with the news broadcast, and the interview will only last a matter of minutes.'

'Very well,' said Helene.

'Yes, all right,' said Bobby. He gave her a little pat. She made a face, much as if she thought he had decided to be a father to her, which was absurd. 'If my mother has got the wireless on, it'll be one way of letting her know I've turned up at last. We'll catch some sleep on the train.'

Jonathan was in the backyard, inspecting the magic of what his dad had made of it, a little garden. This year, among other things, he'd planted peas, and the row of plants was lush and green, the pods swelling. Jonathan thought that was pretty wondrous for a Walworth backyard.

Jemima came out.

'Here you be, Jonathan.'

'So I am,' said Jonathan.

'And looking at your dad's garden peas,' smiled Jemima, attractively buxom and rosy-cheeked. That was pretty wondrous for Walworth too, rosy cheeks. But Jonathan's Sussex mother had always looked what she was, country-born. 'And thinking of what?'

'I'm not thinking of anything in particular,' said Jonathan.

'If you say so, well, I believe you, to be sure I do,' said Jemima. 'Is Emma coming today?'

'No, I'm going there, I'm spending the afternoon with her at her home,' said Jonathan.

'I never did know a sweeter girl,' said Jemima.

'Yes, pity about this damn' old war,' said Jonathan. 'It's bothersome.'

'It's on your mind?' said Jemima.

'It's on everybody's, I should think,' said Jonathan, and Jemima knew then why nothing of a permanent kind had been decided in his relationship with Emma. But if she knew Emma, something would happen before Jonathan's leave was over.

She went back into the kitchen. A few minutes later, just after eleven, she called to him in an excited voice.

'Jonathan, come in quick – quick – the wireless news, you'll never believe!'

Jonathan ran in. He caught the voice of a young woman speaking English with an accent.

'. . . and my father said Sergeant Somers could perhaps get to Switzerland, but no, Sergeant Somers said it would mean him spending the rest of the war making cuckoo clocks. He insisted on Dunkirk and we said no, it is full of Germans now, it would be suicide. Many times I told him he was mad when he spoke of finding a boat not damaged, I said I would not help him to commit suicide. Ask him if that is true.'

Bobby's voice arrived in Jemima's cosy kitchen.

'It was the quickest and shortest way home for me, given a bit of luck.'

'Listen to him,' said the feminine voice. 'A bit of luck? Crazy, I tell you. But he would have it so, yes, and would have stolen my little boat to make the crossing by himself. How could I let him? When I heard my boat had not been damaged, I said to him very well, I will go with you.'

'I did my best to put her off,' said Bobby, with Jemima and Jonathan wide-eyed and rapt, 'but I

299

had to face the fact that she was too obstinate to listen to reason.'

'Jonathan, it's a young Frenchwoman called Helene Oldberg or something,' said Jemima, 'the interviewer gave her name.'

'Obstinate? Myself?' Helene's indignation was obvious. 'Ah, who is calling the kettle black? I have never met anyone more obstinate than Sergeant Somers.'

'There's a difference between obstinacy and duty,' said Bobby. 'Still, I'd never have made it without her, she's a living marvel, and if any of my family are listening, they can write that down for posterity or something.'

The interviewer at Portsmouth had a smile on his face. The broadcast was live, but being recorded for inclusion in the hourly news bulletins, and it was real human stuff, a humdinger of a dialogue between a spirited young Frenchwoman and a British sergeant who had engineered an amazing escape from Dunkirk a week after the massive evacuation had been completed.

Jemima and Jonathan listened fascinated to the dialogue and the unfolding story.

In the kitchen of another home, Susie was staring at the family radio perched on the dresser. Little Paula was beside her, trying to command her attention.

'In a minute, Paula, in a minute. Listen, it's your cousin Bobby talkin' on the wireless, with a French girl. He's come back from France. Listen.'

It seemed to Susie that there was a kind of electricity between those two, Bobby and Helene Aarlberg. Right there on the wireless, they were getting at each other in such a quick funny way while at the same time putting over a marvellous story of courage and enterprise. She could believe that sort of endeavour of Bobby, a young man of initiative who had been a very active peacetime soldier with the Territorials.

Was Lizzy listening? If so, she would be thrilled. And people listening all over the country would be clapping their hands. Susie, enthralled, wondered who she would phone first when the broadcast was over.

Lizzy *was* listening, in company with Edward. Because of the dramatic events of late and the fact that the German and French armies were presently locked in desperate battle, most of the nation's wireless sets were switched on all day. If her sister-in-law Susie was enthralled, Lizzy was doubly so. Bobby said at one point that he and the young lady were flaked out, yet he sounded crisp and perky, and she sounded well and truly alive, especially when she was challenging him to deny that some of his ideas of escape were crazy. Their story was breathtaking to Lizzy and exhilarating to Edward.

Rosie, arriving home, said hello to Chinese Lady and Mr Finch. Mr Finch, still a valuable cog in the machinery of a certain Government department, did not now work on Saturday mornings. He and

Chinese Lady were delighted to see Rosie, who looked as if she had been poured into her tailored uniform. The wireless wasn't on. Chinese Lady had a quarrelsome relationship with what had been coming out of it ever since she had taken a dislike to its frequent mention of what Hitler was up to. She preferred family conversations, as with Rosie now.

'Well, it's that nice to see you, Rosie,' she said, 'it reminds me how much you've been missed these last several years, first at university, then your training college and now in this women's army. Mind you, women's armies shouldn't be allowed. Still, I won't go on about my beliefs as you're only home for the weekend, and I must say that if you had to go into uniform you've chosen one that fits you as if it was made for you.'

'It was, Nana, and you're a sport for not going on about military ladies,' said Rosie. 'My word, Grandpa, aren't we a fortunate family in all our tolerances of each other?'

'We're fortunate on all counts, Rosie, and the whole country's particularly fortunate that our Army is still intact and can profit from the experience of defeat,' said Mr Finch.

'I've never known anything like the experience of watching ships bringing home the Dunkirk men,' said Rosie. 'Where's Mum?'

'She's at the office,' said Mr Finch, 'but she'll be home before one.'

'They're short of staff,' said Chinese Lady by way of tactfully apologizing for Emily's absence.

'Yes, I see,' said Rosie. 'Where's our own young Dunkirk hero?'

'Tim?' said Chinese Lady. 'He's out with a friend, but he won't be long, he's looking forward to seein' you.'

'And Daddy, is he out too?' asked Rosie.

'Only in the garden,' smiled Mr Finch.

'My old reliable,' said Rosie.

'He wanted to see you as soon as you arrived, Rosie,' said Chinese Lady.

Boots was trimming the edge of the grass path that divided two vegetable plots at the bottom of the garden. He had fallen easily into this homely kind of relaxation while awaiting a return to duty, a duty that was going to be exacting. A directive from the very top demanded a complete re-appraisal of command and a total rehabilitation of the demoralized BEF. Prime Minister Churchill further demanded a new and tougher kind of training for every branch of the Army.

'Hello, Daddy old darling.'

He turned and saw Rosie. She was tailored to khaki perfection. He was in an old shirt and trousers, his hair slightly awry, his face lean and brown, his forty-three years sitting very favourably on him and bearing him no malice at all.

'Hello, poppet, glad to see you,' he said.

'Well, give us a kiss, then,' said Rosie. Boots planted a warm kiss on her cheek. 'Bless you, sweetie,' she said, 'and where do we go from here?'

'Where do who go?' asked Boots, who thought that in her looks, her character and her poise she was very much the daughter of her natural father, Major Charles Armitage, a landowner.

'The Army,' said Rosie.

'Back to France,' said Boots.

'Good grief, next week, you mean?'

'Not quite so soon,' said Boots, 'but it's got to be done eventually.'

'When do you finish your leave?' asked Rosie, thinking how much she still liked to have him to herself.

'Next week,' said Boots. 'I believe we'll finish up in Dorset. Sir Henry will let me know. He's still hoping for command of a corps, having handled his division as aggressively as he was allowed to during the fighting. He was sold on aggression, but the overall tactics of the BEF were based on a defensive policy. It played into the hands of the Germans.'

'Well, I'm going to change now and get into something comfy,' said Rosie. 'Then I'm going to sit out here with you and just talk. We haven't seen each other for Lord knows how long.'

'We'll have a chinwag over some coffee,' said Boots. 'This afternoon, we'll throw the war overboard and play some tennis, if you'd like to.'

'Tops with me, Daddy old love,' said Rosie. 'Who else will be playing?'

'Tim and Polly,' said Boots.

'Oh, yes, Polly's home, isn't she?' said Rosie, and guessed that Sir Henry's restless daughter hadn't lost the chance of seeing Boots.

Mr Finch appeared outside the kitchen.

'Boots! Rosie! Bobby's back! He's been heard on the news broadcast. Lizzy's on the phone.'

In that way, by means of Lizzy's excited voice, Boots learned of the astonishing escape performed by Bobby and a young Frenchwoman. Lizzy had already phoned Ned at his work.

The news reached Emma, Emily and Sammy by way of a phone call from Susie to the offices. It reached Tommy at the Shoreditch factory when Vi phoned him from home immediately after she had listened to the wireless broadcast. And it reached Bobby's elder sister Annabelle through a further phone call from Lizzy.

Chinese Lady was content. The family was complete again.

Chapter Eighteen

It was nearly noon by the time Bobby was free to use a phone and make a trunk call home. Lizzy, still in a state of proud excitement, picked up the receiver.

'Hello?'

'Hello yourself, Mum, how's everything at home?' asked a well-known voice.

'Bobby!'

'Yes, it's me, Mum—'

'Bobby, I heard you on the wireless, so did Edward – oh, I don't know if I'm comin' or goin'. You and a French girl, I couldn't believe my ears, nor could Edward. Where are you?'

'I'm at Portsmouth railway station. Be home in a few hours. I'm whacked out but all in one piece. Thought I'd let you know I'm on my way in case you hadn't been listening to the news.'

'Bobby, I feel I'm dreaming or something,' said Lizzy, still giddy. 'Are you bringing the young lady with you?'

'I promised her parents she could make her home with the family, Mum,' said Bobby.

'Yes, of course she can,' said Lizzy. 'After all I heard on the wireless about how she left her own home to help you get back to us, your dad and me will be glad to let her have Annabelle's old room.'

'Well, good on you and Dad,' said Bobby. 'I've got ten days leave, and while I'm home I'll help her to decide what she wants to do. We're catching a train to Waterloo in fifteen minutes. We're both tired out, so would you mind getting Annabelle's old bedroom ready for Helene? She'll probably want to turn in as soon as we arrive. So will I. Listen, what about Tim and Uncle Boots, and yes, Jonathan?'

'They're all home,' said Lizzy. 'Bobby, I still can't believe all this. What's Helene like?'

'She's some girl, believe me,' said Bobby.

'On the wireless, she kept mentioning how crazy you were,' said Lizzy.

'They were all jokes,' said Bobby.

'But she said you were the one who made jokes.'

'She's funny like that,' said Bobby. 'Well, that's all for now, Mum. We must catch this train. See you when we arrive, regards to all.'

He hung up. Helene, fatigue showing, was talking with Lieutenant Woodruffe in his harbour office. She was holding a canvas valise containing the clothes and other items given to her by the Red Cross. At her feet was a new kitbag belonging to Bobby. It held replacements of Army issue lost, including a spare uniform.

'Right, let's get you to the platform,' said Lieutenant Woodruffe as Bobby picked up the kitbag. 'This way, follow me.'

They followed him out into the sunshine.

'What did your mother say?' asked Helene, her

307

gifted dress a colourful cotton print and a very good fit apart from being just a little short for her. Bobby had never seen her in anything colourful before, and as far as he was concerned he minded the knee-length hem not at all.

'You're a nice surprise, she said. Well, mothers are like that. A free pint of milk from the roundsman is a nice surprise to mothers, so's the first snowdrop.'

'But what did she say about me?' asked Helene, who felt she could go to sleep standing up.

'You're a nice surprise too, she said.'

Helene shook her head at him as they entered the station in the wake of the affable Navy lieutenant.

'When are you going to stop making jokes?' she asked.

'It's no joke, Helene, my mother says our home is your home.'

Lieutenant Woodruffe came to a halt beside a standing train.

'Here we are, Sergeant Somers,' he said.

Bobby took a look.

'That's the first-class coach,' he said.

'Yes, and there's a compartment reserved for you and Miss Aarlberg,' said Lieutenant Woodruffe. 'The Combined Services felt they couldn't do less for you. Goodbye, Miss Aarlberg, and I wish you the very best of luck, and hope that the fortunes of war will favour you during your stay in our country.'

'Thank you,' said Helene, as he shook hands with her. Steam hissed and people milled, uniforms predominating. 'Do you know what the news from France is today?'

'Grim, I'm afraid,' he said. The Germans had shattered the French centre and were preparing to cross the Marne on their advance to Paris. Further, Italy had just declared war on France. Helene bit her lip as she received this news. 'It's a swine all round,' said Lieutenant Woodruffe.

'So is Mussolini,' said Helene, 'a fascist pig with a fat belly, yes.'

'I won't quarrel with that,' said Lieutenant Woodruffe. 'Goodbye, Sergeant Somers. If your exploit doesn't earn you a commission, nothing will. Pleasure to have met you both.'

'Same here, sir,' said Bobby, and saluted him. Then he and Helene boarded the train and found the first-class compartment reserved for them.

'My goodness,' said Chinese Lady during the course of a voluble discussion over lunch, 'and Bobby wasn't wounded serious, after all.' The recorded interview had been broadcast on the one o'clock news, and the family had listened. 'I never heard anything more intimate on our wireless—'

'Intimate, Maisie?' queried Mr Finch.

'Intimate, Nana?' said Rosie.

'I'm sure I don't know what else you can call it, my own grandson and all, and sounding like he was only next door,' said Chinese Lady. 'But what made that French girl call him crazy? Yes, and more than once. Bobby's never been crazy in all his life. Sensible, that's what I've always felt Bobby was, and talked sensible too, which not everyone in the fam'ly does, though I won't mention names, not on a nice surprisin' day like this.'

'We know who you've got in mind, Nana,' said Rosie.

'Not me,' said Tim.

'Nor me,' said Emily.

'I, too, exclude myself,' said Mr Finch.

'And I'm innocent,' said Boots. 'It must be the cat.'

'What cat?' asked Chinese Lady. 'We don't have a cat, do we, Em'ly?'

'No, Mum,' said Emily.

'Next door's cat,' said Boots.

'What's your dad talkin' about, Rosie?' asked Chinese Lady.

'His innocence,' said Rosie.

'That was when he was five years old,' said Chinese Lady. 'He was innocent all right then, but not by the time he was six. I wonder how Lizzy's going to manage havin' this French girl living with her? I hope she's not from Paris. Eloise's mother wasn't from Paris, what a blessin'.' Chinese Lady regarded Paris as sinfully French and, accordingly, not a very proper place to come from.

'Has Eloise phoned lately?' asked Rosie.

'Yesterday,' said Boots. 'Unfortunately, she earned herself seven days CB for talking back to an officer, but she sneaked out to call us last night.'

'She'll want to know about Bobby,' said Rosie.

'I'll be phoning a telegram to her after lunch,' said Mr Finch.

'About the girl with Bobby, she's a farmer's daughter,' said Tim. 'The interviewer pointed it out, and I don't think the farm's in Paris.'

Chinese Lady stopped eating scrambled egg on toast. It had been made with imported egg powder from America. She pursed her lips and thought.

'Penny for them, Mum,' said Emily.

'Hasn't this fam'ly had something to do with a farmer's daughter before?' asked Chinese Lady.

'Have we?' said Tim. 'It must have been quick, and I must have missed her in passing.'

'She was a French farmer's daughter too, if I remember right,' said Chinese Lady.

'Oh, you mean when your only oldest son was in the Great War, Nana,' said Rosie, 'and we all know he didn't miss her in passing himself. He dallied.'

'Well, I 'ope Bobby didn't do any dallying with this one,' said Emily.

'Only for a week,' said Tim.

'Mind your words, Tim, there's a good boy,' said Chinese Lady.

'In case you haven't noticed, Grandma,' said Tim, 'I've been wearing long trousers for years, and I do a bit of shaving as well.'

'My, when I think of Bobby and that French girl rowing a boat across the Channel, no wonder they got shipwrecked,' said Chinese Lady.

'Sailing, Maisie, not rowing,' said Mr Finch.

'Well, they still got shipwrecked,' said Chinese Lady. 'Thank the Lord the Navy motorboat rescued them. We'd all best go round to Lizzy's later today and see this French girl for ourselves.'

'Tomorrow, Maisie,' said Mr Finch, 'if Ned and Lizzy would like us to.'

'Yes, better leave them in peace until tomorrow, Mum,' said Emily.

'Well, all right,' said Chinese Lady, 'but what do you think, Boots?'

'Tomorrow,' said Boots.

'Yes, perhaps that would be best,' said Chinese Lady, looking very sprightly in her satisfaction that her grandson Bobby had actually been on the wireless, which was more respectable than newspapers. She just hoped he wouldn't be mentioned in tomorrow's edition of the *News of the World*. 'I'll have a nice talk with Lizzy when we get there. I expect she'd like to unburden herself a bit.'

'Um – unburden herself of what, Maisie?' asked Mr Finch.

'Of her feelings about everything,' said Chinese Lady.

'What's everything?' asked Tim.

'Everything French,' said Boots.

'Is that a clever remark or something?' asked Chinese Lady.

'Just something, old lady,' said Boots.

Rosie's little smile was an appreciation of his whimsical side.

Emma opened the door to Jonathan that afternoon. She bathed him in a sunny and excited smile.

'Jonathan, have you heard about Bobby? Did you hear him on the wireless? Mum did, this morning, and Dad and I heard him on the one o'clock news.

They're repeating it all day. Jonathan, he's got a French girl with him, they crept out of Dunkirk last night in her small yacht—'

'Yes, I heard him on the eleven o'clock news,' said Jonathan.

'Did you?' said Emma. 'Did you jump about? Imagine it, when we all thought he'd been taken prisoner, there he was on a French farm cavorting with the farmer's daughter, just like Uncle Boots did in the last war.'

'How old is this farmer's daughter, then?' asked Jonathan. 'Forty-odd?'

'It's not the same one, you daft thing,' said Emma.

'Well whatever,' said Jonathan, 'it's all a down-right glad piece of news, durned if it isn't. My family send you their happy regards. Are Bobby and the girl here yet?'

'No, not yet, we're expecting them at about three,' said Emma. 'Bobby phoned and told Mum he and the girl Helene were catching a train from Portsmouth about noon. Mum's like a two-year old, and Dad came home from his office with two bottles of champagne. You can join in the celebrations.'

'I'd like that,' said Jonathan. 'Can I come in, then? Only I reckon if I stand on your doorstep much longer, your neighbours will think I'm a Saturday afternoon insurance bloke trying to sell you a policy covering damage to your Sunday hats.'

'Oh, help, ever so sorry, Jonathan,' said Emma, 'only I'm a bit flustered at the moment. Come in, go through to the kitchen and say hello to Mum and Dad and Edward – oh, and Annabelle and Nick and the children will be here later. Anyway, when you've said hello to Mum and Dad and Edward, you can come and meet me.'

'Come and meet you?' said Jonathan, looking cool and casual in an open-necked shirt and dark blue flannels.

'Yes, I'll be in the garden,' said Emma, looking delicious in a simple, unfussy dress of apple green.

'Sounds like summer,' said Jonathan. 'I haven't met you in your garden since Wednesday evening.'

'Oh, dear, what a rotten shame,' said Emma. 'Never mind, we'll make up for it now. We can talk about Bobby and his daring escape. It's just like Bulldog Drummond. Well, *Mademoiselle* Bulldog Drummond in a way.'

Jonathan paid his respects to Lizzy and Ned who, of course, were in a celebratory mood. Edward was present and dying to get a look at Helene. Despite knowing she was a farmer's daughter, Edward felt sure she would have a touch of the 'Folies Bergère' about her.

Then Jonathan joined Emma in the garden, and she made room for him on a bench seat facing the lawn and the flowerbeds. They talked about Bobby and the French girl, and the wireless interview, and Emma said how tickled she was that the young lady had kept insisting Bobby was a crazy man. Jonathan said there was a lot of that sort of thing about. Yes, I know, said Emma, there's some of it sitting next to me this minute.

314

'Caught it when I were a young country chap,' said Jonathan, and Emma thought again that his six months in France really had turned him into a fine-looking man.

'Caught it when you were born, more like,' she said. 'Do you know, I'm so happy I feel I could solve everybody's problems. Except Mr Churchill's. His problems will be awful if the French are defeated. We'll just have to hope for another miracle. Do you have any problems you'd like me to solve for you, Jonathan?'

'I'm feeling fine at the moment,' said Jonathan.

'Yes, but should we keep meeting like this?' asked Emma.

'Pardon?' said Jonathan.

'Well, people are going to talk, aren't they?' said Emma.

'What about?' asked Jonathan guardedly.

'Us,' said Emma.

'Us?' said Jonathan.

'Yes, you and me,' said Emma.

'You and me, yes, see what you mean,' said Jonathan. 'Well, I've been giving it some thought—'

'It?' said Emma.

'And I reckon it's like this,' said Jonathan. 'As there's a war on, and as I'm in the Army, with my prospects uncertain and the pay not very good—'

'Oh, that's it, is it?' said Emma. 'Well, Jonathan Hardy, I'm not wearing that, and you needn't think I will, either. I could sue you, d'you know that?'

'Sue me?' said Jonathan.

315

'Yes, and I've got love letters from you to prove I can,' said Emma.

'I've thought about being practical—'

'Yes, so have I,' said Emma.

'We ought to be practical, Emma,' said Jonathan.

'Yes, so we ought,' said Emma, 'but it doesn't agree with me.'

'Nor me,' said Jonathan, 'but there's no way we can set up a proper home together, Emma. I mean, we couldn't push for more than two rooms somewhere, or think about having children—'

'Oh, a home, a house, children, that's for after the war,' said Emma. 'Until then, it'll just be you and me, and then only when you're home on leave, and perhaps when I'm on leave too, if I join the ATS.'

'But where?' asked Jonathan.

'We could spend all our leaves in a little Devon hotel near Salcombe,' said Emma. 'I know it from the holidays we've spent at Salcombe, and I know the family who run it. It's a lovely retreat, Jonathan, and if being practical now doesn't agree with either of us, then it's just two minds with but a single thought. Don't you remember I told you last year I expected to be engaged this year?'

'Shall I ever forget?'

'Well, I like it that it's now come to pass,' said Emma.

'That's it, is it, Emma Somers?'

'Yes, that be it, Jonathan Hardy,' said Emma, 'and we can start by spending our honeymoon at that hotel.'

'Well, I'm blowed if I know how to say no,' said Jonathan.

'Oh, that's good,' said Emma, 'we'll meet at the altar on your next leave, then.'

They looked at each other, Emma quite sure of her own mind, Jonathan thinking that what a young man fancied didn't have very much to do with being sensible and practical.

'I'm fair gone on you, Emma, and that's a fact,' he said.

'Jonathan, I like it that you are, don't I?' said Emma.

'By the way, what's your single thought?' asked Jonathan.

'It's all about you in sexy pyjamas,' said Emma. 'What's yours?'

'All about you in something silky and not a lot of it,' said Jonathan.

The kitchen window was open, and from the kitchen Ned and Lizzy heard Emma peal with laughter.

The afternoon was beautiful, and in Ruskin Park four people were absorbed in the exhilarating activity of a competitive mixed doubles, Polly partnering Tim against Rosie and Boots. People stopped to watch, some wondering if a game of tennis was in keeping with the serious nature of what was happening in France, and others simply intrigued by the wholehearted way the game was being played. The four contestants, all very good, were completely involved, the older woman quick

317

and supple in her movements, the younger woman extraordinarily lovely and graceful, the young man speedy and dashing, the older long-legged and effortless. The gods of sport, heedless of French disasters, hovered over the public court, and brought forth laughter, yells and lively battle.

Rosie was in her element, loving the fact of being home for the weekend. Twenty-five now, a graduate of Somerville College and academically a world away from that which an elementary education had given to Emily, her adoptive mother, she nevertheless was still at her happiest whenever she was at home and her favourite people were around.

Chinese Lady couldn't understand why Rosie was still single, and not even courting. It was a real puzzle, considering that such a striking young woman must have admirers. Rosie did have, but the simple fact was she hadn't yet found one whom she wanted to marry. Polly had told her it was because she was making the mistake of looking for someone like her adoptive father. If that's a mistake, said Rosie, so's an elephant with four legs. Rosie, there aren't too many men around like your dad, said Polly. There has to be one somewhere, said Rosie.

She played her tennis with swift and skilful athleticism, taking delight in frequently out-matching either Polly or Tim. Polly yelled at her. Tim laughed. Everyone's spirits had been raised by Bobby's extraordinary adventure, and exuberance was easily sustainable.

A watching young bloke made himself heard.

''Ere, you lot, don't yer know there's a war on?'

Polly, always at her liveliest whenever she was with Boots, turned and said, 'Is there, young sport? Well, fetch it here and we'll set about it.'

'It ain't funny, yer know,' said the teenaged lad.

'Who's laughing?' asked Polly, picking up a ball.

'You are. I 'eard yer, all of yer.'

'Oh, sorry about that,' said Polly, knocking the ball back to Rosie for service.

'Mind you,' said the lad sociably, 'I ain't saying I don't like watchin' yer.'

'How kind,' said Polly. Other spectators laughed.

'I like watchin' the other lady as well.'

'We're flattered,' said Polly, 'and just for that we'll all go and join up as soon as the game's over.'

'Service,' called Rosie.

'Same to you, sport,' said Polly and returned the service by hitting it straight at Boots at the net. He ducked and the ball chased madly on through the air and flew out.

'Missed me,' said Boots.

'I'll get you one day,' said Polly with her sweetest smile.

*   *   *

On the landing fields of RAF Fighter Command, fledgling pilots who had just won their wings sat in on lectures delivered by established pilots who had battled with Messerschmitts of the *Luftwaffe* over France. Men from all parts of the Empire were among the newly qualified. They had come to forge links with the British airmen and create the formidable and spirited nucleus of Britain's first line of defence in the event of a *Luftwaffe* invasion of the skies.

Along with Churchill, the chiefs of RAF Fighter Command knew what to expect if France fell, and were preparing for it.

The train was steaming through the soft rolling countryside of Surrey. Farms, hamlets and little woods wound away from the speeding locomotive. Guildford had been left behind and Waterloo was not so far now.

A hand touched Bobby's knee. He woke up from one more catnap.

'How can you sleep?' asked Helene, looking offended.

'I can't,' said Bobby. 'I've been trying to, but my mind's too active.'

'Trying to? You have been asleep, I tell you,' said Helene. 'I can't even close my eyes. I thought I would sleep and sleep, but there's too much to see. All this farmland. I have seen young wheat and barley and huge fields of dairy pasture. How wonderful, oh, and such pretty villages.'

'I know about—'

'I should be sorry if you had no soul,' said Helene. 'Ah, look at you, you are just like any other man. The views from this window are magnificent, but you are only interested in my legs.'

'I've seen all the other views before,' said Bobby. The train rattled over points south of Thames Ditton.

'Why did you let them give me such a short dress?' demanded Helene. 'Look at it, it's hardly a dress at all.'

'Looks fine from over here,' said Bobby, seated opposite her. The hem of the dress was above her knees, her legs splendid in new stockings.

'You should be talking to me, not trying to go to sleep,' said Helene.

'I thought the idea was for both of us to catch some sleep,' said Bobby.

'I have told you, how can I, when everything is so exciting?' said Helene.

'Is it exciting?' asked Bobby.

'Yes, the country, the farms, and what I can do to help in the fight against Hitler. Yes, and speaking on the BBC. Come and sit here.' Helene patted the space beside her.

'I don't want to crowd you,' said Bobby, 'we've still got the whole compartment to ourselves.'

'I want you to talk to me, not sit there looking at this terrible dress,' said Helene.

'It's not terrible,' said Bobby, 'it's quite pretty.'

'Come and sit here,' said Helene again, and Bobby gave in. He moved and sat beside her. 'That is better, isn't it?' she said. 'That is more friendly, isn't it?'

'I'd call it quite cosy,' said Bobby.

'I want to tell you something,' said Helene.

'Go ahead,' said Bobby, liking the feel of her warm body close to his.

'Bobby, I want you to know how sorry I am I was so unkind to you once.' She was looking at him, her blue eyes dark with self-reproach. 'It was disgusting of me to say such things. I was so wrong. So I want to tell you you would make a fine husband for any woman, yes, and there are some women who would especially like to have a husband as brave and crazy as you.'

'Well, I'll go to Bethlehem,' said Bobby, 'what comes next?'

'I am too shy to say more,' said Helene.

'Too shy?' Bobby laughed. 'That'll be the day,' he said.

'No,' said Helene, 'I must leave everything else to you, Bobby.'

Bobby made the only possible start. He kissed her. The train, always superior to the idiosyncracies of passengers, steamed on regardless.

Eventually, it was Lizzy herself who was the first of the family to see them. She was in her front room, frankly watching out for their arrival. From the window, she spotted a taxi pulling up outside the house, and then came the very unusual sight of the cabbie actually getting out and going round to open the door for his passengers. Out they stepped, Bobby first, and then a dark-haired, tanned young woman in a pretty cotton dress, rather short. The cabbie brought out a kitbag and a canvas valise from beside his driving seat. Bobby took the kitbag, and the young woman took the valise. Bobby handed the cabbie some money. The cabbie shook Bobby's hand and said something. Bobby grinned and the young woman laughed, then looked at the gate, the front garden and the house itself.

Lizzy rushed to open the door. Out she came to stand on her step, just as Bobby and the young woman walked through the open gate. Lizzy had thought to see someone a little sad at having exiled herself, and a little nervous about what to expect from the family. But the young lady was smiling.

And she was coming up the path hand in hand with Bobby.

Lizzy opened her arms to Jacob's daughter.

Chapter Nineteen

On 14 June, the Germans took Paris, which the French left undefended as an open city.

A week later, France capitulated and an armistice was signed on 22 June.

The United Kingdom braced itself, and before June had run its dramatic course sporadic air attacks were launched by the Germans on Southern England. Civilian property suffered heavily and the loss of life was a sign of things certain to come in devastating fashion. It was the obvious prelude to an invasion attempt, a prelude of progressively increasing power and menace as Goering's numerically superior *Luftwaffe* swarmed through the skies of July in its endeavour to soften up Britain. Goering had promised Hitler that the *Luftwaffe* would totally destroy the RAF, and leave the way clear for the invasion.

Churchill and the RAF had other ideas, however, and the *Luftwaffe* began to find its own menace neutralized by the menace of the extraordinarily manoeuvreable Hurricanes and Spitfires, which shot down Heinkel and Dornier bombers with alarming regularity, and also took on the fast Messerschmitt fighters in apparent glee.

The battle for command of the skies of Britain was on, and the whole country knew it was fighting for its life. By August the air battles were tremendous in their numeracy and ferocity, the weather as brilliant as it had been since the days of Dunkirk, the skies marked with trails of white vapour and streaming smoke. Churchill was an inspiration in his bulldog defiance, the RAF magnificent in the way it fought every battle.

Bobby and Tim were back with their regiment, which was in Somerset being re-equipped and retrained. Helene was also in Somerset, working on a farm along with other young women, all members of the invaluable Land Army. Helene was in her element, if inclined to be bossy by virtue of her strength of character and her experience of farming. She was also surprisingly happy in her exile, loving the beauty of Somerset and the excitement that came from being able to meet up with Bobby fairly regularly. They wandered fields and meadows together, and dallied in secluded places, where she frequently lost her sense of independence in the face of his initiatives.

'Bobby, when are you going to marry me?'

'Are we engaged, then?'

'No, but if you aren't going to marry me, stop doing things to me.'

'You know I'm going to marry you, but let's see how the war develops first.'

'Oh, that is wise, I suppose, but I did not think Englishmen were as outrageous as you are.'

'It's all this weather, it makes me feel drunk.'

'*Alors*! It is just the weather? I could be any woman?'

'You're not any woman.' Bobby paused, grinned and selected a phrase which he knew would produce fireworks. 'You're a game girl and a jolly good sport.'

'What? I am a horse-faced English college girl with a hockey stick?'

'Not this minute you're not.'

And so on. It was the dialogue of lovers who were a challenge to each other.

The farmer called her in from the fields one afternoon. A strange-looking man was waiting outside the farmhouse for her. Well, he looked very strange in such a rural environment, for he wore an immaculate black bowler hat, a grey suit and gleaming black shoes. Also, he carried a rolled umbrella. Bobby could have told her he was a military executive in traditional mufti. He had come all the way from London. He was a colonel by the name of Ross, and he wished to speak with her. She went into the farmhouse with him, into a parlour with an old-fashioned atmosphere, and there she saw another man similarly dressed. And Bobby was there too. He came to his feet, a smile on his face.

'Hello,' he said.

'Bobby, what is all this about?'

'Come and sit down,' said Bobby.

Colonel Ross, a tall man in his late thirties, introduced his colleague, a Scottish officer, Captain Blair, and then addressed himself at length to Helene and Bobby, making it plain from the start that the matter was highly confidential and asking them to observe this. The promise given, and with Captain Blair making a silent and shrewd study of the potential of this couple, the Colonel outlined the purpose of the meeting. With France out of the war and its Vichy Government hand in glove with Berlin, the time had come to consider encouraging the rise of an underground resistance movement in occupied France, a movement devoted to sabotage, espionage and anything else that would hit at Germany. It was known that there were French people willing to form cells of resistance, but they would need all the help Britain could give, not only in the way of weapons and explosives, but also in the way of specially trained agents from the United Kingdom. *Mademoiselle* was a French citizen of proven worth, Sergeant Somers a man of obvious initiative and enterprise, who spoke excellent French. Would they care to consider volunteering for such work as a team, to be landed in France at some future date? They would receive the special-ized training necessary to turn them into agents and saboteurs. They would also be briefed on how to set up an effective resistance cell of willing French people in some area of occupied France. Sergeant Somers would be commissioned and given charge of the venture, which might entail an initial stay in France of several months.

'He would be leader, that crazy man?' said Helene. 'He would want to blow up a train of German soldiers all on his own.'

'An excellent thing in itself,' said Colonel Ross, 'but not if one goes at it like a bull at a gate. The training is designed to eliminate rash heroics in favour of foolproof security. We shall be against the blowing up of a troop train or any other act of sabotage if it means the capture and destruction of a resistance cell. Our agents and their French resistance colleagues are not to be considered cheap and expendable. I don't expect either of you to be able to decide now if you wish to volunteer for such work. I should like both of you to spend the weekend with us in a house in Taunton, where everything can be discussed at length to help you make up your minds one way or the other. I've brought Sergeant Somers here with me from his training camp, and am now prepared to drive you both to Taunton, if you would care to pack a few things, *mademoiselle*.'

'Are you willing to consider, Bobby?' asked Helene.

'I'm not sure you should,' said Bobby, 'it's not my idea of work for a woman.'

'If you go, I shall go,' said Helene, 'and will fit in easier than you because I'm French.'

'I think from what is known of both of you, that neither will have any difficulty in fitting in,' said Colonel Ross, while Captain Blair continued his study of Bobby and Helene.

'Does what is known of us and does the prop-

328

osition itself relate to our escape from Dunkirk?' asked Bobby.

Colonel Ross smiled.

'Of course,' he said.

'Work like you've mentioned is going to be bloody dangerous for Miss Aarlberg, sir,' said Bobby.

'I can't say it won't be, Sergeant Somers.'

'If you go, Bobby,' said Helene, 'it is no use trying to make me stay behind. It might be just the work for me, in any case, work that will help my country.'

'Let's talk about it,' said Bobby.

'In Taunton, with myself and Captain Blair?' said Colonel Ross.

'Yes, we will come,' said Helene, as fine a figure as ever in her green jersey and her hard-wearing breeches. 'I will change into something nice and pack a few other clothes. Is Mr Beresford to be told?'

Mr Beresford was the farmer.

'I will speak to him,' said Colonel Ross. 'I've already agreed the matter with Sergeant Somers's commanding officer.'

That was Friday afternoon, a day in early August. By Sunday, after all kinds of discussions with Colonel Ross and Captain Blair, Bobby and Helene had made up their minds. It had not been easy, even though there was never any attempt to press-urize them. But Helene had no lack of courage, and eventually the idea of returning to France, of going there as a special agent, took a positive hold of her. Yes, she would go, but only if Sergeant Somers went with her. As for Bobby, the risks, the purpose and the challenge all fired his adventurous spirit and won him over.

They volunteered to commit themselves, to enlist for the specialized training. Colonel Ross said they would be notified, along with other men and women, as soon as the training programme had been set up.

The one drawback they had to face was that not under any circumstances were they to disclose to anyone a single detail of their possible assignments. Not their closest friends nor any family members were to be told. Helene was to enter the select FANY Corps, and Bobby was to become Lieutenant Somers, RA. They would, however, use code names.

Bobby returned to his regiment, Helene returned to the farm, and they began a waiting period.

Jonathan had rejoined his regiment in June, and in July his mother and the rest of the family moved to their new abode in Lorrimore Square. Emma, who had thought about volunteering for the ATS, decided to hold back on that until she and Jonathan were married.

Boots was in Dorset, at 7 Corps headquarters a few miles from Corfe Castle. The training was intense, the divisions equipped with new guns, tanks and other armour, and by August Sir Henry, now in command of the Corps, knew it was eventually destined for Egypt.

Freddy Brown had been called up, and Horace Cooper's application for the job of a PT instructor had been accepted. Their wives and children moved to Wiltshire in July.

Polly beavered away behind the scenes, making typically shameless use of her contacts, and in early August she was transferred, along with Rosie and a small contingent of ATS admin personnel to the headquarters of the 17th Infantry Division in Dorset. The division was a component of the 7th Corps. Sir Henry was not notified of the division's acquisition – he did not have to be, either officially or unofficially. Polly knew of the circulating rumours concerning a Middle East destination for the Corps, and she also knew something else, which was that the ATS staff would embark with the Corps, whose headquarters were to be situated in Cairo. She kept this to herself, not even telling Rosie.

Rosie, at this particular stage was somewhat under siege from the ardent attentions of Captain Clive Gordon, a distinctive and wholly personable Scot, a member of the Brigade H.Q.'s staff. Rosie dealt engagingly, not discouragingly, with his sorties and sallies, for he was a man of wit and humour, qualities which always struck a chord with her. She held him at bay in such a charming fashion that he declared she was positively the most entertaining woman he had ever met, and damned if he wasn't going to pursue her to the bitter end. Rosie asked if a bitter end wasn't too unpalatable to be pursued. Captain Gordon said he wouldn't know until he got there. What, he said, do you say to that? How kind, said Rosie, I'll have a gin and tonic.

*   *   *

On the third Saturday in July, Eloise received a letter.

Dear Private Adams,

I am taking the unusual step of advising you myself that you will be posted to the headquarters of A Battery of the 23rd HFA on the 18th of August, with the rank of sergeant. If you have any objections to this, please notify me in writing. Such objections had better be good. I am, Yours truly, Wm Lucas, Major.

So, he was now a major, and would be in command of his battery. Eloise asked herself if she had any objections to the posting.

No, none.

*　　　*　　　*

The attacks from the air on the RAF fighter stations continued, and the daylight bombing raids on London increased. The fact that the *Luftwaffe*'s fighters and bombers were beginning to pay dearly for their boldness did not cause any diminution of the onslaught, although by mid-August they had lost hundreds of planes. Worse, they had lost an almost unacceptable number of crews and pilots. But Goering, a strange, gregarious man, who combined great good fellowship with a complete adherence to the viciousness of the SS, was so infuriated by the effective resistance of the RAF and the combative 'Tally-ho!' signals of its fighter pilots that he simply threw in more planes, with orders to smash London and its air defences within a week.

Emily wanted new bedroom curtains.

'I don't know why you're worrying about bed-room curtains when we're likely any day now to be blown up by that man Hitler,' said Chinese Lady. 'I never liked him, nor trusted him, either, from the time the wireless first mentioned him, but I never thought he'd get so nasty as to drop bombs on women and children in daylight. It's one air raid after another, and I'm in and out of our air raid shelter so much I might as well take to livin' in it.'

An Anderson shelter had been installed in the garden.

'Still, he hasn't dropped any round here yet, Mum,' said Emily. She was home from her Saturday morning stint at the office, and having lunch with Chinese Lady and Mr Finch. Chinese Lady was not in her best mood. Apart from air raids, there was the fact that the house felt almost empty. It had a sort of hollow ring at times. Home was no real home to Chinese Lady unless its echoes were those of a resident family. Boots, Rosie, Tim and Eloise were all with the Army, and there was only herself, her husband and Emily. And Emily was at work every day except Sundays. Hollow rings in a house just weren't normal. Hollow rings were the sounds of a house complaining it wasn't being properly lived in.

There'd been lovely family years when Tim and

Rosie were growing up, and Boots had made them shout with laughter at some of the things he said. Mind, one didn't always know if some of the things he said didn't have improper meanings. Rosie in her teens would look at him sometimes as she knew exactly what he did mean. Rosie had always been very close to Boots, and how relieved he had been that she had chosen not to break or disturb their relationship when her natural father appeared out of the blue a few years ago.

Chinese Lady missed Rosie. And Tim. And she missed Boots. But there was always Edwin, her second husband and her right arm. Without him she would have been unable to live with the hollow echoes of the house.

Emily was saying something about buying some curtain material that afternoon.

'I'll drive you there, Emily,' said Mr Finch.

'Drive her where?' asked Chinese Lady.

'Didn't you hear me mention that store in Streatham, Mum?' said Emily. 'They're actually advertisin' a range of pre-war curtain material, and it's sort of come and get it while stocks last.'

'Em'ly love, down to Streatham?' said Chinese Lady. 'Suppose there's another air raid?' The skies were clear at that moment and had been all day.

'I'll stop the car, Maisie, and we'll run for cover,' said Mr Finch.

'Anyway, Streatham's not central London,

Mum,' said Emily, 'that's where they mostly drop their bombs.'

'What about petrol for the car?' asked Chinese Lady.

'I've got a good ration in the tank,' said Mr Finch, who had an official allocation of coupons.

'Well, all right,' said Chinese Lady.

'So long, Mum,' said Emily a little later, 'we'll be back in time for a pot of tea in the garden.'

'That's if I'm not stuck in the air raid shelter,' said Chinese Lady.

'Maisie, would you like to come with us?' asked Mr Finch.

'No, I've got letters to write to the fam'ly,' said Chinese Lady. That would mean letters to everyone who was away. 'Edwin, you take care now.'

'Of course, Maisie.' Mr Finch smiled, stooped and kissed her still unlined forehead. 'You know my weakness for a pot of tea in the garden in this kind of weather.'

The Army car pulled up outside the admin block of an artillery camp set in a wild area of the Peak District, Derbyshire. Out stepped Sergeant Eloise Adams. She spoke to the driver.

'Thank you, and will you please hand me my valise?'

'I thought it was sittin' next to you,' said the driver, a lance-bombardier.

'Yes, it's still there,' said Eloise.

'You want me to get it for you?'

'Thank you, I am much obliged,' said Eloise.

What a character, thought the lance-bombardier, she must think she's a colonel. But good-temperedly he got out and pulled the valise off the back seat.

'Crikey, what's in it, the ATS kitchen sink?' he said.

'My kit and my belongings,' said Eloise, 'I don't have anything to do with kitchen sinks. Where is Major Lucas's office, please?'

'Go through the orderly room there.' The lance-bombardier pointed. 'It's—'

'You lead, and I'll follow.'

'Listen, Sergeant, I ain't supposed to leave this here vehicle unattended. This camp is full of old sweats that could nick a standin' elephant and make it disappear in two seconds flat.'

'But someone should escort me to Major Lucas's office,' said Eloise, and smiled.

Crikey, thought the lance-bombardier, what a way of saying 'cheese'. He didn't know any female sergeants who could smile like that. In fact, regular female sergeants could be more bloodcurdling than old Army regulars with three stripes and a crown.

'OK, this way,' he said. He took her into the orderly room and through it. ATS personnel, along with their male counterparts, followed her movements.

Battery Sergeant-Major Dixon, a square-jawed regular, emerged from the OC's office as Eloise and her escort approached.

'Hello, who's this?' he asked.

'Sergeant Adams, new arrival, Sarn't-Major,' said the lance-bombardier. 'I've just collected her from the station. I 'ad to wait a bit.'

The BSM looked Eloise over. She received the survey coolly.

'Sergeant Adams, you're late.'

'The train was late,' said Eloise.

'This unit's out of bounds to excuses,' said the BSM.

'I'm sorry, Sergeant-Major, but you must tell that to the train driver,' said Eloise.

The lance-bombardier coughed, dumped her valise on the floor and disappeared. The BSM eyed the new arrival again, this time with a certain amount of measuring-up.

'When you've seen Major Lucas,' he said, 'report to your immediate superior, Subaltern Forbes.'

'Very good, Sergeant-Major,' said Eloise.

Sergeant-Major Dixon knocked on the door, opened it and stepped in.

'Sergeant Adams of the ATS here to see you, sir,' he said.

'Send her in,' said Major Lucas.

'Step lively, Sergeant Adams, and leave your valise.' said the BSM. Eloise entered and the door closed behind her. The OC's office was pretty basic, but his desk looked formidable, and so did he, with his rugged features and his aggressive jaw. His cap was on, so Eloise advanced to his desk and saluted.

'Reporting, sir,' she said.

The ghost of a smile chased over Major Lucas's face.

'At ease, Sergeant Adams,' he said. 'No objections to the posting, then?'

'None, sir.'

'Good. By the way, I owe you a quid.' He uncovered the banknote by lifting his blotter. He offered it to her. Eloise, however, refused to take it.

'No, sir, not a pound, and I really don't want anything.'

'You did me a favour.'

'You came back from Dunkirk with many of your men, sir, and that did the country a great favour,' said Eloise. 'I should like you to agree we are all square.'

'Fair enough,' said Major Lucas. 'Now, can you drive?'

'Drive?' said Eloise. 'No, sir.'

'That's not a good start, is it?'

'The posting didn't say it was expected of me,' said Eloise.

'Omission noted, Sergeant Adams. Well, we'll have to get you trained. You're going to be my driver, but I'll still require a certain amount of admin work from you. Subaltern Forbes will advise you what it is. But I don't want you fiddling about with forms in triplicate. That stuff's for clerks. You're not a clerk and I don't intend to make you one. Report to Staff-Sergeant Gardner of transport first thing tomorrow morning, and he'll arrange for you to take driving instruction. That's all, Sergeant Adams. Dismiss.'

'Very good, sir,' said Eloise coolly. Really, the way one had to subordinate oneself when one was not an inferior was most exasperating.

Major Lucas spoke again as she reached the door.

'Pleased to see you, Sergeant Adams, good to have you with us.'

'Thank you, sir.' Eloise was smiling as she left. He had acknowledged in his own way that she was not an ordinary young woman, any more than her English father was an ordinary man.

As she retrieved her valise, she realized the little tingles of excitement had come back.

*   *   *

The formidable escort of Messerschmitt fighters was not enough to prevent Hurricanes and Spitfires downing one German bomber after another, but some broke through the air defences to drop explosives on airfields and on London. Suburbs suffered again. Croydon was hit, so were Norbury and Streatham, and Brixton and Kennington. And in Stead Street, Walworth, one bomb demolished an empty house that had only recently been vacated by Jemima Hardy and her family. In Streatham, another hit the main shopping street.

*   *   *

Captain Polly Simms, returning from a scheduled visit of inspection of ATS personnel at a supplies depot, alighted from the staff car, dismissed her driver and entered the admin office where her girls were employed. She had charge of the contingent of ATS at Divisional headquarters, with Rosie as her deputy.

Sergeant Mary James, senior ATS NCO, got up from her desk immediately, and handed Polly a note in a sealed envelope.

'Subaltern Adams left this for you, ma'am,' she said, her expression unhappy.

'Where is Subaltern Adams, then?' asked Polly.

'Ma'am, I – ma'am, she's had to go home, her mother was caught in an air raid. Ma'am, she's dead.'

Polly froze and turned white.

'Oh, my God,' she said, stricken.

She did not know how she got there, but she found herself in the open air again, the late afternoon sun hot, the countryside a bright shimmering green.

Emily? Emily? Dead in an air raid? She thought of Boots. He did not deserve this. In all his years with Emily, he had never let her down, not as far as Polly knew. He had been as attached to his marriage as any man could be, much more than Polly had thought necessary. He had worn his attachment with a smile, with a contented acceptance of its permanency, and it had never wavered, any more than his affection had. To have that attachment smashed and destroyed by a German bomb would be crucifying him.

Polly ripped the envelope open and took out the note Rosie had left.

Polly – I'm devastated – Daddy phoned – the terrible news – he received it from Grandpa – is picking me up to drive me home – What can I do for him – what can anyone do – it's heartbreaking – Rosie.

Polly, a woman whose brittle smile and brittle sense of humour often disguised her true emotions, felt every emotion except grief for Boots drain out of her.

Emily had bought her curtain material, and just as she completed the purchase, the air raid sirens sounded. The alarm bell rang in the store, a signal for all customers to leave and make their way to public shelters. Mr Finch hastened Emily down to the ground floor and to an exit. She ran, dropping her parcel. Mr Finch stopped to pick it up, telling her to go on. She ran out of the store just as a bomb dropped on Streatham High Road. The explosion was massive. Emily was among several people caught by the blast, by flying debris and shattered glass.

Mr Finch, stunned, his ears ringing, was paralysed for a moment. Then he ran, compulsively, out through shattered glass doors and into the sickening chaos caused by the exploding bomb. The sunlit road was littered with glass from shop windows, with torn bricks, lumps of masonry, limp rags and bodies. The quiet was unearthly until it was broken by screams, shouts and cries from people coming to. Men and women appeared,

341

staggering about, their faces ghastly with shock and horror. He saw Emily, lying on her back over the kerb. Appalled, he ran and went down on his knees beside her. Shards of glass dug into his trousers.

Emily lay with her dress in shreds, her body broken, her white face covered with dust, her auburn hair sprinkled with tiny glass splinters, her eyes closed.

'Emily? Emily?' He hardly recognised his own voice. 'Emily?' He touched her shoulder.

She opened her eyes, their green cloudy. She looked up at him.

'Dad?' The merest of husky whispers. 'What – what happened?'

'Emily, my dear—'

'Oh, lor'.' A long sigh. 'Aren't I a silly girl?'

Her eyes closed again, and he stayed beside her on his knees, holding her limp hand and, in grief and helplessness, watching her die. She simply slipped quietly away while the dust of carnage was still floating in the air above her.

Emily, godsend to the family in their years of struggle.

Gone.

Amid the clanging of rushing ambulances, a policeman placed a hand on his shoulder and gently shook him.

Polly went to the funeral with Rachel Goodman. She went in uniform, Rachel in mourning black. They sat together in a rear pew, neither knowing exactly what to say to each other. Each knew the other's weakness, Polly's for Boots, Rachel's for Sammy, but it was not that which made words difficult to come by. It was the tragedy of a life suddenly blotted out, a life that had belonged to a family with whom they had an affinity in their different ways.

They were all there, the Adams and Somers families, although the evacuated children, stayed in the country. Tommy and Vi, Sammy and Susie, Ned, Lizzy, Annabelle and her husband Nick. Bobby, Edward and Emma. Emma had Jonathan beside her, he having managed to get forty-eight hours leave, and Helene sat with Bobby, sharing his silent sadness. In the front pew were Boots, Tim, Rosie, Eloise, Chinese Lady and Mr Finch. The atmosphere seemed unreal, as if no-one could believe in the funeral. An Adams had gone, an Adams who had been a godsend to the family in the years of trial during and immediately after the Great War. Mr Eli Greenberg, also present, kept shaking his head in sad disbelief, like a man who felt every Adams had been destined to live for ever.

But the chosen hymns were about life, not death. Polly wondered exactly who had chosen a particular two, 'Onward Christian Soldiers' and 'All Things Bright and Beautiful'.

She did not attempt to look at Boots during the service, and she stood well apart from the family and their many friends at the cemetery. And when the burial was over, she left. Rachel hastened after her.

343

'Polly, where are you going?'

'Anywhere.'

'Aren't you going to the house?'

'No. How can I? Someone will say, "Look there she is, hovering like a vulture over Boots, waiting to eat him."'

'But my life, Polly, you haven't even spoken to him, nor to any of the family,' said Rachel, distraught.

'Rachel, I shall see the family again, and Boots,' said Polly, 'but not now, not today. Today, Rachel, I don't belong, can't you understand that?'

'Yes, I can understand, Polly, but I think you're wrong. Malice and unkindness are foreign to the natures of Sammy, Tommy, Lizzy and all the others.'

'Rachel, today is all wrong for me,' said Polly, and went.

Rachel sighed.

Everybody had finally gone, and the evening was quiet. The bombers had departed from the skies, and the twilight of double summertime was not yet grey with approaching dusk.

Boots sat in the garden with Rosie and Tim.

'It's a hard one to face, Dad,' said Tim.

'It's an if-only, Tim,' said Boots.

'Yes, if only she hadn't bothered about any new curtains,' said Rosie.

'And if only she had stayed with Grandpa,' said Tim, 'he was still in the store and wasn't even scratched. He's going to take a long time to

344

stop believing he was somehow to blame.'

'Tim, would you like to pour me a little whisky?' asked Boots.

'Anything you like,' said Tim.

'Just a small one,' said Boots, 'and ask your Grandpa if he'd like to join me.'

'Right,' said Tim and got up and went into the house.

'I want to say something,' said Rosie quietly.

'Yes, Rosie?'

'I'd like to have every year with you and Emily my mother all over again,' said Rosie. 'I'd like to be five years old again.'

Dear Mrs Finch

I have to tell you how desperately and sincerely sorry I am that you have all lost Emily so tragically. Also, I want to apologize for not paying my respects to you and your family on the day of the funeral. Please forgive me. I will call one day and make amends.

Yours very sincerely, Polly Simms.

Chinese Lady, troubled and grieving, read the letter twice and put it away. She knew what it meant.

*   *   *

The battle for command of the skies continued into September, and on the 15th the *Luftwaffe* launched 500 aircraft at London in a final attempt to secure victory. But they were met head-on in the skies over the Channel by the now renowned

345

Hurricanes and Spitfires, and by the end of that tumultuous day, the number of German bombers and fighters shot down not only resulted in defeat for Goering, but in Hitler's plans for invasion being cancelled.

*   *   *

In early November, Boots came home again on leave. So did other men serving with 7 Corps. So did some ATS personnel, including Rosie and Polly. Chinese Lady was not only happy to have Boots and Rosie home for a week, she was just as happy to sense they were over the worst effects of Emily's death. She thought Rosie more devoted than ever to her adoptive father, simply because of his tragic loss.

Two days later, she opened the door to a caller.

'Why, Miss Simms,' she said, 'you've come at last. I was beginning to think we'd lost you as an old fam'ly friend. Come in, come in.'

Polly, in civilian clothes, a blue coat and silver-grey costume, stepped into the hall, and Chinese Lady closed the door.

'Mrs Finch,' said Polly, 'do you understand why I've stayed away until now?'

'I think I do,' said Chinese Lady, marvelling at the way Sir Henry's always elegant daughter kept the years at bay. 'Perhaps it was best, even if some of the fam'ly wondered why you disappeared after the funeral.'

'I thought it much the best, Mrs Finch,' said

Polly, 'but I have to see Boots now, and I think you know why.'

'Yes,' said Chinese Lady gently, wondering why it was that this aristocratic woman had such a deep and lasting attachment to a man born in a world very different from her own. 'Yes, I'm sure I know why.'

'Does it offend you?' asked Polly.

'Because Boots lost Em'ly only two months ago?' said Chinese Lady. 'No, it doesn't offend me, Polly.' That was the first time she hadn't addressed Sir Henry's daughter as Miss Simms. 'Boots wasn't born to live alone, he was never made for bein' a widower, not in peace or in wartime.'

'Mrs Finch, you've always been exceptionally kind to me,' said Polly.

'Well, you've always been close to the fam'ly and taught good schoolin' to many of my grand-children,' said Chinese Lady, 'and now you and Rosie are soldiering with your father and Boots and their troops. Bless my soul, I just don't know what this country's comin' to, puttin' young ladies in uniform and probably sendin' them off with the soldiers some day. I'll never understand it, and Queen Victoria wouldn't of allowed it, I'm sure. Still, there it is, and now you'd like to see Boots.'

'Is he here?' asked Polly, pent up.

'Well, no, I'm afraid he isn't,' said Chinese Lady. 'He and Rosie are both home on leave but Rosie's out with her Aunt Lizzy, and Boots has gone to Ruskin Park with Sammy's little girl Paula. Boots is specially fond of little Paula. I think he sees her as he saw Rosie when she was Paula's age. Why don't you go up to the park and meet him there?'

'Mrs Finch, do I have your complete understanding?' asked Polly.

'Yes, my dear, of course,' said Chinese Lady.

'Thank you,' said Polly.

In misty sunshine, little Paula was running about with another small girl. Boots, seated on a bench in the park, was watching them, but thinking of Emily. It was still difficult to believe she had gone. She had always been around, first as the girl next door and then as his wife. She'd been his guide, his mainstay and his unfailing companion during his years of blindness. She'd given him Tim, and been a loving mother to Rosie and Eloise. While she had never been a passionate woman, she had never denied him. Men did have a need, and women perhaps had compliance more than need. Some women, at least. Eloise's mother had been wholly passionate during the few weeks he had known her.

In the misty sunshine, Polly approached, checking in her walk as she saw him, his head turned, his eyes on two small girls dancing and skipping about a little way off. To her, he was the same as he'd always been, in his looks, his good humour, his unaggressive masculinity and his tolerance of fools and idiots. Born of an old-fashioned Walworth mother, he was still the only man she had ever really wanted. She walked slowly up to him. He heard her and turned his head.

'Hello, darling,' she said softly.

'Polly?' he said, and she sat down beside him. His expression was not discouraging, and there was even, perhaps, a hint of a smile lurking. His almost blind left eye had its familiar lazy look, the eye that, for some silly feminine reason, she supposed, she always loved more than his sound right one.

'Darling,' she said, 'I'm desperately sorry about Emily, I truly am. I never wished her dead, never, only that she would share you with me. She never would, and who could blame her? But it's my turn now, isn't it? Oh, not immediately, of course, but not too far away. It is my turn, isn't it?'

'Who else could there ever be but you, Polly?' said Boots.

THE END